Children's
Competence
to Consent

CRITICAL ISSUES IN SOCIAL JUSTICE

Series Editor: **MELVIN J. LERNER**
University of Waterloo
Waterloo, Ontario, Canada

THE JUSTICE MOTIVE IN SOCIAL BEHAVIOR: Adapting to Times of
Scarcity and Change
Edited by Melvin J. Lerner and Sally C. Lerner

CHILDREN'S COMPETENCE TO CONSENT
Edited by Gary B. Melton, Gerald P. Koocher,
and Michael J. Saks

JUSTICE AND THE CRITIQUE OF PURE PSYCHOLOGY
Edward E. Sampson

A Continuation Order Plan is available for this series. A continuation order will bring delivery of each new volume immediately upon publication. Volumes are billed only upon actual shipment. For further information please contact the publisher.

Children's Competence to Consent

Edited by

GARY B. MELTON
University of Nebraska
Lincoln, Nebraska

GERALD P. KOOCHER
Children's Hospital Medical Center and
Harvard Medical School
Boston, Massachusetts

and

MICHAEL J. SAKS
Boston College
Chestnut Hill, Massachusetts

PLENUM PRESS • NEW YORK AND LONDON

Library of Congress Cataloging in Publication Data

Main entry under title:

Children's competence to consent.

(Critical issues in social justice).
   Includes bibliographical references and index.
   1. Children—Legal status, laws, etc.—United States. 2. Informed consent (Medical law)—United States. 3. Consent (Law)—United States. 4. Capacity and disability—United States. I. Melton, Gary B. II. Koocher, Gerald P. III. Saks, Michael J. IV. Series.

KF479.C47 1982	346.7301'35	82-18631
ISBN 0-306-41069-9	347.306135	

© 1983 Plenum Press, New York
A Division of Plenum Publishing Corporation
233 Spring Street, New York, N.Y. 10013

Printed in the United States of America

Contributors

JOEL J. ALPERT • Department of Pediatrics, Boston University School of Medicine and Boston City Hospital, Boston, Massachusetts

DONALD N. BERSOFF • Ennis, Friedman, Bersoff and Ewing, Washington, D.C.; Joint Program in Law and Psychology, University of Maryland School of Law and the Johns Hopkins University, Baltimore, Maryland

THOMAS GRISSO • Department of Psychology, St. Louis University, St. Louis, Missouri

MICHAEL A. GRODIN • Department of Pediatrics, Boston University School of Medicine and Boston City Hospital, Boston, Massachusetts

PATRICIA KEITH-SPIEGEL • Department of Psychology, California State University, Northridge, California

GERALD P. KOOCHER • Department of Psychiatry, Children's Hospital Medical Center (Boston) and Harvard Medical School, Boston, Massachusetts

CHARLES E. LEWIS • Department of Medicine, University of California, Los Angeles, California

GARY B. MELTON • Department of Psychology, University of Nebraska, Lincoln, Nebraska

MICHAEL J. SAKS • Department of Psychology, Boston College, Chestnut Hill, Massachusetts

JUNE LOUIN TAPP • Institute of Child Development, University of Minnesota, Minneapolis, Minnesota

WALTER J. WADLINGTON • School of Law, University of Virginia, Charlottesville, Virginia

LOIS A. WEITHORN • Institute of Law, Psychiatry, and Public Policy, University of Virginia, Charlottesville, Virginia

Acknowledgments

This volume developed from a study group sponsored by the Society for Research in Child Development (SRCD) with funds provided by the Foundation for Child Development. The Foundation for Child Develpment is a private foundation that makes grants to educational and charitable institutions. Its main interests are in research, social and economic indicators of children's lives, advocacy and public information projects, and service experiments that help translate theoretical knowledge about children into policies and practices that affect their daily lives. The contributors to this volume have donated their royalties to SRCD to be used for future study groups on topics in child development research.

The study group met at the University of Virginia in November 1980. Elizabeth Marzo, the administrator of the Institute of Law, Psychiatry, and Public Policy at Virginia, coordinated the arrangements for the meeting, with the support of Richard Bonnie, director of the Institute. Daniel Martell and Edward Mulvey, graduate students in psychology at Virginia, also assisted with local arrangements.

In addition to the contributors to this book, several scholars participated in the study group discussions: Andre Derdeyn (Department of Behavioral Medicine and Psychiatry, University of Virginia); Norma Feshbach (Department of Education, University of California, Los Angeles); Robert Mnookin (School of Law, Stanford University); Dick Reppucci (Department of Psychology, University of Virginia); and Charles Tremper (School of Law, University of California, Los Angeles). Their insights were useful in honing the ideas presented in this volume.

Contents

CHAPTER 3

Social Psychological Perspectives on the Problem of Consent   41

MICHAEL J. SAKS

PART II: CHILDREN'S CONSENT TO TREATMENT: LEGAL,
MEDICAL, AND PSYCHOLOGICAL PERSPECTIVES

CHAPTER 4

Consent to Medical Care for Minors: The Legal Framework   57

WALTER J. WADLINGTON

CHAPTER 5

**Decision Making Related to Health: When Could/Should Children
Act Responsibly?** 75

CHARLES E. LEWIS

CHAPTER 6

Informed Consent and Pediatric Care 93

MICHAEL A. GRODIN AND JOEL J. ALPERT

CHAPTER 7

Competence to Consent: Psychotherapy 111

GERALD P. KOOCHER

PART III: CHILDREN'S CONSENT IN NONMEDICAL AREAS

CHAPTER 8

Juveniles' Consent in Delinquency Proceedings 131

THOMAS GRISSO

CHAPTER 9

Children as Participants in Psychoeducational Assessment 149

DONALD N. BERSOFF

CHAPTER 10

Children and Consent to Participate in Research 179

PATRICIA KEITH-SPIEGEL

PART IV: IMPLEMENTING CONSENT STANDARDS

CHAPTER 11

Preparing Children for Decision Making: Implications of Legal Socialization Research

JUNE LOUIN TAPP AND GARY B. MELTON

CHAPTER 12

Involving Children in Decisions Affecting Their Own Welfare: Guidelines for Professionals

LOIS A. WEITHORN

CHAPTER 1

Children's Competence to Consent

A Problem in Law and Social Science

GARY B. MELTON

The question of children's competence to give or refuse consent[1] is of largely recent origin (see Chapter 9). Until the mid-sixties it was not clear that children were "persons" within the meaning of the Fourteenth Amendment, which makes the Bill of Rights applicable to the states. Although there were several early-twentieth-century "children's rights" cases decided by the United States Supreme Court,[2] each of these could be construed as a vindication of *parents'* liberty interest in childrearing as they saw fit (Melton, 1982). In none of the early cases was there a clear indication of minors' possessing constitutionally protected fundamental liberties independent of their parents. Children were perceived as properly dependent upon their parents who possessed a "right of control" over them.[3] Even though parents' rights in this regard are limited by the fact that they are not "free . . . to make martyrs of their children,"[4] this restriction emanated from the *state's* interest in the socialization of children.[5] Indeed, the Supreme Court had held that it "would hardly seem open to

---

[1] "Competence to consent" will be used generically in this discussion, but with recognition that the standard for particular forms of consent (*e.g.*, consent to treatment, consent to research) may vary.

[2] *E.g.*, Pierce v. Society of Sisters, 268 U.S. 510 (1925); Meyer v. Nebraska, 262 U.S. 390 (1923).

[3] Meyer v. Nebraska, *id.* at 400.

[4] Prince v. Massachusetts, 321 U.S. 158, 170 (1944).

[5] *Id.* at 165.

GARY B. MELTON ● Department of Psychology, University of Nebraska, Lincoln, Nebraska 68588.

question" that the state could impinge on basic freedoms of minors (*e.g.*, freedom of religion) in ways that would be clearly unconstitutional if the same restrictions were placed on adults.[6] Given clear indications that both parents and the state as *parens patriae*[7] could exercise control over minors (see Chapter 9 for additional discussion), the question of the limits of children's *actual* competence to make personal decisions was moot. Simply put, minors were *per se* incompetent (*i.e.*, incompetent on the basis of age alone) to exercise self-determination; no additional inquiry was necessary or even relevant.[8]

Changes in Children's Legal Status

The question of children's competence initially became a clearly live issue in 1967 when the Supreme Court explicitly stated for the first time that "neither the Fourteenth Amendment nor the Bill of Rights is for adults alone."[9] In that landmark case (*In re Gault*[10]), the Court lambasted the juvenile court as a "kangaroo court"[11] and proclaimed that juveniles charged with delinquent offenses were entitled to procedural protections fundamental to due process of law (*e.g.*, rights to notice of the charges, representation by counsel, confrontation and cross-examination of witness, and the privilege against self-incrimination). At the same time, however, the Court recognized that there were

> special problems . . . with respect to waiver of the privilege [against self-incrimination] by or on behalf of children . . . . If counsel was not present for some permissible reason when an admission was obtained, the greatest care must be taken to assure that the admission was voluntary, in the sense not only that it was not coerced or suggested, but also that it was not the product of ignorance of rights or of adolescent fantasy, fright, or despair.[12]

Thus, while the Court reserved judgment as to whether respondents in delinquency proceedings were entitled to *all* of the same due process rights as adult defendants in criminal proceedings,[13] it did acknowledge that recognition of

[6] *Id.* at 169.

[7] Literally "the sovereign as parent," the *parens patriae* power refers to the state's authority and duty to protect the welfare of dependent persons.

[8] *Per se* incompetence need not rely on lack of recogniton of constitutionally protected liberty. In common law, minors are generally considered unable to make binding contracts except for "necessaries" such as food and lodging.

[9] *In re* Gault, 387 U.S. 1, 13 (1967).

[10] *Id.*

[11] *Id.* at 28.

[12] *Id.* at 55.

[13] *Id.* at 10–11. The Court did in fact later hold that juveniles were not entitled to jury trials. McKeiver v. Pennsylvania, 403 U.S. 528 (1971).

some constitutional rights for minors would raise some questions as to the limits of their competent exercise of these rights.

The Supreme Court continued its ambivalent treatment of children's rights with two cases pertaining to the limits of freedom of expression by minors. In 1968 in *Ginsberg v. New York*[14] the Court held that states could constitutionally prohibit the sale to minors of material believed to be obscene on the basis of its prurient appeal to them regardless of whether the material would be obscene to adults. In a concurring opinion, Justice Stewart argued that liberty was contingent upon competence:

> I think a State may permissibly determine that, at least in some precisely delineated areas, a child—like someone in a captive audience—is not possessed of that full capacity for individual choice which is the presupposition of First Amendment guarantees. It is only upon such a premise, I should suppose, that a State may deprive children of other rights—the right to marry, for example, or the right to vote—deprivations that would be constitutionally intolerable for adults.[15]

Even one of the dissenters, Justice Fortas (who had written the majority opinion in *Gault*), agreed that "the State in the exercise of its police power—even in the First Amendment domain—may make proper and careful differentiation between adults and children."[16]

However, in 1969 in *Tinker v. Des Moines Independent School District* the Court reaffirmed that "students in school as well as out of school are 'persons' under our Constitution. They are possessed of fundamental rights which the State must respect, just as they themselves must respect their obligations to the State."[17] Accordingly, the Court held that a school system that had suspended students for wearing black armbands in protest of the Vietnam war had impermissibly invaded the students' exercise of First Amendment rights. The Court seemed particularly concerned that the Des Moines school authorities had attempted to limit behavior akin to "pure speech," although, in the opinion for the Court, Justice Fortas made no effort to distinguish *Tinker* from *Ginsberg*.

In 1972 the Supreme Court decided another case (*Wisconsin v. Yoder*[18]; see Chapter 9 for further discussion of *Yoder*) involving minors' First Amendment rights (in this instance, freedom of religion). *Yoder* is particularly noteworthy in the present context because it is the only case in which a Supreme Court opinion—albeit in a lone dissent by Justice Douglas—included a citation of developmental research to support an assertion about children's capacities. In *Yoder* the Court ruled that Amish parents' First and Fourteenth Amendment

[14] 390 U.S. 629 (1968).
[15] *Id.* at 649–650.
[16] *Id.* at 673.
[17] 393 U.S. 503, 511 (1969).
[18] 406 U.S. 205 (1972).

rights were violated by a state law compelling their children's attendance in school until age 16, in contrast to the Amish practice of removing their children from school upon the completion of eighth grade. The Court majority assumed that the clash of interests was between the state and the parents:

> [O]ur holding today in no degree depends on the assertion of the religious interest of the child as contrasted with that of the parents. It is the parents who are subject to prosecution here for failing to cause their children to attend school, and it is their right to free exercise, not that of their children, that must determine Wisconsin's power to impose criminal penalties on the parent.[19]

In an impassioned dissent, Justice Douglas argued that the key interests at stake were those of the Amish youth themselves:

> It is the future of the student, not the future of the parents, that is imperilled in today's decision. If a parent keeps his child out of school beyond the grade school, then the child will be forever barred from entry into the new and amazing world of diversity that we have today. The child may decide that this is the preferred course, or he may rebel. It is the student's judgment, not his parent's, that is essential if we are to give full meaning to what we have said about the Bill of Rights and of the right of students to be masters of their own destiny. If he is harnassed to the Amish way of life by those in authority over him and if his education is truncated, his entire life may be stunted and deformed. The child, therefore, should be given an opportunity to be heard before the State gives the exemption which we honor today.[20]

Accordingly, "where the child is mature enough to express potentially conflicting desires,"[21] Douglas argued that his or her views should be canvassed. In support of the assumption that Amish eighth graders could be expected to manifest such maturity, Douglas cited Piaget, Elkind, Kohlberg, Gesell, and other developemental authorities as holding that "the moral and intellectual maturity of the fourteen-year-old approaches that of the adult."[22] The validity of such a generalization to Amish youth may be questionable, but the Court majority did not recognize their having significant interests at stake in *Yoder*, so the issue was never reached.

The Court's Assumptions about Minors' Competence

Beyond the incidental discussion of minors' competence to exercise self-determination in *Yoder*, several Supreme Court decisions in recent years have appeared to rest on assumptions about minors' capacities, albeit without the

[19] *Id.* at 230–231.
[20] *Id.* at 245–246.
[21] *Id.* at 242.
[22] *Id.* at 245, n.3.

attempt that Justice Douglas made to ascertain the current state of scientific knowledge on these points. The cases in which such issues have arisen have involved a variety of contexts in which minors might exercise consent: "voluntary" admission to mental hospitals (*Parham v. J. R.*[23]); waiver of the privilege against self-incrimination (*Fare v. Michael C.*[24]); purchase of contraceptives (*Carey v. Population Services International*[25]), and requests for abortions (*Planned Parenthood of Central Missouri v. Danforth*[26]; *Bellotti v. Baird I*[27]; *Bellotti v. Baird II*[28]; *H.L. v. Matheson*[29]).

Parham and *Fare* are particularly interesting because the decisions in these two cases were announced on the same day in 1979—with apparently conflicting assumptions about developmental phenomena. In *Parham* the Supreme Court held that a formal due-processing hearing was not constitutionally required before minors were "voluntarily" committed to mental hospitals by their parents or guardian. Chief Justice Burger's opinion for the Court was replete with largely unsupported empirical assumptions about the workings of the mental health system, interaction in families of disturbed children, and psychological effects of various procedural forms (Slobogin, 1980). Perhaps most basic to the opinion, though, was an assumption that children are generally incompetent and that parents, therefore, should have authority to make major life decisions in their behalf:

> Most children, even in adolescence, simply are not able to make sound judgments concerning many decisions, including their need for medical care or treatment. Parents can and must make those judgments.[30]

Accordingly, formal hearings were perceived by the Chief Justice to be merely "time-consuming procedural minuets"[31] unnecessary to protect minors' interests.

In *Fare* the Court considered the question of whether a 16-year-old boy's request to speak with his probation officer during police interrogation constituted an invocation of his *Miranda* rights.[32] Michael C. was described as immature, emotional, and poorly educated.[33] Moreover, he had declined an attorney apparently because he believed the offer was a police trick: "How I know you

---

[23] 442 U.S. 584 (1979).
[24] 442 U.S. 707 (1979).
[25] 431 U.S. 678 (1977).
[26] 428 U.S. 52 (1976).
[27] 428 U.S. 132 (1976).
[28] 443 U.S. 622 (1979).
[29] –U.S.–, 101 S.Ct. 1164 (1981).
[30] 442 U.S. 584, 603.
[31] *Id.* at 605.
[32] 442 U.S. 707.
[33] *Id.* at 733 (Powell, J., dissenting).

guys won't pull no police officer in and tell me he's an attorney?"[34] Michael C. had been instructed by his probation officer to call him for assistance if he ever got into trouble again, and Michael apparently trusted his probation officer to give him good advice. Nonetheless, in a 5–4 decision, the Court held not only that a request for a probation officer did not constitute a *per se* invocation of the Fifth Amendment, but also that, within the "totality of the circumstances," Michael had made a valid waiver of his rights. The Court ignored both its own recognition of "special problems" with confessions by minors in *Gault* and a large body of decisions by lower courts indicating the need for special attention to the competency of minors to make independent judgments (without parents or counsel) concerning waivers of Fifth and Sixth Amendment rights. Apparently the Court's assumption in *Parham* of minors' incompetence "to make sound judgments" did not extend to the police station, presumably because of the Burger Court's desire to limit *Miranda* applications rather than a careful analysis of minors' capacities in various contexts.

Abortion Cases Concerning Minors

The most extensive, albeit fuzziest, discussions by the Supreme Court of the contingency of minors' constitutional rights on competence has come in a series of case concerning privacy in decision making about sexual matters (*i.e.*, abortions and contraceptives). In the first of these cases (*Planned Parenthood of Central Missouri v. Danforth*[35]), the Court held that a Missouri statute requiring parental consent before minors could obtain an abortion was unconstitutional because it imposed the possibility of "an absolute, and possibly arbitrary, veto [by a third party] over the decision of the physician and his patient to terminate the patient's pregnancy."[36] The Court made clear, however, that "our holding . . . does not suggest that every minor, regardless of age or maturity, may give effective consent for termination of her pregnancy."[37] No standards were suggested for circumstances under which a requirement of parental consent might be permissible or even necessary. That is, "maturity" was left undefined.

The Court in *Danforth* left open the question of whether parental notice or consultation, short of parental consent, might be required before a minor obtained an abortion. There were suggestions, however, that the Court would find such a requirement constitutional. Four justices dissented in *Danforth*. Justice White, joined by Chief Justice Burger and Justice Rehnquist, argued that a

[34] *Id.* at 711.
[35] 428 U.S. 52.
[36] *Id.* at 74.
[37] *Id.* at 75.

requirement of parental consent was justifiable in order to protect minors "from their own immature and improvident decisions."[38] In a separate dissent, Justice Stevens also supported a parental consent requirement as a means of ensuring "that the decision be made correctly and with full understanding of the consequences of either alternative."[39] Moreover, two justices in the majority (Stewart and Powell) indicated that the Missouri law was unconstitutional only because it allowed an *absolute* parental veto of a minor's abortion decision. They concluded that a consultation requirement might be permissible because of many adolescents' immaturity:

> There can be little doubt that the State furthers a constitutionally permissible end by encouraging an unmarried pregnant minor to seek the help and advice of her parents in making the very important decision whether or not to bear a child. That is a grave decision, and a girl of tender years, under emotional stress, may be ill-equipped to make it without mature advice and emotional support. It seems unlikely that she will obtain adequate counsel and support from the attending physician at an abortion clinic, where abortions for pregnant minors frequently take place.[40]

Succeeding cases have concerned the constitutionality of state statutes that involved a parental notice or consultation requirement, following the suggestions made by Justice Stewart in *Danforth*. In 1979 the Court considered a case (*Bellotti v. Baird*[41]) challenging the constitutionality of a Massachusetts law that required parental consent for abortions by minors, but allowed minors who had been denied such consent to appeal to a superior court judge. In the opinion for the Court in *Bellotti*, Justice Powell echoed the logic of the concurring opinion of Justice Stewart which he had joined in *Danforth*. Powell asserted again that parental consultation prior to an abortion decision is often desirable "as immature minors often lack the ability to make full informed choices that take account of both immediate and long-range consequences."[42] He seemed particularly concerned that minors might not make a competent selection of a physician, irrespective of the wisdom of the abortion decision itself.[43] Nonetheless, Powell argued that the Massachusetts statute went too far in limiting minors' options in abortion decisions. If parents refused consent, they might block the minor's access to the court. Powell concluded that the minor must have access to the court without the necessity of first seeking parental consent. Then the court would be required to authorize the abortion if she established either "that

---

[38] *Id.* at 95.
[39] *Id.* at 103.
[40] *Id.* at 91.
[41] 443 U.S. 622.
[42] *Id.* at 640.
[43] *Id.* at 641, n.21.

she is mature and well-informed enough to make intelligently the abortion decision on her own" or that the abortion would be in her best interst.[44]

The most recent Supreme Court decision concerning the restrictions that a state may place on abortions by minors was handed down in 1981 (*H. L. v. Matheson*[45]). *Matheson* involved a test of the constitutionality of a Utah statute that requires physicians to "notify, if possible," the parents or guardian of a minor upon whom an abortion is to be performed. The Court decided the case on narrow grounds. Specifically, it held that H. L. had not established that she or any member of the class that she represented was mature or emancipated. In a 6–3 decision, the Court then held that, as applied to an immature, unemancipated girl living with and dependent upon her parents, the statute serves important state interests and is constitutionally drawn. In the opinion for the Court, Chief Justice Burger asserted that the statute served to preserve family integrity, to protect adolescents, and to provide an opportunity for parents to supply "essential medical and other information to a physician."[46] (As the dissenters pointed out, Burger gave no indication of what information a parent might provide that the adolescent could not.[47]) Burger further asserted that the risks of an abortion are grave:

> The medical, emotional, and psychological consequences of an abortion are serious and can be lasting; this is especially so when the patient is immature.[48]

Burger also made a rather ridiculous assertion that, "if the pregnant girl elects to carry her child to term, the *medical* decisions to be made entail few—perhaps none—of the potentially grave emotional and psychological consequences of the decision to abort."[49]

The Court reserved judgment on the issue of whether a parental notice requirement was constitutional when the minor is mature. There were indications, however, that the Court would find such a requirement unconstitutional. Justice Powell, joined by Justice Stewart, reaffirmed in a concurring opinion his view, previously expressed in *Bellotti*, that a mature minor must have access to an independent decisionmaker without the burden of parental notice. The three dissenters, of course, regarded any notice requirement as an unconstitutional interference with the minor's right to privacy. Thus, as presently constituted, a majority of the Court would appear to view a blanket parental notice requirement as unconstitutional. It remains to be seen how the replacement of Justice Stewart by Sandra O'Connor will tip the balance.

[44] *Id.* at 643–643
[45] –U.S.–, 101 S.Ct. 1164 (1981).
[46] *Id.* at 1172.
[47] *Id.* at 1189.
[48] *Id.* at 1172.
[49] *Id.* at 1173.

Most importantly, the Court again gave little guidance as to the meaning of "mature." In the opinion for the Court, Chief Justice Burger seemed almost to equate maturity with emancipation (*i.e.*, independence from parents of domicile and livelihood), but such an equation was never explicitly stated. The dissenters indicated that they viewed the mature minor rule adopted in *Danforth* as applying to pregnant minors who are "capable of appreciating its [an abortion's] nature and consequences."[50] Even the dissenters, however, gave no clues as to the kinds and amount of knowledge about the abortion procedure that are necessary before a minor may consent independently of her parents.

Conclusions

Although it is clear that children are now considered to be entitled to fundamental constitutional rights, it is also clear that the breadth of these rights, at least as construed by the Supreme Court, is significantly narrower than for adults (see Chapter 9). Shortly after the Court's landmark decision in *Gault*, Judge Lindsay Arthur (1968), a well-known traditionalist on the juvenile bench, asked rhetorically, "Should Children Be as Equal as People?" The Supreme Court seems to have answered, "Not Quite." Nonetheless, by proclaiming minors to be "persons" within the meaning of the Constitution, the Court has opened the door to consideration of the circumstances under which minors might rationally be extended the freedom or protection of constitutional rights.

Examination of the key Supreme Court cases involving children over the past 15 years suggests that the Court's assessment of minors' "maturity" in making various decisions lies heavily in their determinations of the degree to which minors may exercise the rights accorded to adults. It also seems clear that the majority of the current members of the Court (particularly the "conservative" justices who have joined the Court during Burger's tenure as chief justice) have little faith in minors'—even adolescents'—competence to make informed decisions. Moreover, in forming this judgment, the Court appears to have relied exclusively on "the pages of human experience"[51] without any attempt to ascertain the current state of knowledge about children's decision-making prowess.

At the same time, it should be noted that the Court's view of children has not been so uniform as to result in the clear adjudication of social facts by judicial notice. That is, the Court has not stated its assumptions about children's capacities clearly and consistently enough to give these statements of

[50] *Id.* at 1193, n.49.
[51] Parham v. J. R., *supra* note 23, at 602.

social fact compelling precedential value. Indeed, it has appeared at times that the psychological assumptions that the Court has drawn have represented derivations of an "is" from an "ought." Frequently the Court seems to have based its assumptions about child development on a concept of how such processes should operate rather than an examination of how they in fact do. The conflicting assumptions in *Parham* and *Fare* are exemplary. The view of minors as generally incompetent in *Parham* seemed to have been derived from an idyllic view of family life and medical authority and, perhaps, a belief that disturbed adolescents should do what's good for them. On the other hand, the apparently inflated perception of minors' ability to conceptualize and maneuver through police interrogation (*cf.* Chapter 8) in *Fare* probably resulted from the Burger Court's skeptical approach to *Miranda* doctrine, perhaps combined with the sort of belief articulated by Arizona's Supreme Court in *Gault* that "confession is good for the child as the commencement of the assumed therapy of the juvenile court process."[52] Other examples of conflicting psychological assumptions by the Court (apparently based on a desire to reach different results) have come in discussions of child-parent relations in circumstances where family strife might be expected: when the parents seek to institutionalize a child[53] and when the child seeks to have an abortion without parental consent.[54] Moreover, the Court has yet to make clear in any context what it means by "mature." Even in the abortion area where the Court has expressly promulgated a mature minor rule, it has not indicated the standards by which maturity is to be assessed, much less addressed the subtleties of the process by which consent should be obtained (*cf.* Chapter 3). Such ambiguity, absent clear statutory or ethical guidelines, makes professional practice tenuous and, in particular, probably results in deprivation of services to minors who might in fact be "mature" because professionals do not wish to risk liability for working with minors who might not be able to give a valid consent. (In fields where minors do not clearly have a constitutionally protected right to privacy, ambiguity in statutes or regulations concerning minors' consent may of course have similar effects; see Melton, 1981b). Lack of specific substantive standards for competence to consent also makes difficult attempts to provide evidence as to minors' abilities, both as individuals and as a class, to meet various tests for competence. At present, researchers must rely on careful analysis of what standards could be (see Chapter 12) rather than what they are.

While the Court's conflicting assumptions and the vacuum it has left in standards concerning maturity are clearly problematic, this ambiguity at least leaves open the possibility that social scientists might inform the Court (and

---

[52] 387 U.S. at 51, *citing* Applications of Gault, 407 P.2d 760, 767–768 (1965).

[53] Parham v. J. R., *supra* note 23; *see especially* pp. 602–603, 610.

[54] Planned Parenthood of Central Missouri v. Danforth, 428 U.S. 52, 75 (1976).

legislators) as to developmental trends in children's competencies, insofar as standards are based on psychological assumptions. Even if such research does not influence the formulation of standards, it might help to increase intellectual honesty about the values and assumptions underlying the policies that are selected to regulate the lives of children and families.

Problems in Application of Developmental Research

Assuming the opening to present research that might inform the judiciary and lawmakers concerning relevant developmental issues, there are still some issues in the application of such findings to the law that should be addressed. Perhaps the most obvious and most discussed problem is the communication problem resulting from differences in training and jargon. The social scientist who begins discussing "development of social cognitions" or use of "path analysis" is likely to lose his legal audience. Conversely, the lawyer who assumes that a social scientist shares his or her understanding of the concept of "privacy" is likely to leave his listener confused or mistaken. These difficulties, while not trivial, are relatively superficial and presumably remediable through efforts to use plain language and some mutual educative efforts.

There are, however, some basic differences in paradigm or worldview that are much more fundamental in potential clashes between the social sciences and the law. For example, while only the purest Rogerians in psychology base their work on an assumption of free will, that belief is clearly a cornerstone of the law. In the present context, attempts to study the "voluntariness" of consent by children are difficult when the concept is foreign to the paradigm within which psychologists work. Indeed, the clash of paradigms may lead to some paradoxical conclusions. For example, the physicians contributing to this volume (Grodin & Alpert, Chapter 6; Lewis, Chapter 5) argue that children should have the opportunity to exercise greater power of consent to medical treament, particularly when the proposed regimen is complex or long-term, in order to heighten compliance. The psychological expectation is that when children make an affirmative choice, they will be more likely to follow through on that choice in order to avoid dissonance (cf. Chapter 2, Chapter 3). In a sense, the stated purpose is to increase compliance through the exercise of liberty!

In addition to assumptive differences, there are differences in style of analysis of problems between the social sciences and the law that may make application of research difficult. On a practical level, perhaps the most consequential of these differences is the law's reliance on moral or logical analysis versus the reliance of scientists on empirical analysis. Some jurists perceive attempts to inform the law with "hard data" as undermining legal analysis through logic and commonsense. Chief Justice Burger appears to be much more comfortable in making inferences from the "pages of human experience"[55] than from systematic empirical research. A classic example of this bias came in *Ballew v. Georgia*,[56] the most extensive use of social science data by the Supreme Court thus far, In *Ballew*, the Court held that juries of fewer than six persons unconstitutionally deprived criminal defendents of their right to a trial by a jury. In the opinion for the Court, Justice Blackmun relied heavily on small-group research, particularly the work of Saks (1977), to substantiate his arguments concerning the effects of jury size. Nonetheless, in a brief concurring opinion, Justice Powell, joined by Burger and Rehnquist, contended that small juries were unconstitutional essentially because the line has to be drawn somewhere (presumably by intuition). Powell went on to attack the use of empirical evidence:

> I have reservations as to the wisdom—as well as the necessity—of Mr. Justice Blackmun's heavy reliance on numerology derived from statistical studies. Moreover, neither the validity nor the methodology employed by the study was subjected to the traditional testing mechanisms of the adversary process. The studies relied on merely represent unexamined findings of persons interested in the jury system.[57]

As Haney (1980) has noted, the conservative intellectual tradition embodied in the *stare decisis* principle in the law may make "untested" social science evidence appear unreliable: "[D]ata are not always enough: in law, data plus authority are preferable to 'merely' authoritative data" (p. 171). In particular, social science data introduced in appellate briefs (and, therefore, not subjected to cross-examination) may have little credibility, despite the fact that the adversary process is not efficient in assessing scientific truth (Thibaut & Walker, 1978). Haney (1980) suggested that this problem might be alleviated by educating judges informally:

> Psychologists and other social scientists might also *circumvent* the adversary system, without circumventing its decision-makers. That is, they might make more concerted efforts than they have so far to reach judges through judicial conferences, judges' "colleges," and through direct correspondence. In these settings information is not narrowly constrained by rules of evidence and experts are seen less as partisans than sources of potentially useful information. Recognizing the limitations of the adversary system means also seeking alternatives to it. (p. 172, n. 44)

To take an optimistic (perhaps overly optimistic) stance, it also may be that the prejudice against empirical data ultimately will be of relatively little consequence in the courts' examination of the kinds of research presented in this

---

[55] *Supra* note 51.
[56] 435 U.S. 223 (1978).
[57] *Id.* at 246.

volume. Historically, the law has been most open to the behavioral sciences in resolution of questions of juvenile and family law. Indeed, mental health services for children grew up to a large extent with the juvenile court (Levine & Levine, 1970). Moreover, the massive attention given to Goldstein, Freud, and Solnit's (1973) controversial volume on custody standards (*cf.* Crouch, 1979) suggests that the courts may be particulary open to social science research and theory concerning children. It should be noted, however, that clinical input into judicial decisions (and, for the most part, Goldstein *et al.*'s work does not stray from such a model) tends to *serve* the law as the law is presently framed and generally does not challenge the assumptions under which the law operates. Moreover, clinical opinion is compatible with the law's idiographic approach and does not raise the conceptual problems imposed by researchers' nomothetic approach. Indeed, part of the receptivity of many judges and clinicians to Goldstein *et al.*'s work—and the scientific criticism it has evoked (*e.g.*, Katkin, Bullington, & Levine, 1974; Melton, 1978)—may have resulted from their sense of *certainty* about *individual* functioning. They were essentially unconcerned with problems related to the application of probability data to the law (which views "facts" quite differently than do scientists) or of application of finding regarding group differences to individual cases.

Finally, while perhaps obvious, the caveat that social science findings cannot be translated directly into policy bears stating. The question of whether competence should be the determinant of whether children have a right to self-determination in particular situations is an ethical or legal judgment, not a scientific one. Similarly, the standards for competence are legal, not psychological issues, although psychologists might inform legal decisionmakers about the particular results associated with various standards. Perhaps a particularly politically charge example would illustrate this point best. Lewis (see Chapter 5) reports that there were some clear differences based on socioeconomic status of the children in the effects of a system to allow children to make routine health decisions in school. The rate of removing children's privileges to use the system at will was similar (about 3%) in both a university school in which children were from upper-middle-class families and two schools in which children were largely from disadvantage families and the majority were black or Hispanic. However, rates of use were much higher in the low-SES schools, and the children tended to perceive physicians and medicine and as the primary means of health maintenance. Morevoer, although there was a definite shift among white children from nurse to self in perceptions of "who decided" what to do when they made use of the system, this shift did not occur for minority-group children. Lewis suggests that the latter finding may result from a generalization of the overall lack of opportunities for minority groups, such that an actual shift in decision-making power may not seem real. This finding parallels Melton's (1980) observation that development of concepts of rights as entitlements applicable to oneself occurs much later on the average among children from disadvantaged backgrounds than among children from high-SES families.

The implications of the findings of class difference for policy vary widely, depending on one's value preferences. One might, for example, value personal liberty and privacy as a primary purpose of the law, even for children. In that instance, the finding that there is marked variability in the rate at which children come to understand that a right means that they really *can* make a personal decision would imply the need for case-by-case determinations of competency to consent so that youngsters achieving such competence relatively early would in fact have their privacy protected. On the other hand, one might assert equality of opportunity as a primary value. In that instance, one might be offended by the possibility that white, upper-middle-class elementary-age children would enjoy more rights than their less-advantage peers, if a standard of competence is the determinant. Therefore, it might be argued that an age-graded *per se* rule should be used, with the threshold age for competence to consent set high enough that children from diverse backgrounds would be psychologically as well as legally competent to exercise rights. Alternatively, it might be argued that, given evidence that repeated experience in exercising choices might socialize a sense of entitlement (see Chapter 2, Chapter 11) the threshold age for per se competence to consent should be set low so that disadvantaged youngsters might have opportunities to acquire a sense of entitlement. The basic point is that researchers in the area should be careful to distinguish empirical findings from personal normative judgments in discussions of policy reform.

What Do We Know?

While the problems in application of developmental research to the law should not be minimized, it should be noted that, until recently, jurists might have been justified in ignoring developmental research on the ground that research directly on the facts at issue was generally lacking. As several of the contributors to this volume note, developmentalists have frequently avoided the study of children dealing with real-life problems in real-life situations. However, laboratory research on children's general problem-solving abilities and vulnerability to social influence might still be useful in developing guidelines for the consideration of children's competence to consent. In perhaps the most cogent review of this sort, Grisso and Vierling (1978) suggested that there were not grounds on the basis of competence alone to deprive minors aged 15 and older of rights to self-determination, at least in the area of treatment decisions. They suggested further that minors aged 11 to 14 might be thought to be in a transition period in the development of important cognitive and social abilities; they might under some circumstances be competent to consent.

Since Grisso and Vierling's review, there has begun to be a substantial literature on children's competence to consent, especially in the area of consent to treatment (see for reviews: Chapter 7; Melton 1981a; Weithorn, Chapter 12; 1982). Evidence seems to be accumulating that in fact children have the cognitive capacity to exercise rational choices at a significantly earlier age than the law assumes. Weithorn's (1980) work is exemplary. In comparison of 9- and 14-year-olds with adult groups, she found that 14-year-olds reasoned as maturely as the adult groups about hypothetical medical and mental-health treatment decisions. Similar findings have emerged in terms of decision making about abortions (Lewis, 1980) and participation in research (see Chapter 10; Keith-Spiegel & Maas, 1981).

Moreover, although the guidelines Grisso and Vierling proposed continue to make sense in terms of ages at which children demonstrate "knowing and intelligent" information processing, there is evidence to suggest that, at least for relatively uncomplicated, "routine" decisions, even elementary-school children's behavior may be quite reasonable when they are given the opportunity to exercise consent. Lewis's work (see Chapter 5) is exemplary. Similarly, in Weithorn's (1980) study, 9-year-olds tended to reach the same decisions as the older groups that used more skilled reasoning. It should be noted, however, that the actual behavior of 9-year-olds in a medical setting might be different from their statements of what should be done in response to laboratory hypotheticals.

Several caveats are in order as qualifiers to the conclusions stated here. The first is that there are still major areas that are unresearched. While not a "consent" *per se*, children's competence to make or participate in making decisions about their custody has not yet been systematically examined. Similarly, children's understanding of key concepts in particular kinds of decisions (*e.g.*, "risk" of experiments or treatments; the nature of psychological evaluation) has not yet been studied. As implicit in the discussion thus far, most of what we do know has come from children's responses to laboratory hypotheticals rather than from examination of their reasoning processes under real-life conditions and the stress that may accompany them. We also have little direct evidence concerning the validity of assumptions about the effects of children's autonomy on family integrity, although Feshbach and Tremper's (1981) recent study of adolescents' and parents' attitudes concerning the ages at which children should begin making various decisions for themselves suggests that typically adolescents and parents (particularly girls and their mothers) may be in substantial agreement on these points.

Second, the findings thus far may be limited to particular populations. The work of Weithorn, Feshbach and Tremper, and others has used upper-middle-class samples. As already discussed, there is evidence that there are social-class differences in acquisition of important concepts underlying the exercise of rights. Such differences may account for the one major discrepancy in findings thus far. Grisso's work (see Chapter 8) strongly indicates that 14-year-old delinquents are typically *not* as competent as adult defendants in making decsions about waiver of *Miranda* rights. There is, of course, an alternative explanation for the discrepancy. Socialization pressures are strong to "talk" when one has commited a misdeed; moreover, juvenile courts often may not be as adversarial in practice as they are in theory. Accordingly, mean ages of acquisition of competence to consent often may well be a function of expectations. As Bersoff (see Chapter 9) points out, there is evidence that children have the capacity to perform some cognitive operations earlier than they typically do. His suggestion that we need to look at "liberated children and liberating parents" is well taken.

Finally, consent does not occur in a vacuum. It relates not only to the child's capacity for utilizing information but to the nature and quantity of the information presented, the form of presentation, and the source of the information. While Saks (Chapter 3) has made an initial attempt to apply social psychological principles to an analysis of "voluntariness" of consent by children, there generally has been remarkably little attention given to the *procedures* by which consent is sought. Even detailed regulations on children's consent (*e.g.*, proposed federal regulations on children's participation in research) have not included guidelines for the procedures to be used in seeking children's consent. Such guidelines are also unavailable in professional ethical codes. Research is clearly needed in this area. What forms of presentation of information are most likely to facilitate children's processing of information? What effects do prior relationships with the presenter (*cf.* Grodin & Alpert, Chapter 6) have on the consent process? Can clinicians reliably and validly assess children's competence to consent, given various standards? How much time and effort does such assessment take?

A Final Note: The Need for Clear Policy

As the brief preceding review indicates, there has been a burgeoning of research in the last three years on children's competence to consent, probably in response to the increased activity of the Supreme Court in this area. At the same time, there are still some large gaps in the state of knowledge relevant to children's consent. As this knowledge base expands, it should provide the basis for development of a consistent, rational policy concerning children's self-determination. As Wadlington notes (see Chapter 4), even when one looks at the law on a particular topic of consent (*i.e.*, consent to treatment), the existing law is a patchwork of rules without clear underlying purpose. The inconsistencies in the Supreme Court's dicta in this area have already been discussed. It should be noted that state statutes in this area are at least as confused. Even when minors' consent is clarified, typically there has not been attention to related issues of confidentiality and financial liability (Melton, 1981b). When attention has been given, it again typically has occurred with inconsistent logic. For example, the state in which I currently reside (Nebraska) has a statute[58] that permits minors to seek diagnosis and treatment of venereal disease without parental consent or knowledge but then makes parents financially liable for the treatment. It is unclear how access to treatment without parental knowledge is to be maintained if parents may be billed for the minor's expenses. Nebraska law also requires drug and alcohol counselors to attempt to involve parents in the treatment of minors, but then permits counseling without parental consent, provided that the minor himself or herself is competent to consent.[59] There is no similar provision for counseling not related to substance abuse.

Part of the confusion no doubt derives form the fact that the purposes of consent are unclear where minors are concerned. For adults, consent requirements serve clear purposes: to support individual autonomy and to "humanize" the relationship between physician (or other authority) and patient through a mutually-derived contract. For children, there are additional purposes that cloud the issue, especially insofar as power of consent belongs to substitute decisionmakers (e.g., parents). As Mnookin (1978a) noted, such requirements have disparate purposes: to protect the child, to support parental autonomy, and so forth, "but at the root of the common law rule was the narrower notion that parents are legally responsible for the care and support of their children. Among other things, the parental consent requirement protects parents from having to pay for unwanted or unnecessary medical care, and from the possible financial consequences of supporting the child if unwanted treatment is unsuccessful" (p. 343). Moreover, even insofar as one takes a child-centered approach, there is disagreement. Some "child advocates" seek to "liberate" children, others to protect and "save" them (Mnookin, 1978b; Rogers & Wrightsman, 1978). Some of these varying views on children's consent are the result of value preferences that may be outside the purview of social-scientific investigation. To the extent, however, that such preferences are based on empirical assumptions, as they often are, it is hoped that the work presented in this volume—and the research and discussion we hope that it will stimulate—will contribute to the development of a thoughtful, coherent policy concerning the rights of children.

---

[58] Neb. Rev. Stat. § 71–1121 (Reissue 1976).
[59] Neb. Rev. Stat. § 71–5041 (Cum. Supp. 1980).

References

Arthur, L. G. Should children be as equal as people? *North Dakota Law Review*, 1968, *45*, 204–221.

Crouch, R. E. An essay on the critical and judicial receptions of *Beyond the best interests of the child*. *Family Law Quarterly*, 1979, *13*, 49–103

Feshbach, N. D., & Tremper, C. *Attitudes of parents and adolescents toward decision making by minors*. Paper presented at the meeting of the American Psychological Association, Los Angeles, September 1981.

Goldstein, J., Freud, A., & Solnit, A. J. *Beyond the best interests of the child*. New York: Free Press, 1973.

Grisso, T., & Vierling, L. Minors' consent to treatment: A developmental perspective. *Professional Psychology*, 1978, *9*, 412–427.

Haney, C. Psychology and legal change: On the limits of a factual jurisprudence. *Law and Human Behavior*, 1980, *4*, 147–199.

Katkin, D., Bullington, B., & Levine, M. Above and beyond the best interests of the child: An inquiry into the relationship between social science and social action. *Law and Society Review*, 1974, *8*, 669–687.

Keith-Spiegel, P., & Maas, T. *Consent to research: Are there developmental differences?* Paper presented at the meeting of the American Psychological Association, Los Angeles, September 1981.

Levine, M., & Levine, A. *A social history of helping services: Court, clinic, school, and community*. New York: Appleton-Century-Crofts, 1970.

Lewis, C. C. A comparison of minors' and adults' pregnancy decisions. *American Journal of Orthopsychiatry*, 1980, *50*, 446–453.

Melton, G. B. The psychologist's role in juvenile and family law. *Journal of Clinical Psychology*, 1978, *7*, 189–192.

Melton, G. B. Children's concept of their rights. *Journal of Clinical Psychology*, 1980, *9*, 186–190.

Melton, G. B. Children's participation in treatment planning: Psychological and legal issues. *Professional Psychology*, 1981, *12*, 246–252. (a)

Melton, G. B. Effects of a state law permitting minors to consent to psychotherapy. *Professional Psychology*, 1981, *12*, 647–654. (b)

Melton, G. B. Children's rights: Where are the children? *American Journal of Orthopsychiatry*, 1982, *52*, 530–538.

Mnookin, R. H. *Child, family, and state: Problems and materials on children and the law*. Boston: Little, Brown, 1978. (a)

Mnookin, R. H. Children's rights: Beyond kiddie libbers and child savers. *Journal of Clinical Child Psychology*, 1978, *7*, 163–167. (b)

Rogers, C. M., & Wrightsman, L. S. Attitudes toward children's rights: Nurturance or self-determination. *Journal of Social Issues*, 1978, *34*(2), 59–68.

Saks, M. J. *Jury verdicts: The role of group size and social decision rule*. Lexington, Mass.: Lexington Books, 1977.

Slobogin, C. "Voluntary" hospitalization of children: A look at the *Parham* decision. *Division of Child and Youth Services Newsletter*, 1980, *3*(2), 3–4.

Thibaut, J., & Walker, L. A theory of procedure. *California Law Review*, 1978, *66*, 541–566.

Weithorn, L. A. *Competency to render informed treatment decisions: A comparison of certain minors and adults*. Unpublished doctoral dissertation, University of Pittsburgh, 1980.

Weithorn, L. A. Developmental factors and competence to consent to treatment. In G. B. Melton (Ed.), *Legal reforms affecting child and youth services*. New York: Haworth, 1982.

PART I

Psychological Issues in Increasing Children's Self-Determination

CHAPTER 2

Decision Making by Children

Psychological Risks and Benefits[1]

GARY B. MELTON

As noted throughout this volume, the concept of competence to consent has obvious psychological dimensions. Psychologists presumably can inform the law (or at least *potentially* can inform the law) about children's capacity to weigh risks and benefits and to make "mature" decisions in various situations. Underlying the reason *why* there is interest in such developmental research are other less frequently discussed psychological concerns, which are the subject of this chapter. Specifically, a primary justification for denying children the power of consent is that they will be harmed by the consequences of making bad decisions.[2] According to such a theory, self-determination rights are denied

[1] Portions of this chapter appeared previously in an article (Melton, 1980b) in a special issue of *Educational Perspectives* on children's rights (R. Dubanoski & T. Morton, Eds.). Reprinted by permission of the issue editors.

[2] There are, of course, other rationales for depriving children of liberty. Under common law, children were viewed as virtual property of their parents (especially their fathers), because of the economic benefits then inherent in children's labor (see Derdeyn & Wadlington, 1977). Starting from such an assumption, permitting minors to make decisions without parental consent would be a breach of the liberty interests of the child's parents. While the notion of children as chattel may no longer be acceptable, the state remains reluctant to intrude on parental interests, as exemplified by the strong presumptions in favor of biological parents in custody disputes. There also remains a modern analogue of the property-interests argument. That is, minors generally are economically dependent. Fairness may dictate that their providers have a say in choices they make.

Also, it may be argued that, to the extent to which the family is a basic unit in the social order, the state has an interest in preserving the family. If allowing children to make decisions indepen-

GARY B. MELTON • Department of Psychology, University of Nebraska, Lincoln, Nebraska 68588.

incompetent minors because of the state's duty as *parens patriae* to protect dependent persons from harm.[3] Hence, competence becomes an issue as a corollary to the assumption of harm, including psychological harm, resulting from allowing minors to make decisions if they are incompetent to do so. It is not incompetence *per se* that laws restricting children's power of consent are designed to avoid. Rather, the purpose is to enhance children's welfare or at least to minimize harm.

Within such a framework, it is appropriate to move beyond a pure analysis of competence in formulating policies on the limits of decision making by children and to consider other psychological risks and benefits of increasing their autonomy. It is conceivable that children might be able to make to make a competent choice in some situations but that they would be adversely affected by facing the dilemmas involved. Conversely, it is possible that children's competence to make a reasoned choice is marginal but that there are positive benefits from the experience of decision making *per se* that outweigh the risks. One legal authority (Wald, 1976) astutely recognized the psychological questions surrounding increased power for children:

> I have often wondered when I was representing a child in a delinquency or neglect proceeding, what it meant for me to go up to a 9- or 10-year-old and say, "I'm your lawyer. Here I am; tell me what to do. What do you want me to do in representing you?" . . . What are the long-term consequences for a child of being told you have a lawyer, you have rights, and we are going to defend you in court? Does this give children a sense of self-esteem, of controlling their own fate, a sense of powerfulness? Or does it leave them bewildered? How are children different who have gone through such proceedings? (p. 5)

Although with less sophistication about developmental research than Wald has demonstrated, legal authorities sometimes have made explicit their concern about the effects of self-determination on children. Generally, this is expressed in terms of worries about inducing undue stress in children by allowing them (or indeed forcing them) to make major decisions, even if they are competent to do so. One interesting example came in a Pennsylvania case (*In re Green*[4]) in which a teenage boy with severe scoliosis was denied a spinal fusion

---

dently would disrupt the family, childen's liberty interests might be outweighed by the desire to protect the family as an instituion.

[3] A variant of this view that has achieved wide attention among both clinicians and lawyers is Goldstein, Freud, and Solnit's (1979) position, derived from psychoanalytic theory. According to Goldstein *et al.*, children's psychological development is dependent upon a sense of security which they believe requires apparently omnipotent parents (see pp. 8–9). Consequently, they perceive children's liberty interest to be those of their parents (p. 9, footnote).

[4] 448 Pa. 338, 292 A.2d 387 (1972) *See also* Globe Newspaper Co. v. Superior Court,—Mass.—,— n.21, 401 N.E.2d 360, 370 n.21 (1980) (statutory right of child-witness to closed testimony unwaivable because "it would place heavy responsibility on even a mature child"), *vacated per curiam,*

because of the religious objections to blood transfusions of his mother, a Jehovah's Witness. The majority of the Pennsylvania Supreme Court held that the case should be remanded to allow the boy himself to be heard on the issue.[5] However, in an impassioned dissent, Justice Eagen argued that the Court should have reached the decision on behalf of the boy without involving him:

> The mandate of the Court presents this youth with a most painful choice between the wishes of his parents and their religious convictions on the one hand, and his chance for a normal, healthy life on the other hand. We should not confront him with this dilemma.[6]

The situation in which Ricky Green was placed also raises questions about the voluntariness of his decision.[7] How should this opinion have been sought and how should it have been evaluated if the goals were both to generate a competent decision and to minimize the stress on him in making it? These questions are raised in a more mundane but perhaps no less dramatic way in other settings, most notably custody determinations, in which a youngster has to make a decision that may place him or her at odds with people important to and having authority over him or her (Benedek & Benedek, 1979; Siegel & Hurley, 1977).

It is such questions that will be examined in this chapter. Competence issues aside, what actually happens when autonomy of children is increased? It should be emphasized that this discussion consists primarily of speculations based on research that is tangential to the questions of effects of increased autonomy. There have been few systematic evaluations of natural settings in which children have been given a clear measure of autonomy. Those studies that are available sometimes have involved trivial increases in freedom. For example, a frequently cited model of self-government by adolescents is the Achievement Place program for delinquent boys (Fixsen, Phillips, & Wolf, 1973: Phillips, Phillips, Wolf, & Fixser, 1973). In that program, residents were found to prefer an elected manager to administer a behavior-modification points system. The specific task for which residents were given control was

---

101 S.Ct. 259 (1980), *remanded for consideration in light of* Richmond Newspapers, Inc. v. Virginia, 448 U.S. 555 (1980) (press has right of access to criminal trials), *aff'd on remand,*—Mass.—, 423 N.E.2d 773 (1981), *rev'd on other grounds,* —U.S.—, 50 U.S.L.W. 4759 (6/23/82).

[5] *See also* Wisconsin v. Yoder, 406 U.S. 205, 241 (1972) (Douglas, J., dissenting in part). In a case involving religious exemption of Amish 14-year-olds from compulsory school attendance, Douglas argued that the case should have been remanded to obtain the opinions of the youngsters themselves.

[6] 448 Pa. at 355, 292 A.2d at 395.

[7] "We are herein dealing with a young boy who has been crippled most of his life, consequently, he has been under the direct control and guidance of his parents for that time. To now presume that he could make an independent decision as to what is best for his welfare and health is not reasonable." 448 Pa. at 355, 292 A.2d at 395 (dissenting opinion).

maintenance of cleanliness of the bathroom, questionably significant self-government to say the least.

The Nature of Freedom

In considering the effects of autonomy, it is important to examine the psychological meaning of this concept. Behavior ultimately may be determined by external contingencies, and in that sense freedom and autonomy in fact may be illusory (Skinner, 1971). Nonetheless, there is ample evidence that the *experience* of autonomy, irrespective of its antecedents, is an important mediating variable and motivating force. Indeed, the social-psychological literature is filled with research on the effects of the experience of power and perceived control (see Perlmuter & Monty, 1979). Such heavily researched concepts as locus of control (Lefcourt, 1976; Rotter, 1966), personal causation (deCharms, 1968), and learned helplessness (Seligman, 1975) are obviously relevant.

Even from a behaviorist perspective, "freedom" can be conceptualized meaningfully (see, for example, Mahoney & Thoreson, 1974). The degree of personal autonomy one has can be defined as the breadth and efficacy of his or her behavioral repertoire: the range of alternative behaviors an individual possesses in a given situation. Also relevant is the strength of available counter-controls: the degree of control an individual has over his controllers. That is, does the individual have any power to reinforce or punish those who are in authority?

The significance of this psychological conceptualization of autonomy is that is implies that freedom and autonomy are not all-or-none variables. Even if children possess rights (whether legal or "natural") to self-determination in particular contexts, it does not necessarily follow that individual children will experience having real choices. As Saks points out in Chapter 2, authorities can structure the consent-seeking process using social-psychological principles (whether knowingly or not) so that refusal becomes highly improbable, even by adult clients.

In the present context, children (particularly young children) are unlikely to perceive themselves as having rights, regardless of the "objective" reality of their legal status (Melton, 1980a, in press). As Keith-Spiegel (1976) put it, children learn that they should "obey thy father and mother—and anyone else bigger than they are" (p. 56). Children's history of punishment for non-compliance is likely to render them disbelieving (at least initially) of gestures designed to increase their autonomy. The probability of experiencing rights as applicable to oneself decreases further if a child has experienced entitlement rarely. Thus, lower-class children tend to persist until early adolescence in an understanding of rights as those things that one can in fact concretely have to do without being punished. Development of concepts of rights as part of "fair" interpersonal relations occurs several years later on the average than among upper-middle-class children (Melton, 1980a, in press).

The implication of the discussion thus far is that changes in children's legal status may actually have minimal impact on the level of autonomy that they in fact experience. Such changes often may be psychological moot, particularly for children from disadvantaged groups. Furthermore, the freedoms that are introduced may not be salient to the children affected and consequently of little effect. For example, children rarely mention civil liberties as rights that they should have (Melton, in press). While such rights may simply be unimaginable to children cognitively bound by concrete reality, it also may be that they are unimportant to them. It is unsurprising that children are more concerned about "rights" with regard to family rules than due-process rights and freedom of expression. It is quite possible that most minors would not exercise civil liberties even if they were available to them. At present, for example, few juveniles charged with delinquent offenses assert their Fifth and Sixth Amendment rights (Grisso & Pomicter, 1977; see Chapter 6).

Additionally, legal rights may be practically moot simply because children do not have knowledge of them. A good example comes from the implementation of a Virginia statute[8] extending to minors the right to consent as adults to outpatient psychotherapy. In a survey of Virginia's community mental health centers approximately nine months after the statute went into effect (Melton, 1981b), almost all clinics reported that there had been no change in the rate of minors seeking treatment without parental consent. Essentially, they had not made an effort to inform youngsters in their catchment area of the availability of the service to them. An indication of the possible effect at least on adolescent behavior[9] of such information came from one center serving several rural counties that did make an effort to disseminate knowledge of the change in the law. That clinic reported that it had increased its total caseload by 3% (10 minors seeking treatment independently per month) by such an outreach effort.

One implication of the Virginia data is that, before one even reaches the problem of setting the situation so that rights to self-determination are psychologically meaningful, there is a problem of dissemination of knowledge about recognition of new legal rights for minors. Actually, in fact, the latter problem is really two problems: dissemination of the law to adults who are affected by the change and dissemination (often by these same adults whose interests may

---

[8] Va. Code Ann. § 54–325.2(d)(4) (Cum. Supp. 1979). *See* Cogbill (1979) for commentary on this statute.

[9] Forty percent of the community clinics were still unaware of the new statute (*see* note 8) more than a year after its passage.

be directly at stake) of the law to minors who might assert their rights. There are, of course, psychological problems involved in the efficacy (or lack of it) of these processes (see Havelock, 1969).

Psychological Effects

As indicated in the discussion thus far, specific measures to increase autonomy for children need not translate into increased psychological freedom and, therefore, need not have any significant behavioral or experiential effects (either positive or negative). However, such an experience is likely to be more probable if the new freedom does not occur in isolation. A child who has had a variety of experiences of active participation in decision making would be less likely to generalize an expectation for compliant behavior to a situation in which he or she really *can* make a free choice. Therefore, the discussion that follows will be concerned with effects of broad, affirmative attempts to design systems that feature minors' self-determination.

It should be noted in this regard that the effects of freedom may be differentiated on the basis of the degree of control that the child in fact has over a particular decision. Lacey (1979), for example, has suggested a dichotomy between control over agenda and control over outcome. For example, the slave driver, through his control of most of the reinforcements and punishments, may set the agenda of laying stones for a pyramid, but the slave may maintain control over whether the stones are laid from left to right or right to left. There also may be a third form of control, closely related to control over outcome: *i.e.*, "owning" the goals of others as one's own. DeCharms (1979) describes this form of control as a "realistic" form of "origin" behavior (perceiving oneself rather than external forces as the origin of one's behavior):

> In the idealistic-type origin story the hero may want a bicycle (goal) and sets out to earn money to get it (activity). In the realistic-type origin story, an authority (teacher or parent) or the context (a dangerous setting) specifies major goals. The hero accepts the inevitablility of the setting and the imposed goal (taking an exam), takes the ownership of the goal (to do well), and works for it. Note that in both cases, pawn alternatives are clear. The pawn dreams of a bicycle but does nothing to obtain it. The pawn reacts against the situation or authority in negative ways rather than either accepting the imposed goal of making his or her own. (pp.36–37)

While there is no research directly on point, control over agenda might be expected to have the most pronounced effects because it implicitly involves some control over the distribution of reinforcements. At the same time, however, to the extent to which the three types of control described form a hierarchy, it may be that efforts to teach children to assert freedoms and to do so responsibly might follow such a hierarchy. These hypotheses are worthy of investigation.

Legal Socialization

Perhaps the clearest possible effect of increased autonomy for children would be a facilitation of moral development and of legal socialization in particular (Levine & Tapp, 1977; Melton, 1982; Tapp & Levine, 1974; Torney, 1977). Both cognitive-developmental and social-learning theorists emphasize the significance of participation in role-taking in determining the rate of moral development (for example, Selman, 1976). Essentially, moral-development theorists conceptualize achievement of milestones in cognitive development as necessary but not sufficient for progress in moral development. For example, from a cognitive-developmental perspective, formal-operational thought (the capacity to think abstractly) is necessary for the attainment of principled moral reasoning. However, attainment of such reasoning based on abstract ethical principles also requires extensive experience with resolving ethical problems in social interaction and exposure to diverse, "higher" points of view (Kohlberg, 1976). From a more social perspective, development of such principled reasoning requires a pluralistic cultural setting in which there is an opportunity to attempt to integrate diverse expectations and to choose among a variety of means of access to social and economic goals (Garbarino & Bronfenbrenner, 1976).

The implication of these analyses is that a requisite of enhanced moral development is the opportunity for democratic resolution of social conflicts and for independent moral decision making by children. For example, in his classic text on moral development, Piaget (1932/1965) advocated schools based on "self-government" and interpersonal cooperation. From Piaget's perspective, schools based on a primary value of respect for authority are unlikely to facilitate moral development on an individual level. Rather, such disciplinary systems confirm the young child's egocentric view of morality as the avoidance of punishment for violation of rules established by authority.

On a moral social level, the child's acquistion of democratic ideals is postponed by education within authoritarian systems:

> The essence of democracy resides in its attitude toward law as a product of the collective will, and not as something emanating from a transcendent will or from the authority established by divine right. It is therefore the essence of democracy to replace the unilateral respect of authority by the mutual respect of autonomous wills. (Piaget, 1932/1965, pp. 362–363)

Expressed more concretely, it is unsurprising that children do not acquire a sense of personal involvement in a democratic political system when the student "government's" authority is limited to choosing the band for the dance in the school gym. Conversely, political socialization is likely to be enhanced if freedom of the press is not simply taught as an empty platitude but is *experienced* by the school newspaper staff. "Due process" is much more meaningful when actively applied to school disciplinary procedures.

The long-term political cost of a system in which socialization is based on an experience of lack of participation and of a "law-and-order" morality is a populance who do not apply democratic principles to concrete situations. There is ample evidence that, while most Americans support civil liberties in the abstract, large percentages of American adults would not extend freedom of speech to unpopular groups or due-process rights to criminal defendants (Prothro & Grigg, 1960; see studies reported in Zalkind, 1975). While this lack of tolerance is in itself disturbing, one of the related issues is that many citizens probably do not exercise their rights because they neither perceive themselves as really having rights nor understand the application of rights. Of concern here is that these views are most common in disadvantaged groups who have little experience in diverse social role-taking (Note, 1973; Williams & Hall, 1972; Zellman, 1975). Perhaps an initial step toward these groups' use of their rights under the law as a "mobility belt" (Levine & Tapp, 1977) is the development of socialization systems that foster the experience of autonomy.[10]

Reactance and Power

There may be immediate affective and behavioral consequences of increasing freedom for children. Perhaps most directly relevant here is reactance theory (J. Brehm, 1966; Wicklund, 1974). Briefly, reactance theory predicts that, when an established or expected behavioral freedom is eliminated or threatened with elimination, reactance is aroused and the individual is motivated to restore the freedom. There are several ways in which this motivation can be expressed behaviorally. Most obviously, the individual can act directly to restore the freedom. The classic example of this means of expression of reactance is the phenomenon of "reverse psychology." That is, if told *not* to make a particular choice, the individual will in fact do so. Secondly, there can be an indirect attempt to restore freedom, such as disobedience of the next request made. Third, the individual may not take action to restore freedom, but

---

[10] There are also shorter-range analogous issues in juveniles' exercise of their rights that are currently available to them. Arguably, one of the factors involved in many juveniles' inability to apply their rights in delinquency proceedings is again the lack of experience that children usually have in the exercise of rights. *See* the discussion by Grisso in Chapter 8.

(if not) reactance will result in a perception of increased attractiveness of the lost freedom.

Reactance motivation has been observed experimentally in children as young as two years old (S. Brehm & Weinraub, 1977).[11] Given the relevance of this social-psychological concept to children, it might be predicted that increased freedom would reduce reactance. Correspondingly, one might expect a reduction in oppositional behavior which was principally motivated by desire to assert freedom of choice.

However, such predictions are overly simple. There are several factors that affect the strength of reactance, one of which is the importance of the threatened freedom. One of the considerations in making predictions about reactance in children is that, as discussed previously, they may not feel that they have freedom initially. Obviously, one cannot restore a freedom that was not there. Studies using first- and fifth-grade children, unlike earlier research with college students (Worchel & J. Brehm, 1971), have shown that direct attempts at social influence by adults produce compliance. Only when another adult creates or restores the freedom does the direct influence produce observable reactance behavior (S. Brehm, 1977).[12]

The initial predictions of decreased reactance with increased freedom may be valid, however, for older children and adolescents, who are usually provided with more opportunites for independent behavior than younger children. At least one study corroborates this hypothesis. Wicklund and J. Brehm (1967; reported in Wicklund, 1974) informed junior-high students that they would be having an assembly with a speaker who would advocate lowering the voting age from 21 to 18. Four days later, the students were told that the assembly had been canceled because a school administrator objected to their hearing the speech. As predicted by reactance theory, the majority of students in the "Censorship" condition expressed more positive attitudes toward lowering the voting age. Presumably the freedom to hear diverse opinions was in fact salient to the junior-high students.

In addition to reactance, other social-psychological constructs may be useful in explaining or predicting responses of children to increased freedom. The best researched of these concepts is probably locus of control (Lefcourt, 1976; Rotter, 1966), the degree to which an individual perceives reinforcement as being under his or her control. Although there is probably some relationship, it is important to note that there is not a direct parallel between increased opportunity for autonomous decision making and locus of control and the

---

[11] Among two-year-olds there was a marked sex difference. Boys preferred objects behind barriers (as predicted by reactance theory), whereas girls preferred accessible toys. One possible explanation is that girls may not perceive themselves free to choose initially.

[12] Freedom was restored by another adult's saying, "Wait a minute, I think you should choose whichever one you want."

relationship may be a weak one. To reiterate, locus of control involves perceived control over *reinforcements*. It is conceivable that a youngster might have control over decision making but still not feel that his behavior had systematic consequences. In other words, a child might believe that his being rewarded or punished was not contingent on the quality of decision that he made.

To the extent to which increased autonomy implies an increase in control over contingencies of reinforcement, an increase in internal locus of control would be expected, however. Such an increase was reported in an evaluation of an "Open Campus" high school in northwestern Georgia (Rosen, 1977). Students were given the same freedoms that they would have if they were attending a community college. Locus of control of the students became more internal, especially for blacks, who arguably had less previous experience of control.

The concept of "personal causation" (deCharms, 1968) may be more promising than locus of control as an outcome variable in studies of effects of increased autonomy. While the concepts are superficially similar, reported correlations between personal causation and locus of control are quite low (deCharms, 1979). The difference may simply be one of measurement techniques. Locus of control is typically measured by degree of agreement with statements of belief about internal or external causation. On the other hand, personal causation is typically measured by projective stories in which the outcome measure concerns the degree to which the hero is involved in goal setting and planful behavior. More conceptually, deCharms understands the difference as being between perception and experience. Personal causation refers to the global experience of being in control: a dimension ranging from feeling that one is the Origin of his or her own behavior to feeling that one is a Pawn, pushed around by the environment. Of interest in the present context are the efforts of deCharms and his associates (deCharms, 1976; Koenigs, Fiedler & deCharms, 1977) to develop school settings that are based on increasing children's sense of themselves as Origins. Through teacher training, deCharms *et. al.* have helped teachers to increase the "origin climate" in their classroom, to increase fifth- to eighth-grade students' sense of personal control and responsibility. Such attempts to vest control in the students result in increased academic achievement as well as increased Origin scores. Long-term effects have also been demonstrated: students who participated in the program were more likely to graduate from high school eventually.

Performance

As suggested by the deCharms findings, there is reason to believe that increased autonomy would increase children's performance in those spheres in which they had the opportunity to make choices. For example, the affirmitive act of making a choice might induce cognitive dissonance if a child did not follow through on an educational or treatment program to which he or she had consented. Choice results in increased perceived value of the chosen object or event (J. Brehm, 1956). Consequently, the freedom to decide might increase the child's motivation to perform well in the program. Furthermore, to the extent to which such programs are in themselves stressful, participation in the decision-making process might serve as an "innoculation" (Meichenbaum, 1977) against the stress to follow and increase the probability of the child's sustained involvement in the program. In this regard, Holmes and Urie (1975) found that a preparatory interview to establish and discuss expectations for psychotherapy reduced premature terminations among children aged 6 to 12.

The significance of choice as a factor in performance has been examined most extensively in a series of studies by Brigham (1979) involving elementary-school and preschool children. In these studies, response rate in working arithmetic problems was markedly accelerated when the children had had the opportunity to choose among enjoyable math games as reinforcers (compared with teacher-selection of the consequence). Choice itself was also demonstrated to be a positive reinforcer. That is, response rate was further increased if the child had the opportunity to choose whether the child or the teacher would select the consequences. Response rate was also accelerated, although not to a statistically significant extent, by the opportunity to set goals within the contingencies. Even though the student-set goals were substantially the same as had been set by the teacher, most children preferred to set the goals themselves. In short, Brigham's results suggest that children like to make choices and that they will be more highly motivated to perform well if they are allowed to do so.

Privacy

Another factor in the calculus of risks and benefits of decision making by children is the effects of maintenance of privacy. Discussion of this factor is complicated by the fact that privacy has several different dimensions, both psychologically and legally. There are at least three identifiable privacy interests: protection from bodily intrusion, including arguably protection from intrusion into the privacy of one's thoughts; management of access to one's personal space (i.e., physical space at least psycholgically under one's control); management of access to information about oneself.[13] While the content of the claim to privacy in each of these broad types is different, the ethical basis for

---

[13] A somewhat different conceptualization of the behavioral dimensions of privacy is described in Laufer and Wolfe (1977). For discussion of the legal parameters of privacy, including the relevance of psychology to these determinations, see Levin and Askin (1977).

their assertion is essentially the same. Privacy is grounded in respect for personal dignity, for the integrity of the self. Obviously, the relevance of the concept then depends at least in part on whether one views minors as "persons" owed such respect. Starting from such an assumption, it follows that privacy of mature minors should be protected where possible. This section is concerned with the psychological implications of such a philosophical stance.[14]

The best researched form of privacy is management of access to personal space. Developmental sequences have been observed in the degree of physical privacy that children have and expect (Parke & Swann, 1979; Wolfe, 1979). While this line of research tells us something about day-to-day parent-child relations and also has some legal relevance.[15] it is only tangentially relevant to a consideration of the risks and benefits of children's decision making. Consequently, this brief discussion of privacy in childhood will center on protection from bodily intrusion and on management of access to information.

Privacy has been most clearly explicated as a basic societal value in the Supreme Court's decisions concerning the privacy of sexual behavior. Thus, a constitutional right to privacy was first articulated in cases involving access to contraceptives[16] and reiterated in the Court's celebrated opinion overturning state statutes proscribing abortion.[17] This right has been variously held to emanate from the penumbras of the Bill of Rights,[18] the Ninth Amendment,[19] or the concept of personal liberty embedded in the Fourteenth Amendment.[20] The right to privacy, at least insofar as sexual matters are concerned, has been extended to mature minors in a series of opinions concerning minors' access to abortions and contraceptives.[21] While the limits of the right to privacy have not

---

[14] Another philosophical conflict here concerns the relative weight of individual privacy and family privacy. *Compare* Goldstein, Freud, and Solnit (1979) with Melton (1982). *See also* Feshbach & Feshbach (1978) (overemphasis on family privacy interferes with societal goal of child protection and nuturance)

[15] Such research is relevant to cases involving the legality of searches and seizures, particularly concerning the issue of the breadth of reasonable expectation of privacy under the Fourth Amendment. Special problems arise when minors give access to their home to police officers. Does control over such access actually belong to children in a household? At what age? *See* Weinreb (1974, p. 60). Similar problems arise when minors' own personal space is invaded, as in searches of school lockers. Under what circumstances do youngsters in fact have a reasonable expectation of privacy? What are the psychological norms in this regard?

[16] Eisenstadt v. Baird, 405 U.S. 438 (1972); Griswold v. Connecticut, 381 U.S. 479 (1965).

[17] Roe v. Wade, 410 U.S. 113 (1973).

[18] Griswold v. Connecticut, 381 U.S. 479, 484–485.

[19] *Id.* at 486 (Goldberg, J., concurring).

[20] "Liberty" under the Fourteenth Amendment includes "a right of personal privacy, or a guarantee of certain areas of zones of privacy." Roe v. Wade, 410 U.S. at 152.

[21] Bellotti v. Baird II, 443 U.S. 622 (1979); Carey v. Population Services International, 431 U.S. 678 1977); Bellotti v. Baird I, 438 U.S. 132 (1976); Planned Parenthood of Central Missouri v. Danforth, 438 U.S. 52 (1976).

been made clear, they are more limited for minors than for adults.[22] In theory, though, the right of personal privacy includes "the interest in independence in making certain kinds of decisions."[23] For minors, this interest may be construed as applying only to bodily privacy in sexual matters and then only if the minor is mature. The Supreme Court has held, for example, that minors do not have a constitutional right to privacy in decisions concerning mental hospital admissions.[24] While the latter holding is difficult to reconcile with the abortion decisions[25] (see Annas, 1979), it does suggest that privacy as protection from intrusion in personal matters concerning one's body and mind may be quite limited. Given these limitations, the behavioral effects of the right to bodily privacy might be expected to be more or less limited to increased demand for contraceptives and abortions and perhaps increased frequency of sexual intercourse among adolescents, specific but certainly not trivial effects.

More general effects might be expected to result from recognition of rights to control of information about oneself (*e.g.*, medical, psychiatric, and educational records), particularly among adolescents. Concepts of privacy become more complex as children reach adolescence; information management espe-

---

[22] Carey v. Population Services International, 431 U.S. 678, 693, n. 15.

[23] Whalen v. Roe, 429 U.S. 589, 599–600 (1977).

[24] Parham v. J. L. & J. R., 442 U.S. 584 (1979); Secretary of Public Welfare v. Institutionalized Juveniles, 442 U.S. 640 (1979)

[25] *Compare* the following quotes from *Planned Parenthood* and *Parham*:

> One suggested interest [in conditioning abortions by minors on parental consent] is the safeguarding of the family unit and of parental authority. . . . It is difficult, however, to conclude that providing a parent with absolute power to overrule a determination, made by the physician and his minor patient, to terminate the patient's pregancy will serve to strengthen the family unit. Neither is it likely that such veto power will enhance parental authority or control where the minor and the nonconsenting parent are so fundamentally in conflict and the very existence of the pregnancy already has fractured the family structure. (Planned Parenthood, 438 U.S. at 75.)

> Our jurisprudence historically has reflected Western Civilization concepts of the family as a unit with broad parental authority over minor children. Our cases have consistently followed that course; our constitutional system long ago rejected any notion that a child is "the mere creature of the state" and, on the contrary, asserted that parents generally "have the right, coupled with the high duty, to recognize and prepare their [children] for additional obligations." . . . Surely, this includes a "high duty" to recognize symptoms of illness and to seek and follow medical advice. The law's concept of the family rests on a presumption that parents possess what a child lacks in maturity, experience, and capacity for judgment required for making life's difficult decisions. More important, historically it has recognized that natural bonds of affection lead parents to act in the best interests of their children. . . .
> Simply because the decision of a parent is not agreeable to a child or becauae it involves risks does not automatically transfer power to make that decision from the parents to some agency or officer of the state. The same characterizations can be made for a tonsillectomy, appendectomy or other medical procedure. Most children, even in adolescence, simply are not able to make sound judgments concerning many decisions, including their need for medical care or treatment. Parents can and must make those judgments. (Parham, 442 U.S. at 602–603)

cially develops new importance (Wolfe, 1979). Furthermore, the nature of reported invasions of privacy shifts to disruptions of information management:

> Our respondents' descriptions of invasion experiences also change with age, with the interruption of activities being cited less often and the inability to manage information cited more often as the child enters adolescence. More of the adolescents, as compared to children 12 and younger, describe being questioned about their behavior and/or having someone find out something they did not want known. And compared to younger children, when adolescents describe these invasion experiences, the information they have not been able to manage is more likely to be related to sex, smoking, and drugs—all "deviant" activities. (Wolfe, 1979, p. 199)

Independent access to services—without a requirement of parental notice—might increase adolescents' use of medical and psychological services when they become involved in such "deviant' activities." State statutes allowing independent access to treatment for pregnancy, drug abuse, and emotional disorders are founded in part on a belief that adolescents would not seek treatment for these conditions without a guarantee of privacy. By adolescents' self-report at least, there are some data supporting such a premise (Melton, 1978, 1981a).

Wolfe (1979) has hypothesized more generalized personality effects of maintenance of privacy. She and her colleagues have argued that experiences of privacy are important in development of sense of self. Specifically, in the present context, successful information management by adolescents might be important in keeping a close relationship with peers beyond the limits of the family and in developing intimacy and sense of oneself as an independent person. One might add that respect for information managment might increase sense of oneself as an independent person. One might add that respect for information management might increase sense of interpersonal trust and self-esteem (as a respected person). While these possible personality effects are important ones, they are at this point essentially intuitive hypotheses based to a large extent on clinical theory. They might be researched through interventions designed to increase privacy of thought in home or school situations.

Some Questions

Brigham (1979) added an important caution to interpretation of the results of his studies of effects of choice:

> [I]t must be noted that choice is not an unlimited blessing. All our research has been conducted in fairly structured situations where the response alternatives were positive and where individuals were limited in the opportunity to make choices that might have long-term detrimental effects on their lives. This obviously is not the case in every situation where the individual has a choice of multiple response alternatives. (pp. 139–140)

Although there is reason to believe that increased autonomy for children would have a number of positive psychological effects,[26] it is probable that these variables would interact with task difficulty and age. To the extent to which children are not predisposed to make "good" decisions in difficult situations, the negative consequences of these decisions might actually increase the children's discomfort. Furthermore, where the choice is between aversive events or one of such complexity that is an impossible choice, the necessity of making a choice itself may be quite anxiety-provoking. It is well established in personality research that ambiguity fosters anxiety (Dibner, 1958). Complex choices are likely to present particularly ambiguous stimulus-situations to children who do not have the cognitive structures available to sort out the options but who are sufficiently sociocentric to be aware of their lack of cognitive capacity. Moreover, "little people's" assertion of rights is likely to arouse reactance in adults who are insecure in their own power (Melton, in press). As such, attempts to increase children's autonomy without first changing attitudes and behavior of their caretakers may well be a "set-up" which will result in punitive response for expressions of autonomy. Additionally, there may be individual differences, to date unexplored, in response to increased autonomy. Quite possibly, even some "normal" children (perhaps those who function better with more "structure") dislike having choices and become anxious in response to autonomy.

In order to identify factors predicting these potential negative effects as well as to test other hypotheses suggested in this Chapter, there is a need for field research evaluating systematic attempts to increase children's autonomy. There are now many programs that include some measure of youth autonomy,[27] but these programs have seldom been evaluated.

One of the few relevant evaluation studies was an examination of the effects of allowing elementary-school children access to health care on their own initiative through the school nurse (Lewis, Lewis, Lorimer, & Palmer, 1977).[28] Lewis et al. related use-patterns to variables which had been found to be relevant to adults' use of the health-care system (e.g., class, sex, locus of

---

[26] There is ample evidence from social-psychological research with adults to indicate that control— or at least *perceived* control—is related to life-satisfaction and both psychological and physical health. *See, e.g.*, reviews in Perlmuter & Monty (1979), especially the chapter by Strickland.

There may be other more subtle positive effects. A disruptant's having had an opportunity to have a say in the resolution of a dispute—and to have had some control over the outcome— increases perception of fairness of the proceeding. It is possible that children's involvement in decision making would result in their perceiving greater justice in institutions of which they are a part (Melton & Lind, 1982).

[27] The National Commission on Resources for Youth operates a clearinghouse that contains descriptions of more that 1,500 projects involving youth participation (not necessarily youth control). Information is available from the Commission at 36 West 44th Street, New York, New York 10036.

[28] This research is described in detail in Chapter 5.

control, perceived vulnerability, etc.). They also studied effects of the program on health-related beliefs, actual use rates, etc. Briefly, Lewis *et al.* found that variables affecting utilization were essentially the same as those predicting adult health-care use (for example, greater use by females). Furthermore, the program was effective in reducing perceived severity of health problems and increasing the value placed on self-care. Actual patterns of utilization of health care were not changed, however. Lewis *et al.* concluded that "the lack of behavioral change should not be a surprise, since the children are still immersed in a real-world system that removes them from a decision-making role with regard to their own health care" (p. 506).

Lewis *et al.*'s study is instructive in at least two ways. First, it is indicative of the kind of research that needs to be done: conceptually based evaluations of attempts to increase children's autonomy in natural settings. Second, the results of this study lend emphasis to the point that a sense of autonomy may not be easily engendered when most of the children's experiences indicate that they have very little choice. Isolated attempts to increase autonomy are likely to have effects that are at most situation-specific, although the degree of generalizability of various experiences of autonomy has not yet been examined empirically. It might be expected that basic control over one's fate (*i.e.*, control over outcome) in a particular sphere would have the broadest effect.

A Practical Irony

As a final note, it is worthwhile to consider the irony that it will be difficult to conduct program evaluations of the kind advocated here as long as decision-making authority and responsibility is vested by statute and custom in adult caretakers. For example, even if a school principal is sympathetic to providing children more autonomy (or at least testing the effects of such measures), he or she may find a divestiture of authority too risky and perhaps a dereliction of duty. Thus, it may not be possible to evaluate the effects of children's being given power of consent before there is actually significant legal change.

One alternative obviously is to create settings in which minors voluntarily (*i.e.*, with substitute consent by their parents) enter model programs in which they will be allowed to make many or all decisions for themselves. There are two problems with such a strategy. The first and less significant is the irony that the final decision in such a situation will be that of the parent and that the "autonomy" of the youngster may therefore be quite circumscribed. This problem may be resolved more or less satisfactorily by requiring consent from the child as well and by documenting as carefully as possible the range of choices in fact available within the program. The second problem perhaps represents a more serious methodological hurdle. That is, parents who choose to send their children to alternative programs are possibly quite unrepresentative of parents generally. Therefore, the sample of participants is likely to be skewed significantly, and it may be difficult to obtain a comparable control group, through either matching or random assignment.

Given these difficulties in establishing and evaluating programs allowing some measure of autonomy to children, the best alternative may be to evaluate increasingly greater levels of autonomy, beginning, for example, with mere participation by the child in making relatively routine and minor decisions in natural settings. For example, the focus might be initially on effects of participation in decision making about a particular treatment rather than of a broader system of health care in which minors have considerable autonomy. Such a strategy also is probably the strongest ethically, given that we really do not know at this point the range of potential harm, if any, of permitting children to make decisions.

At the same time, however, until more evaluation research is completed, there seems to be ample reason for practitioners to support, at a minimum, children's participation in planning their educational and treatment programs (see Melton, 1981a) even if not full power of consent. The available research and theory suggest that there are positive psychological effects of such participation, at least in relatively routine decisions. As noted previously in the discussion of privacy, in making such a recommendation I am also starting from value judgments that children fully qualify as "persons" ethically and legally and that they have discernibly separate interest that should be examined and respected where reasonable. Given these assumptions, it makes sense to support children's autonomy insofar as harm is not done and certainly insofar as substantial benefits accrue.

References

Annas, G. Law and the life sciences: Parents, children, and the Supreme Court. *Hastings Center Report*, October 1979, *9*, 21–41.

Benedek, R. B., & Benedek, E. P. The child's preference in custody disputes. *American Journal of Family Therapy*, 1979, *7* 37–43.

Brehm, J. W. Post-decision changes in the desirability of alternatives. *Journal of Abnormal and Social Psychology*, 1956, *52*, 384–389.

Brehm, J. W. *A theory of psychological reactance*. New York: Academic Press, 1966.

Brehm, S. S. The effect of adult influence on children's preferences: Compliance versus opposition. *Journal of Abnormal Child Psychology*, 1977, *5*, 31–41.

Brehm, S. S., & Weinraub, M. Physical barriers and psychological reactance: 2-year-old's responses to threats to freedom. *Journal of Personality and Social Psychology*, 1977, *35*, 830–836.

Brigham, T. A. Some effects of choice on academic performance. In L. C. Perlmuter & R. A. Monty (Eds.), *Choice and perceived control*. Hillsdale, N. J.: Lawrence Erlbaum, 1979.

Cogbill, J. V. III. Outpatient mental health services: A minor's right. *University of Richmond Law Review*, 1979, *13*, 915–926.

deCharms, R. *Personal causation: The internal affective determinants of behavior*. New York: Academic Press, 1968.

deCharms, R. *Enhancing motivation: Change in the classroom*. New York: Irvington, 1976.

deCharms, R. Personal causation and perceived control. In L. C. Perlmuter & R. A. Monty (Eds.), *Choice and perceived control*. Hillsdale, N. J.: Lawrence Erlbaum, 1979.

Derdeyn, A. P., & Wadlington, W. J., III. Adoption: The rights of parents versus the best interests of their children. *Journal of the American Academy of Child Psychiatry*, 1977, *16*, 238–255.

Dibner, A. S. Ambiguity and anxiety. *Journal of Abnormal and Social Psychology*, 1958, *56*, 165–174.

Feshbach, N. D., & Feshbach, S. Child advocacy and family privacy. *Journal of Social Issues*, 1978, *34*(2), 168–178.

Fixsen, D. L., Phillips, E. L., & Wolf, M. M. Achievement place: Experiments in self-government with delinquents. *Journal of Applied Behavior Analysis*. 1973, *6*, 31–47.

Garbarino, J. The price of privacy: An analysis of the social dynamics of child abuse. *Child Welfare*, 1977, *56*, 565–575.

Garbarino, J., & Bronfenbrenner, U. The socialization of moral judgment and behavior in cross-cultural perspective. In T. Lickona (Ed.), *Moral development and behavior: Theory, research, and social issues*. New York: Holt, Rinehart & Winston, 1976.

Goldstein, J., Freud, A., & Solnit, A. S. *Before the best interests of the child*. New York: Free Press, 1979.

Grisso, T., & Pomicter, C. Interrogation of juveniles. An empirical study of procedures, safeguards, and rights waiver. *Law and Human Behavior*, 1977, *1*, 321–342.

Havelock, R. G. *Planning for innovation through dissemination and utilization of knowledge*. Ann Arbor, Mich.: Center for Research on Utilization of Knowledge, Institute for Social Research, 1969.

Holmes, D. S., & Urie, R. G. Effects of preparing children for psychotherapy. *Journal of Consulting and Clinical Psychology*, 1975, *43*, 311–318.

Keith-Spiegel, P. Children's rights as participants in reseach. In G. P. Koocher (Ed.), *Children's rights and the mental health professions*. New York: Wiley, 1976.

Koenigs, S. S., Fiedler, M. L., & deCharms, R. Teacher beliefs, classroom interaction, and personal causation. *Journal of Applied Social Psychology*, 1977, *7*, 95–114.

Kohlberg, L. Moral stages and moralization: The cognitive-developmental approach. In T. Lickona (Ed.), *Moral development and behavior: Theory, research, and social issues*. New York: Holt, Rinehart & Winston, 1976.

Lacey, H. M. Control, perceived control, and the methodological role of cognitive constructs. In L. C. Perlmuter & R. A. Monty (Eds.), *Choice and perceived control*. Hillsdale, N. J.: Lawrence Erlbaum, 1979.

Laufer, R. S., & Wolfe, M. Privacy as a concept and a social issue: A multidimensional developmental theory. *Journal of Social Issues*, 1977, *33*(3), 22–42.

Lefcourt, H. M. *Locus of control*. Hillsdale, N. J.: Lawrence Erlbaum, 1976.

Levin, H. A., & Askin, F. Privacy in the courts: Law and social reality. *Journal of Social Issues*, 1978, *33*(3), 138–1532.

Levine, F. J., & Tapp, J. L. The dialectic of legal socialization in community and school. In J. L. Tapp & F. J. Levine (Eds.), *Law, justice, and the individual in society*. New York: Holt, Rinehart & Winston, 1977.

Lewis, C. E., Lewis, M. A., Lorimer, A., & Palmer, P. P. Child-initiated care: The use of school nursing services by children in an "adult-free" system. *Pediatrics*, 1977, *60*, 499–507.

Mahoney, M. H., & Thoreson, C. E. *Self-control: Power to the person*. Monterey, Calif.: Brooks/Cole, 1974.

Meichenbaum, D. *Cognitive-behavior modification: An integrative approach*. New York: Plenum Press, 1977.

Melton, G. B. Children's right to treatment. *Journal of Clinical Child Psychology*, 1978, *7*, 200–202.

Melton, G. B. Children's concepts of their rights. *Journal of Clinical Child Psychology*, 1980, *9* 186–190. (a)

Melton, G. B. Psychological effects: Increased autonomy on children. *Educational Perspectives*, 1980, *19*(4), 10–14. (b)

Melton, G. B. Children's participation in treatment planning: Psychological legal issues. *Professinal Psychology*, 1981, *12*, 246–252. (a)

Melton, G. B. Effects of a state law permitting minors to consent to psychotherapy. *Professional Psychology*, 1981, *12*, 647–654. (b)

Melton, G. B. Teaching children about their rights. In J. S. Henning (Ed.), *The rights of children: Legal and psychological perspectives*. Springfield, Ill.: Charles C Thomas, 1982.

Melton, G. B. Children's rights: Where are the children? *American Journal of Orthopsychiatry*, 1982, *52*, 530–538.

Melton, G. B. *Child advocacy: Psychological issues and interventions*. New York: Plenum Press, in press.

Melton, G. B., & Lind, E. A. Procedural justice in family court: Does the adversary model make sense? In G. B. Melton (Ed.), *Legal reforms affecting child and youth services*. New York: Haworth, 1982.

Note. Legal knowledge of Michigan citizens. *Michigan Law Review*, 1973, *71*, 1463–1486.

Parke, R. D., & Swann, D. B. Children's privacy in the home: Developmental, ecological and child-rearing determinants. *Environment and Behavior*, 1979, *11*, 84–104.

Perlmuter, L. C., & Monty, R. A. *Choice and perceived control*. Hillsdale, N. J.: Lawrence Erlbaum, 1979.

Phillips, E. L., Phillips, E. A., Wolf, M. M., & Fixsen, D. L. Achievement place: development of the elected manager sytem. *Journal of Applied Behavior Analysis*, 1973, *6*, 541–561.

Piaget, J. *The moral judgment of the child*. New York: Free Press, 1965. (Originally published, 1932.)

Prothro, J. W., & Grigg, C. W. Fundamental principles of democracy: Bases of agreement and disagreement. *Journal of Politics*, 1969, *22*, 276–294.

Rosen, C. E. The impact of an Open Campus program upon high school student's sense of control over their environment. *Psychology in the Schools*, 1977, *14*, 216–219.

Rotter, J. B. Generalized expectancies for internal versus external control of reinforcement. *Psychological Monographs*, 1966, *80* (1, Whole No. 609).

Seligman, M. E. P. *Helplessness: On depression, development, and death*. San Francisco: Freeman, 1975.

Selman, R. L. Social-cognitive understanding: A guide to educational and clinical practice. In T. Lickona (Ed.), *Moral development and behavior: Theory, research and social issues*. New York: Holt, Rinehart & Winston, 1976.

Siegel, D. M., & Hurley, S. The role of the child's preference in custody proceedings. *Family Law Quarterly*, 1977, *11*, 1–58.

Skinner, B. F. *Beyond freedom and dignity*. New York: Bantam, 1971.

Tapp, J. L., & Levine, F. J. Legal socialization: Strategies for an ethical legality. *Stanford Law Review*, 1974, *27*, 1–72.

Torney, J. V. Socialization of attitudes toward the legal system. In J. L. Tapp & F. J. Levine (Eds.), *Law, justice, and the individual in society: Psychological and legal issues*. New York: Holt, Rinehart & Winston, 1977.

Wald, M. S. Legal policies affecting children: A lawyer's request for aid. *Child Development*, 1976, *47*, 1–5.

Weinreb, L. L. Generalities of the Fourth Amnendment. *University of Chicago Law Review*, 1974, *42*, 47–85.

Wicklund, R. A. *Freedom and reactance*. Hillsdale, N. J.: Lawrence Erlbaum, 1974.

Williams, M., & Hall, J. Knowledge of the law in Texas: Socio-economic and ethnic differences. *Law and Society Review*, 1972, *7*, 99–118.

Wolfe, M. Childhood and privacy. In I. Altman & J. F. Wohlwill (Eds.), *Human behavior and environment: Advances in theory and research* (Vol. 3). New York: Plenum Press, 1979.

Worchel, S., & Brehm, J. W. Direct and implied social restoration of freedom. *Journal of Personality and Social Psychology*, 1971, *18*, 294–304.

Zalkind, S. S. (Ed.). Civil liberties. Issue of *Journal of Social Issues*, 1975, *31*(2).

Zellman, G. L. Antidemocratic beliefs: A survey and some explanations. *Journal of Social Issues*, 1975, *31*(2), 31–54.

Chapter 3

Social Psychological Perspectives on the Problem of Consent

MICHAEL J. SAKS

The chapters in this volume approach the problem of consent from a variety of perspectives. Some view it as a problem of understanding principles of child development, of clinical assessment, or patient management. Others attend to specific programs to study or enhance children's decision making or examine consent as a moral-ethical-legal problem: what rights and duties shall govern seeking and granting consent; how shall the power and responsibility to decide be distributed? The present chapter brings yet another set of concerns, methods, and substantive knowledge to this interdisciplinary effort to cope with the problem of consent. It begins by introducing readers to social psychology, then discusses the ways in which this subfield may aid physicians, lawyers, and mental health professionals in dealing intelligently and effectively with the problem. It offers several concrete examples of such contributions and concludes by noting lines of further research and application suggested by the perspective presented. The discussion and examples center about the problem of consent in medical settings, notably transplants from minor donors. I have no doubt, however, that the various propositions made about the role of social psychological knowledge, research, evaluation strategy, and so on, are applicable in other settings where competence to consent is at issue.

MICHAEL J. SAKS ● Department of Psychology, Boston College, Chestnut Hill, Massachusetts 02167.

What is Social Psychology?

Generalizations should be offered with a generous helping of apology to those who will be misinformed or offended by what the generalization leaves out. With apologies, then, I offer the following definition of social psychology, shaped to emphasize those of its features that are most relevant to the problem of consent.

Social psychology is composed of those parts of psychology and sociology that look at causes residing in the social and physical environment of people: situational variables, organizations, social structure, the behavior of other people, the products of society, the natural and built environments, etc., and effects that constitute experience and behavior at the individual level. Issues that evolve within this broad framework typically are studied with a potent concern for rigorous empirical verification. Many spheres of life vie for the title of Most Myth Ridden:— health, economics, political behavior, and others. If social behavior does not win the gold medal, surely it will come close. Social psychology is one of numerous social sciences concerned with sorting out reliable generalization from myth. In so doing it has developed a notable capability in research methodology, having pioneered the use of true experiments (randomized controlled trials) in the study of social behavior (*e.g.*, Lewin, Lippitt, & White, 1939; Murchison, 1935), as well as developing quasi-experiments (Campbell & Stanley, 1963), and certain statistical techniques (see, *e.g.*, Winer, 1971; Kenny, 1979; Harmon, 1967).

The substantive areas social psychologists have spent most of their time working on include attitude formation and change, social perception, interpersonal influence, group dynamics, organizational behavior, and decision making (Lindzey & Aronson, 1968). This is not to say that social psychology is alone or even preeminent in the study of these areas, and it certainly is not the leading applier in these areas. But these are areas relevant to the problem of consent and from which interdisciplinary problems around the question of consent can profit.

The Contribution of Social Psychological Findings and Theories to Consent Issues

One major assumption links the substantive knowledge and methods of social psychology to the problem of consent. That assumption is that the goals of consent granting may be better or worse served by the procedures and circumstances under which consent is sought. These procedures and circumstances are matters that physicians and other hospital staff of necessity have direct and continuous control over and which legal abstractions barely touch, except in specific litigated cases,[1] and then, obviously, not in a representative, aggregated form.

As is noted not infrequently, physicians and other hospital staff need not usurp from patients their decisions; they are in a position to "manage" patients' decisions. The most obvious way is by control of the information given to patients and their families. The law is not so interested in the content of the decision as it is in ensuring that the procedures through which decisions get made do not usurp the patients' right to self-determination. In short, the law is interested in the management of the management of decision making. In several ways—methodological and substantive—social psychology ought to be able to make some contribution to the easing if not the resolution of the dilemmas that surround the granting of consent by minors.

The role in which I would like to cast social psychology is as a true consultant. The task of the consultant here is to alert the "clients" to information that will assist them in intelligently and effectively balancing the best interests of patients with the right to those patients to determine what those best interests are. The clients are health professionals, lawyers, legislators, judges, and anyone else concerned with these questions. The true consultant's job, to the degree that it can be accomplished, is to advise a client about alternative strategies for achieving the goals sought by the client. This does not preclude questioning the goals. It does, however, require ultimate deference to those goals.

An early task would be to take a close look at what actually goes on in the usual process of obtaining consent. The balancing of the patient's interest in accurate diagnosis and expeditious, effective treatment against the requirements of ultimate patient control probably depends in part upon the actual distribution of cases of various kinds. The tough decision areas, where risk–benefit decisions are close calls, may highlight ethical and legal problems. They may not, however, serve as the best model for developing procedures for managing what appear to be the majority of routine decisions—those for which diagnosis is clear, the benefits of the treatment of choice are clear and universally desirable, and the problem of harmful side effects borders on nonexistent. For these kinds of choices the role of informed consent is a different sort of problem; consent granting here is a virtual epiphenomenon because there is no real choice to be made. The kinds of consent seeking and granting procedures that will serve the patient's right to control his or her own life may vary with

---

[1] *E.g.*, Planned Parenthood of Central Missouri v. Danforth, 428 U.S. 52 (1976); Parham v. J.L. and J.R., 442 U.S. 584 (1979); Lacey v. Laird, 166 Ohio St. 12, 139 N.E.2d 25, 30 (1956). Indeed, the judiciary sometimes even seems to have some problems coming to grips with the workings of legal institutions, *e.g.*, Fare v. Michael C., 442 U.S. 707 (1979).

such background data on the nature of diagnoses and treatments and may need to change as diagnostic and treatment procedures change.

The details of the consent seeking and granting process must then be scrutinized because it is in the implementation of principles and operation of procedures that the decision is controlled or controlling. We are familiar with abstract legal pronouncements that never make themselves felt in practice (*e.g.*, Lipsitt, 1980; Saks & Miller, 1978). Judges and lawmakers are likely to be unaware of the actual specifics of consent seeking practices in medical settings. Their orders and statutes, therefore, do not connect effectively with the events they seek to manage or, by dealing with certain salient but relatively rare problems, they fail to manage the bulk of instances effectively. Practitioners are likely to be unaware of the differential effects of various procedures for obtaining informed consent, and of course their agendas are not entirely consistent with those of patients and advocates of the rights of patients. The lack of awareness can result from the simple fact of using one general set of procedures and having no comparison conditions for observing patient decision making under different informational and procedural circumstances. A second reason is that practitioners lack the conceptual tools to know what to look for. As the next section of this chapter illustrates, there are procedures that are recognizable as decision-management strategies having predictable influences, but "seeing" them is facilitated by having concepts from theoretical and experimental work. These form lenses through which the organization and effect of a set of procedures may be seen. The ability of physicians to recognize disease dynamics in a set of signs and symptoms and lawyers to see the legal implications of certain fact situations is analogous to the ability of a social psychologist to see behavioral consequences of certain organizational structures or procedures.

What the social psychologist may contribute is to identify procedural options that may not have been recognized as options, and to help inform the decision-management choices by allowing them to be tested against the agreed upon goals. Moreover, new decision-management procedures can be devised, compared to existing procedures, and ultimately result in strategies that evolve to more effectively achieve the desired goals. Guessing at what will work will not do it. Moreover, the balancing of medical efficiency and effectiveness and the norm of patient control may not be a zero-sum problem. Certain organizational or procedural inventions may permit greater achievement of both goals. For example, surgical patients given more prior information and decision-making opportunity recuperate more quickly from their surgery (Egbert, Battit, Welch, & Bartlett, 1964).

The final contribution of social psychology to this effort is really one that has grown to be the tool of numerous of the social, behavioral, and biomedical sciences. that is *evaluation research* or *program evaluation*. Even the most laboriously developed plans and procedures, however well informed, conflictually or collaboratively resolved, cannot be known in advance to achieve the goals sought. The establishment of programs and procedures, whether by litigation, legislation, professional association codes, or informal norms is not the achievement of the goals, however satisfying it may be for people to reach such a state of agreement. Whether the procedures work is an empirical question. Evaluation research provides the feedback loop that informs one of the extent to which desired goals are or are not being achieved and whether unanticipated undesirable consequences have occurred. No one would assume that the administration of a treatment will *ipso facto* cure an illness or have no harmful side effects. Some monitoring of effects is necessary. In social or organizational—as opposed to individual—treatments, the monitoring and feedback is more difficult to obtain. The goals, the purposes, and their operationalizations need to be specified so they can be measured. People often are vague about goals, or goals are anatgonistic, and the link between a particular set of procedures and its goals often is not clear. Evaluation research ideally would measure the program's implementation as well as its consequences. A conclusion that "it doesn't work" should not be reached because a certain approach was not tried. Elements found to be working in the service of the agreed-upon goals would be retained; those that were not working would be modified or replaced. Rarely if ever does a program or set of procedures succeed without a certain (if not considerable) amount of trial-and-error evolution. Even less often do people try to gather systematically the information necessary to provide feedback for shaping the program into one that works and is known to work (See generally, Guttentag & Streuning, 1975; Gilbert, Light, & Mosteller, 1975).

In brief, whatever is contemplated as a solution to the dilemmas of consent might be further enlightened by the empirical findings, concepts, and theories of social psychology. And whatever is attempted as a solution ought to be evaluated empirically for its efficacy.

Illustrations

My closest encounter with the issue of consent involving children was when I served as a member of a subcommittee of a special legislative commission of the Massachusetts legislature, formed to deal with the legal and ethical problems of using children as donors in organ and tissue transplants. (My role and experiences in that capacity are described in more detail in Saks, 1978.) What I learned of the process of consent seeking and granting in Boston hospitals I learned secondhand through the testimony of lawyers and medical personnel. Thus, I was limited to their skill as observers and candor as witnesses. Although not as close to the process as I have suggested one ought to be, this encounter nevertheless will serve the present purpose of providing some illustrations of what social psychological knowledge can add to the understanding of the issue.

Preparing a Patient for Granting Consent

The subcommittee was told that the actual request that a person, child or adult, make the decision to grant or withhold consent to be a donor is put to the person only after a period of extensive tests and briefings. The rationale was that a person should understand fully what he or she is deciding before being asked to decide, and that it be established that the prospective recipient and donor be compatible before the prospective donor is asked to decide. Indeed, one physician told the subcommittee that the only "morally" acceptable time to ask a person to be a donor was after the biological possibility of donorship had been established. These procedures had prospective donors making numerous visits to the hospital for tests and briefings by various medical personnel and afforded them an opportunity to meet with past donors and their families so, presumably, they could learn what it was like from people who had gone through the experience.

Let us examine the effect of such a pattern on the prospective donor's decision whether to consent. Research on the effect of induced action-taking on subsequent compliance suggests that under conditions of self-perceived voluntariness, the small prior acts of compliance reliably increase the likelihood of ultimate compliance with the target behavior (*e.g.*, Freedman & Fraser, 1966; Bandura, 1969; Abelson, Aronson, McGuire, Newcomb, Rosenberg, & Tannenbaum, 1968). Thus, it ought to be the case that if a person is asked to submit to a physical examination and give blood and tissue samples, that person also has been psychologically readied to make a positive consent decision. Indeed, Schwartz (1970) obtained precisely this effect in an experimental study of the determinants of consenting to the donation of bone marrow. Different blood donors were asked either (1) whether they would consent to donate some of their bone marrow if a suitable recipient were found, or (2) whether some already-donated blood could be tested and then whether they would consent to the bone marrow donation, or (3) if more blood could be drawn for a sample, etc. The more small acts of compliance obtained, and the more they successively approximated the target decision, the more people agreed to donate bone marrow when the consent question was finally asked.

The supplying of information is certainly necessary to obtaining "informed" consent. But when does education become advocacy or manipulation? Interviews with organ and tissue donors suggest that they do not behave as the rational calculators of costs and benefits that live in the imaginings of common law. In part a social influence process is operating. Fellner and Marshal (1970) found that many donors report that they decided immediately and impulsively, as soon as the issue arose, and before they were given any further information. Information received prior to making a decision is used in a more or less rational way to reduce predecisional conflict between choices. Information received subsequent to making a decision is used "irrationally" to reduce postdecisional dissonance: Information that supports the already-made decision is given more weight or attended to selectively, sometimes even to the exclusion of contrary information. Thus, the procedural lengthiness of the informing process (at least for these prospective donors) helps to reduce dissonance, so that by the time the "official" decision is required, they are stable and committed.

> Donors who did not decide impulsively could not recall ever really having made a clear decision, yet they never considered refusing to go along either, and as it became clear toward the end of the selection process that they were going to be the person most suited to be the donor, they finally committed themselves to the act. (Fellner & Marshall, 1970, p. 272)

For these donors, the decision-shaping process discussed earlier is at work. Even the simple transmittal of information is automatically selective and skewed. Virtually all (if not all) of the medical personnel to whom prospective donors and their families are exposed are part of the transplant team. Those with serious reservations either do not become or do not remain part of the enterprise, or they do not express those views to patients. Nor are past donors and their families a representative group of similarly situated decision makers. They are people who decided to consent. The process of being informed seems to have been a process of being persuaded and prepared, with prospective donors exposed to unanimous conformity pressure (Asch, 1951), modeling (Bandura, 1969), social comparison (Festinger, 1954), and expert influence (French & Raven, 1968). Rodin and Janis (1979) discuss the various forms of power—expert, legitimate, coercive, reward, and referent—physicians can bring to bear in influencing the choices and behavior of their patients and the relative efficacy of the different forms of power. It is interesting to consider the alternative possibility that physicians may arouse oppositional responses unwittingly or, failing to appreciate in concrete detail the differences in children's oppositional behavior, exert more influence than they intend. Brehm (1981) discusses such oppositional behavior in children from the viewpoint of reactance theory, highlighting differences and similarities between children and adults in reacting against control techniques that threaten perceived freedom to choose.

The timing of the actual (as opposed to the official) decision, and the number, nature, and sequencing of events leading up to the actual and official decisions has an effect upon the decision; if done "right," it can reduce noncompliance to a minimum. Alternative procedures that allow for more balanced informing and less compliance-inducing actions may be more facilitative of "free and informed" consent.

Making Decisions for Minors

If someone else's judgment is to be substituted for that of another (*e.g.*, a minor), how and through what process is that judgment to be made? Should parents or doctors simply decide whether a child should become a donor? Should a guardian *ad litem* be appointed since parents and doctors are in a classic conflict of interest?[2] Should the guardian make the decision for the child, or should it be endorsed by some agency, or argued before a court and a judge asked to decide? Some people advocate the minimization of adversariness, since the families and children are already under considerable stress from the medical and personal problems that plague them. Why add more? Others fear the loss of concern with the prospective donor's interests in the rush to help the prospective recipient, and look to the adversary process to insure attention to those interests (Saks, 1978). Some research has been done on people's reactions to having their interests decided through adversary versus nonadversary procedures (Thibaut & Walker, 1975). In general the more adversarial the structure of the forum, the more the people whose interests are at stake are satisfied with the fairness of the process. Subsequent research examined the limits of that generalization. (Thibaut & Walker, 1978; see also McGillis, 1980, for a discussion of the unsuitability of formal adjudication for resolving certain kinds of disputes, and the search for alternatives). Moreover, specific research could be done testing what procedure for substituted judgment would best serve the subjective and objective well-being of prospective donors in the kinds of situations we have been discussing. Different procedures have differential power to protect or undermine interests, produce more or less balanced fact distributions, and generate more or less subjective stress or well-being.

Manipulating Attributions of Responsibility

Suppose a child is found to be compatible with a sibling who needs a transplant, but the child, or adult for that matter, refuses to consent to or cooperate with the transplant. How will the parents and others concerned for the welfare of the prospective recipient feel toward the person who has refused to be a donor? Intrafamily conflict over both refusals and consents has been

---

[2] *See* cases cited in Levine, Camitta, Nathan, & Curran (1975).

reported (Bennet & Harrison, 1974; Eisendrath, Guttman, & Murray, 1969; Kemph, Bermann, & Coppolillo, 1969). Medical personnel have sought to protect those who refuse to donate due to repercussions within their families by representing to the family not that the prospective donor declined but, rather, that the prospective donor turned out not to be compatible. Furthermore, prospective donors are informed in advance of the formal decision that this subterfuge will be available to them should they decide not to donate. I am going to pass over the obvious ethical problems raised by this tactic; they are more ably addressed by ethicists and lawyers than by social psychologists. I will focus instead on the practical prospects and dangers of this procedure.

In the language of attribution theory (Heider, 1958; Jones & Davis, 1965), what the physicians are doing to accomplish the manipulation of perceived intentions and dispositions is to convert personal causation into impersonality. To attribute personal causation several conditions must hold—including local causality—which is removed by shifting the "cause" to sources (in the present situation, biology) that are not under an individual's control. Individuals are held accountable for what appear to be free choices. But if their genes determined the result, they cannot as easily be blamed. (Obviously, the perception of causality or responsibility is something that lawyers defending accused criminals and tortfeasors regularly try to manipulate.) Some of the social psychological research on attribution processes has focused on the development of attributions, and they appear to be in place, at least in primitive forms, at very young ages (Kassin, 1981). More to the present point, however, is whether the young age of a behaver deflects the making of dispositional attributions by adults; on this there appears to be no research. Most likely, the prospective child donors who would be invited to participate in the ruse described would be above whatever age threshold is required for one to be blamed for one's choices.

To the extent that people other than the prospective donor know about the possibility of such a ruse, it more than fails. If more than one prospective donor is made aware of the available ruse, word could leak out. Or if the family learns from other sources that such subterfuges are practiced, a situation is created whereby the only way an unambiguous internal attribution of intent can be made is by the making of a donation. If a person does not donate, families will be told, "the prospective donor was not compatible," whether the failure to donate truly was due to biological incompatibility or whether it was due to a decision by the prospective donor. Families will thus always be burdened with some suspicion. Truly incompatible donors will be deprived of being unambiguously seen as such. If the ruse does succeed entirely, then the nondonor has to carry the knowledge that he or she has entered into a conspiracy with the doctors to deceive the rest of the family. And, as an aside, we might consider that the existence of awareness of such institutionalized dishonesty cannot improve anyone's perception of the trustworthiness of the medical profession.

Are Children Competent to Consent?

Much of the rest of this volume directly addresses the question of children's competence to consent and its legal and psychological implications. In this subsection I will try to emphasize the more social and situational aspects of what is largely a cognitive developmental issue.

Undoubtedly, nervous systems and cognitive structures mature. Children who at one time cannot comprehend the facts and issues on which consent must be granted do become able, or at least as able as adults, by some time in their adolescence. Piaget and Kohlberg have lent clarity and detail to our understanding of such cognitive development and the nature of the cognitive manipulations and transformations that become possible with growth and experience with the physical and social world. What can this knowledge contribute to solving the dilemmas of children's consent? None of the major developmental theories—cognitive, social learning, psychoanalytic—purport to predict or explain the content, but only the process, of a (consent) decision at various stages of development. Nor do they prescribe where fine lines should be drawn when the question is whether a given person is competent to make a particular decision. Even if such advice were forthcoming, the best the law is likely to do is to lower the age for effective granting of consent. With more adolescents thus considered "mature minors," the problem would be reduced, at least numerically. The matrix of problems involved in consent, though affecting fewer people, would still be intact.

While the law finds it most convenient to specify age cutoffs that create presumptions, there is measurable age variation in the abilities that are supposed to correlate with the age cutoffs, as well as variations due to subject matter and situation. If case-by-case competence judgments are to be made, the specificity of subject matter and situation become important considerations. Similarly, in addition to the issue of developmental changes in decision-making competence, we might note that consenting to donate organs or tissue is an altruistic or at least "prosocial" act. This has been studied as an issue in its own right and is also subject to developmental phenomena. Moore and Underwood (1981) review the literature on prosocial behavior in children, its relation to age, and its mediation by cognitive and situational variables, including social norms (which may vary over families and subcultures), socialization practices, perspective taking, and empathy; and they examine methods of inducing change in these variables. Again, specificity of situation and information is of importance in explaining or controlling the child's behavior.

Research and Applications

Contributions to clarifying these problems, and making the granting of consent more workable, meaningful, and just, might come from three kinds of work. One would be research that sought to specify the important variables that determine the interaction among such organismic variables as age and socialization with content and situational variables. A second kind of work would be identifying the most effective ways to inform young people (as well as adults), so that informational-educational methods are best suited to the person who has the need to know. Third, the components of "comprehension" could be specified and identified and measures developed so that in particular cases evaluations of competence could be made with something more valid and reliable than guesswork, impressions, and intuition.

This chapter has suggested, or at least adverted to, potentially useful research. Some of the research would result in knowledge at a fairly high conceptual level, lending itself to deductive applications, as with the basic research I described in the Illustrations section. At present, this basic research is the most substantive contribution that social psychology has to offer. But it is not enough. Some of the work would have to be highly situation-specific, studying particular decision-making areas and settings. The waiver of rights in a police station (see Chapter 8) may not be the same as the granting of consent in a medical setting (see Chapter 12). It will be valuable to identify robust variables that hold across situations, persons, and subject matters, in order to know whether the conclusions hold parametrically, especially with the age variable, and to know the limits of external validity (Campbell & Stanley, 1963; Cook & Campbell, 1979) so that findings are not transferred to circumstances where they do not hold. And there it will be of value to know what variables interact with the major variables of interest to limit their generality.

Research needs to develop some measures of "free and informed consent." How would we know it if we saw it? Or may it only be inferred from the procedures through which it is sought? Perhaps subjective feelings of reactance could be tapped (cf. Brehm, 1981). Alternative methods of informing and managing the decision process will actually have to be developed, implemented, and examined. The findings could then be used to inform policy and practice in seeking informed consent. At that point evaluation research would be appropriate and would, ideally, serve two purposes. One would be the usual function of assessing the extent to which a program or set of procedures is meeting its intended goals. The second would be the function that is usually regarded as that of basic research—the generation of knowledge at a more abstract level that can be generalized to other questions, in other settings, with other people. Benefits could then accrue to basic research and to those interested in questions of the development of human decision making and the effects of neurological development, cognitive structure, and situational influences and their interactions. Although this problem area may be an annoyance to physicians and a cause célèbre for lawyers, to those who wish to understand its nature and how to modify it to serve competing values effectively, the problem is one of formidable complexity.

References

Abelson, R. P., Aronson, E., McGuire, W. J., Newcomb, T. M., Rosenberg, M. J., & Tannenbaum, P. H. (Eds.), *Theories of cognitive consistency: A sourcebook.* Chicago: Rand McNally, 1968.

Asch, S. E. Effects of group pressure upon the modification and distortion of judgements. In H. Guetzkow (Ed.), *Groups, leadership and men.* Pittsburgh: Carnegie Press, 1951.

Bandura, A. *Principles of behavior modification.* New York: Holt, Rinehart & Winston, 1969.

Bennett, A. H., & Harrison, J. H. Experience with living familial renal donors. *Surgery, Gynecology, and Obstetrics,* 1974, *139,* 894–898.

Brehm, S. S. Oppositional behavior in children: A reactance theory approach. In S. S. Brehm, S. M. Kassin, & F. X. Gibbons (Eds.), *Developmental social psychology.* New York: Oxford University Press, 1981.

Campbell, D. T. & Stanley, J. C. *Experimental and quasi-experimental designs for research.* Chicago: Rand McNally, 1963.

Cook, T. & Campbell, D. T. *Quasi-experimentation: Design and analysis issues for field settings.* Chicago: Rand McNally, 1979.

Egbert, L., Battit, G., Welch, C., & Bartlett, M. Reduction of postoperative pain by encouragement and instruction of patients. *New England Journal of Medicine,* 1964, *270,* 825–827.

Eisendrath, R. M., Guttmann, R. D. & Murray, J. E. Psychologic considerations in the selection of kidney transplant donors. *Surgery, Gynecology, and Obstetrics,* 1969, *129,* 243–248.

Fellner, C. H., & Marshall, J. R. Kidney donors. In J. Macaulay & L. Berkowitz (Eds.), *Altruism and helping behavior.* New York: Academic Press, 1970.

Festinger, L. A theory of social comparison processes. *Human Relations,* 1954, *2,* 117–140.

Freedman, J. L. & Fraser, S. C. Compliance without pressure: The foot-in-the-door technique. *Journal of Personality and Social Psychology,* 1966, *4,* 195–202.

French, J. R. P., & Raven, B. The bases of social power. In D. Cartwright & A. Zander (Eds.), *Group Dynamics.* New York: Harper & Row, 1968.

Gilbert, J. P., Light, R. J., & Mosteller, F. Assessing social innovations: An empirical basis for policy. In C. A. Bennett & A. A. Lumsdaine (Eds.), *Evaluation and experiment: Some critical issues in assessing social programs.* New York: Academic Press, 1975.

Guttentag, M. & Streuning, E. L. (Eds.), *Handbook of evaluation research.* Beverly Hills: Sage, 1975.

Harmon, H. H. *Modern factor analysis* (2nd rev. ed.). Chicago: University of Chicago Press, 1967.

Heider, F. *The psychology of interpersonal relations.* New York: Wiley, 1958.

Jones, E. E. & Davis, K. E. From acts to dispositions: The attribution process in person perception. In L. Berkowitz (Ed.), *Advances in experimental social psychology* (Vol. 2). New York: Academic Press, 1965.

Kassin, S. M. From "laychild" to layman: Developmental causal attribution In S. S. Brehm, S. M. Kassin, & F. X. Gibbons, (Eds.), *Developmental social psychology.* New York: Oxford University Press, 1981.

Kemph, J. P., Bermann, E. A., & Coppolillo, H. P. Kidney transplant and shifts in family dynamics. *American Journal of Psychiatry,* 1969, *125,* 1485–1490.

Kenny, D. A. *Correlation and causation.* New York: Wiley, 1979.

Levine, M. D., Camitta, B. M., Nathan, D., & Curran, W. J. The medical ethics of bone marrow transplants in childhood. *Journal of Pediatrics,* 1975, *86,* 145–150.

Lewin, K., Lippitt, R., & White, R. Patterns of aggressive behavior in experimentally created "Social climates." *Journal of Social Psychology*, 1939, *10*, 271–199.

Lindzey, G., & Aronson, E. (Eds.), *Handbook of social psychology*. Reading, Mass.: Addison-Wesley, 1968.

Lipsitt, P. M. Emergency admission of civil involuntary patients to mental hospitals following statutory modification. In P. D. Lipsitt & B. D. Sales (Eds.), *New directions in psycholegal research*. New York: Van Nostrand, 1980.

McGillis, D. Neighborhood justice centers as mechanisms for dispute resolution. In P. D. Lipsitt, & B. D. Sales (Eds.), *New directions in psycholegal research*. New York: Van Nostrand, 1980.

Moore, B., & Underwood, B. The development of prosocial behavior, In S. S. Brehm, S. M. Kassin & F. X. Gibbons (Eds.), *Developmental social psychology*. New York: Oxford University Press, 1981.

Murchison, C. (Ed.). *Handbook of social psychology*. Worcester, Mass.: Clark University Press, 1935.

Rodin, J., & Janis, I. L. The social power of health-care practitioners as agents of change. *Journal of Social Issues*, 1979, *35*(1), 60–81.

Saks, M. J. Social psychological contributions to a legislative subcommittee on organ and tissue transplants. *American Psychologist*, 1978, *33*(7), 680–690.

Saks, M. J. & Miller, M. L. A systems approach to discretion in the legal process. In L. E. Abt & I. R. Stuart (Eds.), *Social Psychology and Discretionary Law*. New York: Van Nostrand, 1979.

Schwartz, S. H. Elicitation of moral obligation and self-sacrificing behavior: An experimental study of volunteering to be a bone marrow donor. *Journal of Personality and Social Psychology*, 1970, *15*, 283–293.

Thibaut, J., & Walker, L. *Procedural justice: A psychological analysis*. Hillsdale, N.J.: Erlbaum, 1975.

Thibaut, J. & Walker, L. A theory of procedure. *California Law Review*, 1978, *66*(3), 541–566.

Winer, B. *Statistical principles in experimental design*. New York: McGraw-Hill, 1971.

PART II

Children's Consent to Treatment

Legal, Medical, and Psychological Perspectives

Chapter 4

Consent to Medical Care for Minors

The Legal Framework

WALTER J. WADLINGTON

Whether minors should be accorded greater authority to make binding decisions on matters involving their personal welfare is a subject of considerable dispute today. After the 26th Amendment to the U.S. Constitution in 1971 assured that 18-year-olds could vote, many states lowered the general age of majority under their laws to conform with the voting age. Another catalyst for change was the concern that many statutes were vulnerable to constitutional challenge because they maintained differing ages for majority, or for marriage, based on sex.[1] Some states lowered the general age of majority but retained (or added) higher minimum age requirements for acts such as purchasing alcoholic beverages. (Virginia, for example, permits a person to marry without consent at age 18 but not to purchase champagne—even for the wedding—until age 21.[2]) As a result of this somewhat haphazard process, the rules regarding majority today are a melange of legal anachronism and contemporary expediency which reflect only minimally our current understanding about the intellectual and emotional capacities and interests of young persons.

Allocation of authority to make decision about health care for minors

---

[1] *See, e.g.*, Phelps v. Bing, 58 Ill.2d 32, 316 N.E.2d 775 (1974) (sex discriminatory minimum marriage age unconstitutional); Stanton v. Stanton, 429 U.S. 501 (sex distinction impermissible for determining majority age for child support purposes).

[2] *See* Va. Code Ann. §§ 4–62, 20–48.

WALTER J. WADLINGTON ● School of Law, University of Virginia, Charlottesville, Virginia 22903.

provides a good illustration of the confusion and inconsistency about the appropriate age at which children can or should be allowed to make choices for themselves without ratification by or notice to their parents. This chapter will examine the contours of state law in this area today, along with the emerging movements toward reform.

The rules that govern medical decision making for minors derive chiefly from (1) tort law, which controls the civil liability of physicians or other health care practitioners for unauthorized treatment or violation of the privacy rights of patients, as well as liability for substandard treatment; (2) specific legislation providing for general or limited emancipation of children in the field of medical decision making; (3) common law or statutory rules of general emancipation; (4) abuse, neglect, and dependency statutes establishing parental duties to supply necessary medical care to children; and (5) the law governing financial responsibility for medical services, which includes a mixture of contract law, family law, and special statutory provisions such as those in (2), (3), and (4).

The Tort Law Background

The law of torts governs civil liability to compensate for personal injury or other harm through money damages. It is still heavily rooted in judicial decisions that provide legal precedents for application in future cases. Each state controls its own tort law, except to the extent that it involves infringement on basic liberty or property rights guaranteed by the U.S. Constitution. Basic rules and principles are common among many jurisdictions, however, and cases from one state often will be cited with approval in another even though they are not binding precedents in the latter. Although some persons consider tort actions for medical malpractice to be an important quality control measure as well as an avenue to compensation for injured patients, there is concern by many that the threat of tort liability may lead clinicians to practice "defensively"—that is, to take measures designed as much or more to protect themselves from liability as to promote the health and welfare of their patients. This might consist of unwillingness to accept a patient or proceed with treatment when there is any uncertainty about the legal adequacy of consent in a specific case. Whether or not defensive medicine poses a serious problem in health care delivery today, concern about potential tort liability seems to play an increasingly significant role in influencing physician conduct, for better or worse. The recent movement toward more clearly delineating the rights of patients in the medical decision-making process specifically, and in the hospital setting generally, is in large measure dependent on availability of a tort remedy.

The Basic Requirement of Consent

Most medical malpractice actions are based on negligence. This requires proof that the actor (the physician or other person delivering health care) failed to conform to the minimum standard of care legally owed to the patient, and that this breach of duty resulted in damage or harm of sufficiently close causal connection to justify imposition of liability in the form of money damages.

Unauthorized or unprivileged interference with some legally protected personal interest, such as the right to be free from invasion of one's body, also can be tortious without regard to a negligence standard. Such acts usually are known as intentional torts;[3] it is the actual invasion of a protected interest that provides the basis for the civil action, whether or not identifiable physical harm results. When intentional torts are committed with malice on the part of the actor, some jurisdictions permit the award of special or punitive damages that can serve deterrent or punitive function similar to the criminal law.[4] Punitive damages are relatively rare in medical liability cases,[5] but the potential for such an award poses a threat that can influence physician conduct.

The basic requirement of patient consent to medical treatment derives from the characterization of bodily invasions without consent as tortious.[6] In most instances little risk to the patient is involved, and consent ordinarily will be implied legally in cases of medical emergency when a patient, because of incapacity, lacks competence to agree even to immediate needs for protecting life and health.[7] In other cases, however, express consent should be obtained; for such major intervention as surgery, or for other procedures having the potential for severe or dangerous side effects, consent ordinarily will be reduced to writing.

If it is to be binding, consent to medical treatment must be obtained from a person who has legal capacity to give it. It is this requirement which raises problems for treatment of minors. Until a child reaches the legal age of majority, is emancipated generally, or is specifically empowered by legislative or judicial action to consent to medical treatment, the child's parent or guardian usually has legal capacity to give or withhold consent to treatment.[8] If consent is withheld arbitrarily, contrary to the needs of the child, a course of action may

---

[3] For further discussion of this concept, *see* Restatement (Second) of Torts §§ 18–20 and Explanatory Notes.

[4] *See* W. Prosser, *Law of Torts* 9 (4th ed. 1971).

[5] For an illustration of the problems of seeking punitive damages in a medical malpractice case, *see* Smith v. Courter, 575 S.W.2d 199 (mo. App. 1979).

[6] Restatement (Second) of Torts § 15.

[7] W. Prosser, *supra* at 103.

[8] *See* R. W. Bennett, Allocation of child care decisionmaking authority: A suggested interest analysis, *62 VA. L. REV.* 285 (1976).

be available against the parent under the abuse and neglect statutes; courts generally are empowered either through such laws or under the broad scope of *parens patriae* jurisdiction to appoint a guardian for the purpose of consenting to treatment of an incompetent. But without consent from some competent person or agency, a physician who renders treatment not falling within the exception of the emergency doctrine risks a legal action. Two key developments, one largely judicial, the other legislative, have served to lessen the problems, but the clinician's position still may be uncertain in many cases.

The Mature Minor Doctrine

Some states recognize a "mature minor" doctrine in deciding whether medical intervention effected with the consent of an older child, but not the child's parents or guardian, should be deemed tortious. The doctrine was developed initially through judicial action, but in recent years it has been codified by legislatures in some states, particularly where courts had not already announced its existence.

A decision of the Kansas Supreme Court[9] illustrates how the mature minor doctrine can work. Parental consent had not been obtained to take a skin graft from the forearm of a 17-year-old girl to repair an injury sustained when her finger was caught in a door at the hospital where her mother had just undergone surgery. The mother, not fully conscious after a general anesthetic, was not competent to give consent, and no other legally authorized person was available. Negligence was alleged but not proven with regard to the quality of the medical care; however, an action against the hospital was also asserted because of its having undertaken treatment without parental authorization. Finding that consent both to the emergency repair operation and the skin graft had been given by the daughter, the court decided that the facts brought the case

> within an exception to the general rule requiring consent of the parent to a surgical operation on a child. The exception applicable is that under the circumstances the daughter was mature enough to understand the nature of the consequences and to knowingly consent to the beneficial surgical procedure.[10]

Invoking the mature minor doctrine had the practical effect of avoiding imposition of liability for what some would describe as a "technical" battery. The doctrine seems most likely to be applied when a consenting minor is near majority and able to comprehend clearly the nature and potential impact of

[9] Younts v. St. Francis Hospital and School of Nursing, Inc., 205 Kan. 292, 469, P.2d 330 (1970).
[10] *Id.* at 205 Kan. 301, 469, P.2d 330 (1970).

the particular medical treatment. Appellate cases clearly delineating its scope outside the specific framework of abortion and contraception still are relatively few in number; often they have involved situations not far from those in which the general emergency doctrine might have been invoked to imply consent.[11] Thus the doctrine, which seems to be rooted more in a sense of judicial or legislative pragmatism than in any careful conceptualization of minors' rights to self-determination, addresses only a limited segment of the minor consent cases.

Some Specific Statutory Approaches

During the past two decades there has been wide enactment of statutory provisions focusing on specific aspects of consent to medical treatment for minors. One approach establishes a hierarchy of persons, usually commencing with parents or guardians, whose consent can be relied upon by health care personnel seeking to assure conformance with legal requirements.[12] Another type of statute fixes an age below majority at which some minors can consent to medical care generally.[13] Such provisions may extend only to married minors, or to those who meet some specified test for emancipation, or to emergency care.

In recent years many legislatures have adopted provisions which permit a minor to consent to treatment, couseling, or procedures for diagnosis of certain enumerated illnesses or conditions.[14] These statutes commonly contain an age floor, but this is by no means universal. Problems or conditions to which such statutes typically extend are drug abuse or addiction; alcoholism; family planning or maternity care; venereal disease; various contagious diseases; and, to a limited extent, mental illness. Abortion ordinarily is dealt with in a different statute.

Such "condition specific" consent provisions seem to reflect a policy of expedience on the part of legislatures that have adopted them. They probably stem from belief in, or recognition of, widespread contemporary breakdown in family communications and relationships involving adolescents. The statutes are directed toward problems that legislatures acknowledge as presenting serious medical difficulties among minors; they abrogate the historical legal in-

---

[11] *See* W. J. Wadlington, Minors and Health Care: The age of consent, *73 Osgoode Hall. L.J.*, 115, 117, *et. seq.* (1973).

[12] *See, e.g.*, Va. Code Ann. § 54–325.2; Miss. Code Ann. § 41–41–3.

[13] *See. e.g.*, Alaska Stat. § 0.9.65–100; Minn. Stat. Ann. §§ 144.341–342.

[14] Such provisions often are in addition to those dealing with limited emancipation of certain minors. Examples of condition-specific consent statutes are N. J. Stat. Ann. § 9:17A–4; Va. Code Ann. § 54–325–2.D.

capicity of minors to consent to treatment for fear that if parental consent were required in the specifically enumerated instances many adolescents would refrain from or delay treatment, to the detriment of themselves and their community.

The degree to which the goal of encouraging timely treatment at the initiative of minors who do not wish to communicate with their parents will be achieved through the statutes often may depend on how well (or whether) they explain the rights and duties of a physician regarding consultation or communication with the parents of a minor who is being treated with only the child's consent. Whether a clinician wishes to communicate with the parents of an adolescent under treatment may vary according to individual views about the family, the nature and seriousness of the minor's medical needs, and the perceived need for parental cooperation. Unfortunately, the latitude for physician disclosure often remains unclear even after adoption of specific consent statutes. Some laws are silent on the subject, thus assigning to the courts the task of resolving whether a minor's individual right of privacy takes precedence over a larger right of family privacy. One can contend strongly that a minor patient capable of consenting to treatment should be entitled to the same protection of confidentiality that would be accorded an adult patient. Although the number of cases is not large, damage actions against physicians for breach of the duty of confidentiality owed their patient have been recognized generally; such actions sometimes are regarded as subject to certain public policy exceptions, however, and one can imagine how the courts might shape such an exception to encompass disclosure to parents if the proper case were before them.[15] Aware of these various concerns, some legislatures have specifically addressed the problem of consulting with or informing parents. These newer statutes may provide specific guidelines for the physician, or they may give the clinician discretion to communicate with the minor patient's parents, sometimes under prescribed limitations. They even may preclude giving information to a parent without the child's permission in most, if not all, instances. The various statutory approaches obviously reflect differing conclusions about the way of balancing the interests of unduly discouraging treatment and avoiding unnecessary state usurpation of traditional parental roles.[16]

[15] *See, e.g.*, Horne v. Patton, 291 Ala. 701, 287 So. 2d 824 (1974); Hague v. Williams, 37 N.J. 328, 181 A.2d 345 (1962); Berry v. Moench, 8 Utah 2d 191, 331 P.2d 814 (1958).

[16] For various provisions regarding physician duty or discretion, *see, e.g.*, Del. Code tit. 13, § 708 (physician has discretion to provide or withhold information from parents, "having primary regard for the interests of the minor"); Minn. Stat. Ann. § 144.346 (physician may inform parents where "in the judgment of the professional, failure to inform . . . would seriously jeopardize the health of the minor patient"); Mass. Gen. Law Ann. ch. 112, § 12F (information to be kept confidential between minor and physician except that when attending physician "reasonably

The Juvenile Justice Standards Relating to the Rights of Minors,[17] approved by the House of Delegates of the American Bar Association in 1979, contain detailed standards and guidelines that may have significant impact on future legislation dealing with minors' consent to health care. The standards start from the premise that parental consent should be required for treatment of unemancipated minors,[18] but they recognize specific exceptions in cases of chemical dependency;[19] venereal disease; pregnancy; and services, therapy, or counseling for family planning, including contraception or birth control by procedure other than sterilization.[20] In addition, a minor age 14 or older may consent to three sessions with a "psychotherapist or counselor for diagnosis and consultation" regarding mental or emotional disorders.[21]

The Juvenile Justice Standards regarding notification to parents about treatment of their minor children are relatively elaborate.[22] They begin with the proposition that even when prior consent of parents is not required, the health care provider should notify the parent or custodian about such treatment promptly and obtain consent to further treatment. Again, the Standards include a number of specific exceptions. If the services are for treatment of chemical dependency, venereal disease, contraception, or pregnancy, the physician should first seek consent from the minor to notify the parent. If the minor objects, the physician should not tell the parent about the treatment without concluding that failure to inform could seriously jeopardize the minor's health. Factors listed for consideration about whether to reach such a conclusion include the potential impact that notification would have on treatment of the minor; medical considerations requiring notification; the "nature, basis, and strength" of the child's objections; and the need for or desirability of parental involvement in the course of treatment. A physician who concludes that parental notification is "medically required" should state the medical justifications in the patient's file and advise the parents only after proceeding with "all reasonable efforts" to persuade the minor to consent to such notification.

The Standards also deal specifically with mental or emotional disorders. As stated earlier, a minor who is 14 years or older may consent to three sessions with a "psychotherapist or counselor for diagnosis and consultations." Following three sessions for "crisis intervention and/or diagnosis," however, notifica-

---

believes the condition of said minor to be so serious that his life or limb is endangered," the parent shall be notified and the minor shall be told of the notification).

[17] *IJA/ABA Juvenile Justice Standards, Standards Relating to Rights of Minors* (1980) (hereafter, *Standards Relating to Rights of Minors*).

[18] *Standards Relating to Rights of Minors*, § 4.1, at 50.

[19] *Id.*, § 4.7, at 70.

[20] *Id.*, § 4.8, at 72. This section also includes abortion.

[21] *Id.*, § 4.9, at 85.

[22] *Id.*, § 4.2, at 54.

tion of such sessions should be given to the parent and parental consent should be obtained for further treatment. The Commentary to the Standards explains that this will allow youth counseling agencies, hot lines, and the like to provide limited counseling services but no long-term psychotherapy without parental involvement.[23] However, some minors age 16 or older might be involved in longer term counseling or treatment under the provisions dealing with chemical dependency.

Also included in the Juvenile Justice Standards is a broad statement of the "mature minor" doctrine.[24] One who has reached the optional age of 16 "and who has sufficient capacity to understand the nature and consequences of a proposed medical treatment for his or her benefit" may consent as an adult. Nevertheless, the physician who treats such a minor should notify the parents, subject to the previously described exemptions and criteria in cases of chemical dependency and other expected conditions. The Standards also deal with the emancipated minor, for whom neither parental consent or notification is necessary.[25] Because a determination of whether a minor is "emancipated" can be difficult even for lawyers, the emancipation exception may be of limited use to physicians in many jurisdictions. The Standards respond to this concern by providing that in a damage action against a physician based on treatment without parental consent it is a defense that such treatment was given in good faith reliance on the minor's representation that he or she was emancipated.

The Doctrine of "Informed Consent"

The requirement that a health care practitioner obtain patient consent in order to avoid potential action for an intentional tort of battery already has been discussed. Physicians and other health practitioners also must take care to assure that the consent is "informed"—*i.e.*, that the consenting patient has received adequate information about the risks associated with the particular treatment and the alternatives that might be selected in place of it. One might assume that if a consent were not "informed" then the law would determine that there had been no legal consent and thus a battery action might be initiated. However, recent judicial evolution of the informed consent doctrine generally has placed it within the ambit of negligence rather than intentional tort.[26] A physician is said to have a duty to disclose sufficient information and details so that the patient can decide whether or not to consent to the recom-

---

[23] *Id.*, at 85.

[24] *Id.*, § 4.6, at 68.

[25] *Id.*, § 4.4, at 64.

[26] *See* Cobbs v. Grant, 8 Cal.2d 229, 104 Cal. Rptr. 505, 502 P.2d 1 (1972); Canterbury v. Spence, 464 F.2d 772 (D.C. Cir. 1972).

mended treatment. If minimum disclosure requirements are met, in order to prove the necessary element of causation it still must be established that different (or no) treatment would have been selected had the patient been fully informed. The causation element is important in distinguishing the action for failure to obtain informed consent from one for an intentional tort, such as battery. In the latter, the unauthorized invasion itself constitutes a tort; in the informed consent/negligence action, it must be established that failure to disclose caused the patient to choose an alternative that otherwise would not have been selected.

A damage suit for failure to obtain informed consent sometimes is described as a "parasitic action." This refers to the fact that it seldom will be brought alone; usually it will accompany an allegation that the health care practitioner negligently violated some standard of care with regard to the quality of the specific treatment procedure, thereby causing harm.

Physicians have experienced considerable anxiety over the potential effects of the informed consent doctrine in its present shape. Much of their concern centers on uncertainty about what information must be conveyed to a patient. Another worry focuses on the difficulties of proving exactly what a patient was told before a procedure calling for informed consent. The latter evidentiary concern has caused some practitioners to tape or otherwise record preoperative discussions with patients; to have witnesses present for such discussions; or to include elaborate written descriptions of risks and procedures in basic operative consent forms. Some two dozen state legislatures have sought to define the scope of the duty to disclose by adopting specific legislation; some such laws even include model consent forms.[27] A key difference among the judicially shaped or legislatively defined rules centers on whether the standard of disclosure is a matter to be established by expert testimony of physicians and thus based on customary practice, or whether it is a matter for lay determination of what is appropriate for the patient to know in order to make an "informed" decision.[28] Courts generally have been willing to engraft certain exceptions such as those for the person who clearly professes the desire not to know more about a procedure but wishes to trust the physician's judgment. But in states without clear legislation (and many existing statutes are incomplete or ambiguous) a significant number of "close-call" issues remain to be answered by the courts.

In speculating about the special problems of informed consent with regard to minors, it seems appropriate first to examine the specific language of the statutes on minor consent, and then to determine the extent to which the

---

[27] *See* Meisel & Kabnik, Informed consent to medical treatment: An analysis of recent legislation, *41 U. Pitt. L. Rev.* 407 (1980).

[28] *See* W. Wadlington, J. Waltz, & R. Dworkin, *Cases and Materials on Law and Medicine* 502 *et seq.*

minors' individual capacities to understand the nature of the proposed procedures and to make reasoned decisions should be "read in" to such provisions. For the most part, statutes authorizing minors to consent to specific medical procedures merely specify an age floor at most. Though such a statute may be satisfactory to avoid a battery action against one who relies on it in treating a minor patient, the threat of a negligence action for failure to disclose to the patient sufficient information to make an informed decision can remain. If disclosure has not been made in such a manner that it will be understood clearly by the minor, potential problems of liability may exist. It must be recalled that the "mature minor doctrine," discussed earlier, was predicated on the minor's understanding and ability to make decisions.

An example of a minor consent statute that seems to reflect a legislative concern for these problems is found in Nevada.[29] In addition to permitting consent to medical treatment by some minors (those who have been living separate and apart from parents for more than four months), the statute extends consent authority to a minor who is "in a physician's judgment, in danger of suffering a serious health hazard if care services are not provided." The section makes parental consent unnecessary for treatment or examination of such a minor "who understands the nature and purpose of the proposed examination or treatment and its probable outcome, and voluntarily requests it."

A special aspect of the informed consent doctrine noted by some courts is that disclosure requirements may be tempered by a fear that they will be counterproductive. As stated by the Supreme Court of California:

> A disclosure need not be made beyond that required within the medical community when a doctor can prove by a preponderance of the evidence he relied upon facts which would demonstrate to a reasonable man the disclosure would have so seriously upset the patient that the patient would not have been able to dispassionately weigh the risks of refusing to undergo the recommended treatment.[30]

This exception could be of special concern for minor children. In states that in effect permit the disclosure standard to be set by physician custom, a practice may develop among clinicians that the disclosure required for younger minors is more limited than that for older minors and adults. However, it is plausible to argue that if the true goal of the informed consent doctrine is to be reached, then the disclosure requirements should be higher for younger minors, or at least that greater care should be taken to make the explanations clear to them. Whether either approach is susceptible to a workable formula for clinicians is open to serious question.

In summary, it seems that there has not been enough recognition of the

---

[29] Nev. Rev. Stat. § 129.030.
[30] Cobbs v. Grant, 104 Cal. Rptr. 505, 516, 502, P.2d 1, 12 (1972).

fact that simply enacting legislation that permits minors to consent to treatment for certain problems, or to treatment generally, does not adequately address serious questions posed by the informed consent doctrine. So far there is little case law on informed consent with regard to minors outside of the cases on the "mature minor" doctrine which are only partially relevant. It is possible that if the implications of the informed consent doctrine were fully understood by practitioners, the practical effect might be a diminished willingness to treat minors on their own request without parental involvement, despite specific legislation authorizing consent by minors. This point is worthy of research (perhaps using time–series designs) in jurisdictions adopting such laws.

Consent and Financial Responsibility

As a general rule, contracts by minors are considered to be voidable at common law, and thus subject to either ratification or disaffirmance when the child reaches majority.[31] This sometimes has been offered as a reason for not lowering the age for consent to medical care more broadly. Parents ordinarily are liable for "necessaries" supplied to their minor children based on their basic support obligation.[32] They usually also will be contractually liable if they have given express consent to treatment whether or not the particular care is deemed "necessary." An additional statutory duty to provide medical treatment or meet other health care needs often is placed on them by statutes defining neglect.[33]

Some legislatures that have lowered the age for minors to consent to medical treatment, either generally or specifically, also have dealt expressly with the issue of financial responsibility. One common provision makes it clear that the minor cannot disaffirm the agreement on reaching majority.[34] Another provides that if the extension of medical care is based on the minor's and not the parent's consent, then it is the minor who has the obligation to make payment. Unfortunately there seems to be room for confusion in the construction of such provisions; if the treatment is necessary, it seems inconsistent to relieve a parent from the normal legal duty to provide it. Other questions remain about the applicability of medical or health insurance coverage, though these often may be dealt with in specific contractual provisions.

---

[31] *See* Halbman v. Lemke, 99 Wis.2d 241, 298 N.W.2d 562 (1980); Gardner v. Flowers, 529 S.W.2d 708 (Tenn. 1975).

[32] The minor also may be liable for the cost of such "necessaries," however. *See* Gardner v. Flowers, *supra* note 30.

[33] *See, e.g.,* Ind. Code Ann. § 31–6–4–3; Va. Code Ann. §§ 17.1–241, 63.1–248.2.

[34] *See, e.g.,* La. Rev. Stat. 40:1095. In some instances a statute acknowledges the obligation of both child and parent. *See* Del. Code tit. 13, § 707(b).

The Juvenile Justice Standards on the Rights of Minors adopt the traditional approach that a parent should be liable for medical treatment to which he or she consents, as well as for emergency services provided to an unemancipated minor child. The Standards further provide that a minor who consents to medical treatment under authority of any of the exceptions discussed previously should be liable for payment,[35] and that health insurance under which a minor is covered should allow the child to file claims and receive benefits in those instances where only his or her consent is necessary for treatment. Protection of the minor's confidentiality rights under such circumstances would be effected by barring the insurer from informing the parent or other policy holder that the minor has claimed or received a benefit under the policy unless the attending physician has previously notified the parent of the treatment.[36] The latter proposal is regarded by some as impractical, or at least highly difficult to implement.

Parental Consent to Medical Procedures Not for the Minor's Primary Benefit

In one special group of cases courts have been asked to review the decision or wish of a parent or guardian to consent to a minor child's participation in a medical procedure for the benefit of some person, usually a sibling of the child. Although some state statutes specifically allow minors to consent to the donation of blood and the penetration of tissue,[37] the cases reaching the courts usually have involved much riskier and more invasive procedures such as donation of healthy tissue or organs. Parental consent for such a nontherapeutic purpose has been permitted in almost all of the reported decisions.[38] One court has indicated that not only should judicial approval be obtained, but that there should be community representation in the proceeding.[39] Because of such a caveat and the general rule that a parent or guardian is limited to acts consistent with the interest of the child, it is likely that such problems will be brought to court in most instances in order to protect all persons concerned. One way for the court to permit such treatment is to rationalize a benefit to the healthy child. For example, a court permitting parental consent for donation of a kidney from a healthy child to a sibling might consider it to be in the benefit of the donor who otherwise would be concerned in the future that he or she could

---

[35] *Standards Relating to Rights of Minors*, § 4.3B.

[36] *Id.*, § 4.3D.

[37] *See, e.g.*, La. Rev. Stat. 40:1097.

[38] *See* Little v. Little, 576 S.W.2d 493 (Tex. Civ. App. 1979) and cases cited therein.

[39] *See* Hart v. Brown, 29 Conn. Sup. 368, 280 A.2d 386 (1972).

have kept a sibling alive but did not do so.[40] This approach also might be regarded as a form of sustituted judgment" in which the parent and the court make the decision that they think the minor would make if he or she were legally competent and capable of reasoning maturely. This is not, however, what the courts usually have asserted that they were doing.

One might well raise the question of whether a "mature minor" could consent to such procedures without parental or judicial concurrence. As a practical matter it seems unlikely that many physicians would risk the potential threat of a damage action that seems substantial in such cases in the absence of advance approval by a legally qualified person or agency. This is reinforced by the fact that in the past, physicians or hospitals have sought judicial approval of such procedures involving younger minors even when their parents consented.

Special Problems of Mental or Emotional Disorders of Children

The problems of consent to treatment for emotional or mental disorders of children generally have focused on one of two issues: (1) the degree to which the child may give valid consent to initial, short term, or longer term therapy; and (2) the degree to which a minor can be committed to an institution by parents for treatment without according the child safeguards similar to those that would be extended to an adult.

The first issue has been discussed previously in connection with the general status of minors and consent under the law today. The second recently was the subject of a U.S. Supreme Court decision in *Parham v. J. R.*,[41] which upheld Georgia's law permitting parents to commit minors "voluntarily" to state mental hospitals. Deciding that the Georgia medical factfinding processes were "reasonable and consistent with constitutional guarantees," the court rejected arguments that the constitutional rights rights of children, coupled with the likelihood of parental abuse, were sufficient to require a formal adversary hearing before such voluntary commitments. It explained:

> Our jurisprudence historically has reflected Western Civilization concepts of the family as a unit with broad parental authority over minor children. Our cases have consistently followed that course; our constitutional system long ago rejected any notion that a child is "the mere creature of the state" and, on the contrary, asserted that parents generally "have the right, coupled with the high duty, to recognize and prepare [their children] for additional obligations." . . . Surely, this includes "high duty" to recognize symptoms of illness and to seek and follow medical advice. The

---

[40] *See* Little v. Little, *supra* at note 38.
[41] 442 U.S. 584 (1979).

law's concept of the family rests on a presumption that parents possess what the child lacks in maturity, experience, and capacity for judgment required for making life's difficult decisions. More important, historically it has recognized that natural bonds of affection lead parents to act in the best interest of their children.[42]

In reviewing what process would adequately protect the constitutional rights of a child without unduly restricting parental authority, the court concluded that a "neutral factfinder" should make some sort of inquiry to determine whether statutory requirements for admission are satisfied, and that there be periodic review, by some independent procedure, of a child's continuing need for commitment. This did not mean, however, that the deciding physician must necessarily conduct a formal or quasi-formal hearing. A state is free to require such a hearing, but due process is not violated by use of informal traditional medical investigative techniques.

Because some of the children in the class involved in the *Parham* case were wards of the state at the time of their admission, the court also was called upon to determine what process was due them. The majority stated that they could not assume that the state having custody would act so differently from a natural parent in seeking medical assistance as to require different procedures or further safeguards.

Parental Consent Overruling Child

Another consent issue that can arise involves disagreement between parent and child as to a decision made by the latter under circumstances in which only the child's consent seems legally necessary. This problem was confronted in *In re Smith*,[43] a Maryland case involving an unmarried, pregnant 16-year-old who refused to terminate her pregnacy despite her mother's demands that she do so. A Juvenille Court adjudicated the minor to be a person in need of supervision and ordered her to submit to medical procedures for terminating her pregnancy. The court's order provided that the mother's instructions would be sufficient authorization for any doctor or hospital. At that time Maryland had a minor consent statute that extended to treatment or advice concerning pregnancy. In overruling the Juvenile Court's order, an appeals court explained:

Under the conditions set out, the minor, having the same capacity to consent as an adult, is emancipated from the control of the parents with respect to medical treatment within the contemplation of the statute. We think it follows that if a minor may consent to medical treatment as an adult upon seeking treatment or advice concerning pregnancy, the minor, and particularly a minor over 16 years of age, may not be

---

[42] *Id.* at 602.
[43] 16 Md. App. 209, 295 A.2d 238 (1972).

forced, more than an adult, to accept treatment or advice concerning pregnancy. Consent cannot be the subject of compulsion; its existence depends upon the exercise of voluntary will of those from whom it is obtained; the one consenting has the right to forbid.[44]

The law regarding minors' decision making with regard to abortion has been the subject of significant constitutional interpretation since the *Smith* case. But the Maryland court's rationale that minors should be able to effectuate medical care decisions which they have been legally declared capable to make should have applications to many situations aside from abortion.

The Supreme Court and Abortion

The decisions on abortion handed down by the U.S. Supreme Court during the past decade could provide the base for a separate chapter (or book). They will be discussed here briefly, and only in the context of their significance regarding consent to medical treatment for minors.

It is important to understand that in these cases the Court was called to delineate the scope of state power to limit abortion and regulate its practice. Specific state legislation was reviewed to determine whether it violated individual rights guaranteed under the federal Constitution. In focusing on the limitations that could be placed on abortion for minors, the Court thus was determining whether their rights would be protected just as if they were adults, or whether special restrictions could be maintained for them. This conceptualization in terms of protection of enforcement of minors' rights represents an approach that many states have yet to take in formulating rules regarding minor consent to medical care in cases other than abortion, and whether patient-physician confidentiality should be protected for minor patients just as it is for adults.

In *Roe v. Wade*,[45] the U.S. Supreme Court described the rights of women generally with regard to abortion and spelled out some limitations that states could impose on abortion practice. The Court said that during the first trimester of pregnancy abortion is a matter between a woman and her physician. During a second stage, said to correspond with viability of the fetus, abortion procedures can be regulated by the state, but only in ways "reasonably related to maternal health." After the second stage, abortion can be proscribed except when deemed medically necessary to protect the life or health of the pregnant woman. Since 1973, when *Roe v. Wade* was handed down, a series of cases has reached the Court dealing with various statutes adopted by states that sought

[44] 16 Md. App. 225, 295 A.2d 246 (1972).
[45] 410 U.S. 113 (1973).

to limit abortion to the maximum extent permitted by *Roe v. Wade*. Only some of those cases, dealing with the special problems of minors, will be discussed here.

In 1976, in *Planned Parenthood v. Danforth*, the Court reviewed a post-*Roe v. Wade* statute adopted by Missouri.[46] Among provisions of the statute declared unconstitutional was one requiring parental or *in loco parentis* consent for non-lifesaving abortions performed on unmarried women less than 18 years of age during the first 12 weeks of pregnancy. But by explaining that what the State lacked was power to give a third party "absolute, and possibly arbitrary, veto over the decision of the physician and his patient to terminate the patient's pregnancy," the Court left open the possibility of some lesser requirement of communication to or consultation with parents that might be valid.

The same day that *Danforth* was decided, the Supreme Court returned the case of *Bellotti v. Baird (Bellotti I)*[47] to a U.S. District Court for certification to a state appeals court of certain questions about interpretation of a Massachusetts statute dealing with parental involvement in a child's abortion decision. When the case reappeared before the Supreme Court in 1979 (*Bellotti II*), Justice Powell, in a plurality opinion, stated:

> [I]f the State decides to require a pregnant minor to obtain one or both parents' consent to an abortion, it also must provide an alternative procedure whereby authorization for abortion can be obtained.
>
> A pregnant minor is entitled in such a proceeding to show either: (1) that she is mature enough and well enough informed to make her abortion decision, in consultation with her physician, independently of her parents' wishes; or (2) that even if she is not able to make this decision independently, the desired abortion would be in her best interests. The proceeding in which this showing is made must assure that a resolution of the issue, and any appeals that follow, will be completed with anonymity and sufficient expedition to provide an effective opportunity for an abortion to be obtained. In sum, the procedure must ensure that the provision requiring parental consent does not in fact amount to the "absolute, and possibly arbitrary, veto" that was found impermissible in *Danforth*.[48]

The statute in *Bellotti II* was held unconstitutional because (1) it allowed judicial authorization to be withheld from a minor found by the court "to be mature and fully competent to make this decision independently," and (2) because it required parental consultation in every case, without allowing the minor to establish her maturity to consent or that the abortion would be in her best interest.

In 1981 a Utah statute requiring physicians to "notify, if possible," parents of a minor seeking an abortion was upheld by the Supreme Court in *H. L. v.*

[46] 428 U.S. 52 (1976).

[47] 428 U.S. 132 (1976).

[48] 443 U.S. 622, 643–44 (1979).

Matheson.[49] The Court was careful to explain that in the particular case they considered themselves only to be dealing with an unemancipated minor living at home and dependent on her parents. Because the facts before them were deemed to lack the basis for finding that the minor plaintiff was either emancipated or "mature" in the technical, legal sense, the court found that she was precluded from arguing that the statute was overbroad by possibly extending to such persons. The Court also pointed out that the statute in question gave neither judges nor parents a veto over a minor's abortion decision. The narrow decision sheds little new light on the Court's prior decision. In a short opinion for the Court, Chief Justice Burger concluded:

> That the requirement of notice to parents may inhibit some minors from seeking abortions is not a valid basis to void the statutes as applied to appellant and the class properly before us. The Constitution does not compel a State to fine-tune its statutes so as to encourage or facilitate abortions.[50]

The parade of abortion cases will probably continue before the Supreme Court. Certainly there remain for determination a number of important issues, including whether it is permissible to require notification to the parents of a mature minor, and what restrictions can be placed on decision making by pregnant women in this category. A clear, workable definition of who will be considered a mature minor also is needed.

Conclusion

The law regarding consent to medical treatment for minors, like many areas of family law, still varies significantly among the states. Probably the greatest degree of uniformity lies in the basic tort law regarding the need for parental consent to avoid potential tort liability for treatment of minors in the absence of some specific exception. This in turn has led many legislatures to enact exceptions authorizing minors to consent to treatment for specific illnesses, problems, or conditions. Such statutes probably have been based more on expediency than on desire to protect minors' rights of privacy or self-determination, and they do not seem to reflect considered legislative determination that all minors are qualified to understand fully the decisions that they are ostensibly authorized to take. Nor do they adequately take into consideration the problems of the physician in complying with informed consent requirements widely imposed by judicial or legislative action. Often the statutes have even generated confusion among physicians about their rights and duties regarding

[49] 450 U.S. 398 (1981).
[50] *Id.* at 1173.

maintaining the confidences of minor patients as opposed to notifying their parents that a treatment course has been commenced. This not only has the potential for placing the physician in an unclear legal position, but also can be counterproductive to the practical goal of condition-specific statutes by discouraging minors from obtaining care through their own consent for fear of what might be communicated to their parents.

These issues and uncertainties point up the need for reexamination and careful conceptualization of the entire area of consent to medical care for minors. Such a review might well be expanded to other areas such as minors' contracts or wills, where current limitations often can be explained only through resort to anachronistic views about the capacities as well as the social and economic roles of children.

The development of a "mature minor" rule in many jurisdictions reflects recognition of the problems of using majority age arbitrarily as the factor for determining legal capacity to consent. Expansion or clarification of this doctrine is one possible avenue for reform. This however, would require careful formulation of the criteria for determining "maturity" and some clear safeguards for the physician who acts in accord with such announced guidelines.

Studies about the capacity and effectiveness of decision making by minors at various ages could provide better starting points for legislators than the "gut reactions" that one strongly suspects have formed the basis for legislative declarations of capacity based on age in the past. And finally, questions about the impact on the family of allowing independent decision making by minors in an area which affects them so vitally as health care should be faced squarely in any deliberations. Failure to do this has invariably led to problems, as the current confusion about physician-parent communication indicates.

Chapter 5

Decision Making Related to Health

When Could/Should Children Act Responsibly?

CHARLES E. LEWIS

In the literature related to health, references to decision making usually are concerned with the actions of physicians. Simulations of clinical decision making have been developed to assist in the instruction and practice of physician's assistants and nurse practitioners. Decision analysis is employed in studying diagnostic problem-solving. In contrast, the health-related actions of individuals—their lifestyles, risk-taking, and use of health services—are studied as behaviors affected by beliefs, attitudes, and social norms. Although people are seen as making decisions about when to seek care and which option to select for treatment (if any options are presented), the general impression to be gained from this literature is that people behave and physicians decide.

The scope of potential decision making or actions taken representing choices by individuals with regard to their own health care is determined largely by their role or location—in or out of the formal health care system—and their age. Individuals *can* choose or select from a variety of options related to their own lifestyle. They can decide to smoke or not smoke. They can decide what and how much to eat. They can determine, to a large degree, their degree of physical activity. As indicated however, most of these behaviors have not been studied as decisions made consciously among choices. Adults do, however,

CHARLES E. LEWIS ● Department of Medicine, University of California, Los Angeles, California 90024.

decide when and for what reasons to seek attention from health professionals (at least for initial visits).

When individuals assume the role of the patient, the number of decisions available to them in most cases is reduced. Despite concern with informed consent, except when dealing with high-risk interventions likely to have poor outcomes or when required by hospital regulations, most physicians fail to present options for treatment to patients. If they do, they often describe the alternatives in such a way that the probability of an individual concurring with the physician's recommendation is greatly enhanced.

If adults have little involvement in decision making related to their own care (except for the selection of personal lifestyles that are important determinants of health), then children have almost none. While there are a variety of articles in the literature describing "children's use of health services," these only serve to perpetuate the myth that children are more than passive participants in this process. Children are taken to physicians by adults whenever the child has a problem or the adult has a problem. In the office, many physicians limit their verbal interactions to the adult caretaker, viewing the child primarily as the bearer of pathology (if any is present).

The care of children represents transactions between adults. Physicians spend much of their effort assessing the competencies of mothers, both as historians and as administrators of therapeutic programs to be carried out under the doctor's orders. Children are seldom involved in the processes related to their own care. There are some noteworthy exceptions. Several studies have demonstrated the reduction in psychological effects and postoperative complications of hospitalization and surgery by involving children in the processes of care (Gellert, 1958). This may include "innoculating" them against emotional trauma by explaining what they may expect when they wake up after anasthesia, allowing them to participate in certain noncritical decisions related to care, etc.

To date, with the exception of our own work to be discussed, public concerns with children's involvement in health-related decisions have been concentrated around some rather rare problems. These lie within the intersect of the fields of law and medicine (or more precisely, psychiatry). The specific questions that seem to represent the most urgent concerns of courts, psychologists/psychiatrists, and some physicians, are derived from relatively rare phenomena. Questions are *not* being raised about when children can/should seek routine health care on their own, or when they can/should be involved in giving consent for routine surgical procedures such as tonsillectomy or herniorrhaphy.

The treatment of children in the legal system seems no different: Children are not judged by their peers; they are not allowed to present their own perspectives on issues; adults speak for (and impose adult norms on) children. Medicine does not have a monopoly on paternalistic practices.

For the past two decades, there has been increasing concern over the rights of individuals as they relate to health services. This includes the right to have access to care, and the right to be informed of the consequences of any treatment procedure. Most individuals view the practice of involving patients in their own care as desirable from an ethical point of view. Patients now have their own Bill of Rights.

More recently there has been discussion of the role/responsibility of the individual in maintaining his/her own health. This rhetoric has increased as the costs of health services have risen, often without demonstrable evidence of equivalent increases in the efficacy of care.

Some now advocate patient participation in care for a different reason. It may be the best means available for enhancing patients' abilities to adhere to professional recommendations (Steckel & Swain, 1977). There is no evidence that those advocating increased patient control to improve outcomes of care are less "ethical' than those promoting it as a personal right. However, many see this tactic as "blaming the victim," *i.e.*, suggesting to individuals that whatever happens to them is largely their own fault and not that of the profession.

Children's Health-Related Beliefs and Behaviors

Our own research has not been concerned with any of the relatively uncommon medical/legal problems faced by courts and attorneys. Since 1971, we have been examining the origins of children's health-related beliefs and behaviors, and the extent to which children can make responsible decisions about the more trivial problems (as defined by professionals) that afflict them as they go about their work of attending school, playing, and growing up.

Our orientations should be clear; we are not primarily interested in increasing children's rights for political or ethical reasons alone. Our objectives have been to test the hypothesis that by participating in decisions related to health, children will learn to choose courses of action that benefit their health. We are interested in the processes of children's decision making as a means to an end.

Our interest in this research grew out of the experiences of my colleague, Mary Ann Lewis. While serving as a public health nurse in a child and youth project in the mid-1960s, she began to see as "patients" an increasing number of children from disadvantaged families. Her office was adjacent to a public school, and children, having seen her make home visits to their families, began dropping in to talk about their problems. Her panel of patients grew, and they began to make regularly scheduled appointments (which they kept) to see her. Her observations suggested that this experience seemed to have a positive effect on many of the children, who began to have a greater interest in being responsible for their own health.

At this time, my principal research interest was the health and illness behaviors of adults, which represents the principal barrier to the achievement of improved health status in the population. A significant proportion of adults (most often males) delay in seeking care in the face of complaints that have ominous consequences (Hackett, Cassem, & Baker, 1973). Approximately one-third of all individuals who gain access to the health care system and receive an appropriate treatment for their illness, comply with the regimen prescribed (Marston, 1970). For example, an individual with hypertension may be placed on a diet low in salt, asked to exercise regularly, and prescribed a drug to take on a regular basis. Studies suggest that about one-third of such individuals follow very little of this advice, about one-third comply with all the recommendations, and the other third are intermittently compliant. Also, 10–15% of the people in any defined population make over half of all ambulatory visits to doctors (Avent, 1967). These individuals have been termed the "worried well"; they have no detectable disease.

Involving Children in Decision Making

In 1971 we began a project entitled "Child Initiated Care" which addressed two questions:

1. Given the passivity of children in an adult-oriented health care system, what behaviors would children exhibit if they were free to initiate care on their own (without adult control)?

2. Would participation in the decision-making processes related to their own care have a positive impact on children's health-related beliefs and behaviors?

To create an adult-free system we established a "care card system" in the University Elementary School at the University of California, Los Angeles. Cards were placed in boxes throughout the school and on the playground. Children were told that whenever they wanted to see the nurse (who was present whenever school was in session) all they had to do was take a card, make a mark or write their name on the top, leave it on the teacher's desk, and go directly to the nurse. There a history was taken, they were examined, and the nurse's findings presented to them. They then were asked to formulate options for the treatment and disposition of their own problems. They were subsequently asked to decide among those options and their choice was honored.

There were, of course, certain ground rules and assumptions important to the operation of this system. One of these was that the system described would operate *only* when there was no threat to the health or welfare of the child. For example, if a child came to the office with a temperature of 102° or a severe cut, the child was not placed in the decision-making role with regard to the treatment and disposition of that problem. We also assumed that all complaints were *real* to the child, regardless of how trivial, and that each encounter presented a "teachable moment" for affecting future health-related beliefs and behaviors of the child.

The results have been presented elsewhere, (Lewis, Lewis, Lorimer, & Palmer, 1977). Children rapidly learned the rules of this system. There is evidence that they were quite aware of the nature of the intervention. Despite some initial concerns voiced by them, (such as "But, *you* are supposed to tell me what to do!"), almost all displayed ability to participate, and even nonusers were aware of the changes in the nature of the transaction.

Increasing access to care altered the patterns of utilization. Among boys, a twofold increase in access to care was followed by a twofold increase in use. However, among girls, and particularly younger girls, there were more striking increases in the rates of visitation. The proportion of children, during the school year, who did not seek care from the nurse decreased, and the proportion of high utilizers changed also. In both cases, girls exhibited an increased tendency to use services compared to boys.

In the "adult-free" health service system in the experimental school, the use of services by children ages 5 to 12 closely resembled that of adults. The actual rates of visiting by boys and girls (3.25 and 4.83 visits per year) were not too dissimilar from those reported for adults 35 to 54 years of age (3.7 and 5.6 visits per year). The ratio of female/male utilization for children under 14 is 0.90 in the "real world." That is, more boys are taken to doctors than girls. Approximately the same ratio was found for the utilization of pediatric services by this population. In the experimental school the sex ratio of utilization was 1.62 and 1.48 for the two years of observation. The sex ratio of utilization for adults 35 to 54 years of age is 1.55.

The frequency distribution of utilization among these students was quite similar to that observed in adult populations, and the same variables influenced use. Children from more affluent backgrounds made more visits, and girls came more often than boys. Psychological orientations were associated with patterns of use. Children with higher perceived susceptibility and who perceived the benefits of care to be greater were significantly higher users of services.

The higher rate of use of services by young males in the health care system of the United States may be explained in terms of the role of the mother as a controller of the use of services. Mothers are important in many other ways with regard to children's use of services. The child's health status, as perceived by the child and as reported by the mother, were found to be highly associated.

Significant associations also were found between a mother's tendency to seek care for herself and for her child, and the child's pattern of use of services at UES and his/her frequency of being taken to a physician. The mother is not only the principal decisionmaker in child care, but also an important role model for the social learning of health and illness behavior.

The behaviors observed were to some degree predictable through interviews designed to determine the child's health-related beliefs, *i.e.*, their perceived vulnerability and perceptions of the benefits of care. After this "treatment," children who were high utilizers (without medical cause) demonstrated significant shifts in their health beliefs. They had lower estimates of personal susceptibility and the benefits of care. However, they continued to be high users of services. The children who constituted the high users group were perceived by us to have problems with basic self-esteem and self-concept. They were viewed by the teachers as children who had problems making decisions about *anything*, *e.g.*, what to do when they had lost or forgotten their lunch. There was no doubt, based upon sequential interviews with the students, that they perceived that they were involved in the decision-making processes related to their care.

Informed Consent by Children

In 1975, investigators from the Department of Pediatrics approached the experimental school with regard to involving school children in a trial of swine influenza vaccine. The question was referred to us. We suggested that since the children were accustomed to being involved in decision making related to their own care, they should be the first ones to be involved in the consent process.

Since the study was limited to children between 6 and 9 years of age (by the pediatricians and virologists), only classrooms with children of this age range were included. We went to each of these classrooms on the same morning, informing the children that a study was to be conducted and that they were going to be asked to participate. The nature of the study was described, but few details were provided. After a brief pause, questions were invited. This was done to permit the children to initiate inquires about the experiment. An effort was made to conduct these discussions in a completely neutral tone. The process was tape recorded so that the sessions could be reviewed for possible bias in terms of suggestions by the presenters that the trial was either "good" or "bad."

Following the question-and-answers period, risks and benefits were reviewed as outlined in the protocol and children were given individual consent forms. They were told that if they wanted to participate in the study, they should indicate yes, and if they did not want to do so, they should write no. However, if they felt that this was a decision they were unprepared to make by themselves, they would be allowed to share this decision making with their parents.

They were further instructed that *only* those children who indicated they would like to participate, or who felt unable to make a decision, would have a letter sent home to their parents describing the trial. It was emphasized that in these cases parents would participate and make the ultimate decisions, and only those children whose parents agreed, could be given the vaccine. The parents of those children responding no would *not* be sent any letter inviting them to give consent for their children to participate. Any child saying no, in essence, made the final decision. While the discussions involved groups, children were not allowed to review their decisions with others until the forms were collected.

Subsequently, letters were sent home with children indicating yes or "?" accompanied by a cover letter from the principal of the school stating that parental consent was required for children to receive the vaccine. The study and its risks and benefits were described in detail as required by the protocol for the study. Pressures of time did not permit mailing these letters to the homes, but contact with a sample of parents indicated that essentially all letters arrived at their intended destination. Sending communications home with the children is a common procedure at this school.

Informed Consent by Question and Answer

The presentation in each classroom lasted approximately five minutes. Question-and-answer sessions took from 15 to 30 minutes. All presentations were made on the same morning. The form of the question-and-answer sessions was remarkably similar. All questions were initiated by the students; the presenters' only question was, "Anything else you'd like to know? Children verified that the study would involve getting "shots." They asked about lthe side effects; these were described. They asked how soon the side effects might occur and how likely these were to occur. They also asked why blood samples (to determine antibody responses) would be taken. Younger children (age 6) often asked the presenter to demonstrate how much blood would be taken (two teaspoonfuls) and the size of the needle to be used.

Children asked about the magnitude of the side effects with such questions as, "Will I be sick enough to have to stay home from school?" Children in more than one class asked if "it" (the vaccine) had been tried on anyone else and why *they* in particular had been chosen for this study. They also asked if the presenter had taken the shot (answer: no). With regard to benefits, they asked what would happen if they were exposed to, or got influenza.

A review of the tape recordings provided no evidence of any classroom variation in the introductory statements or biased responses to questions.

Differences by Age and Sex

There were only two differences noted among age groups. In all but one class—composed only of six-year-olds—the question and answer period clarified the potential future benefits to the subjects, *i.e.*, the vaccine, if effective, would keep them from getting influenza, if exposed. Older children more often asked about the likelihood of influenza occurring in their community this year. (Obviously, several of these epidemiologic questions could only be answered honestly by saying, "We don't know.") There were no differences in the type of questions asked by boys and girls.

The final step in each classroom before asking children to decide was the reading of the risks and benefits associated with the project, as enumerated in the protocol. This amounted to a reiteration of the material generated by the children themselves in the question and answer period—with the exception of the one class of 6-year-olds.

Of the 213 children "at risk," 54% said either 'yes' or felt that they could not make the decision without their parents. Of those parents who received letters, only 15% agreed that their child should participate in the trial, and all but two of this group received the vaccine. Two children had mild febrile reactions.

While from 70 to 90% of the children in each class (N = 20–30) participated in the discussions about the vaccine, there was no opportunity to relate the nature of the child's participation or questions posed and the decision made. Thus, it was not possible to examine the child's level of information at the time he/she decided about participation.

Under the system of Child-Initated Care, utilization patterns have been found to be quite similar to those of adults, *i.e.*, approximating a negative binomial distribution. During the year 1975–76, approximately 30% of the 376 children in the school made no visits to the school nurse, while 18% made seven or more visits and accounted for over 50% of all visits recorded. The members of the latter group have been termed "high users." The cut-point was placed at seven visits in order to define, for statistical purposes, children who compose that portion of the population making about one-half of all visits.

There was a statistically significant association between patterns of use and the decisions made, with high users being more likely to volunteer. In this setting using the care card system and in other public schools where the study has since been replicated, high users have been found *not* to have significant illnesses or medical problems.

When the responses were examined on the basis of age, younger children more often declined to give consent. Among 6-year-olds, 80% said no, while for 7-, 8-, and 9-year-olds the figures were 56%, 46%, and 27% respectively.

More girls were unable to decide than boys, and when patterns of use and decision making were examined for each sex separately, among girls, higher users more often volunteered for the trial ($\chi^2 = 25.6, p < .001$). Among boys, a similar trend was observed; this, however, was not statistically significant (Lewis, Lewis, & Ifekwunigue, 1978).

Child-Initiated Care in Public Schools

In 1976 we began a replication of the child-initiated care study in a public school system. The design permitted the assignment of schools to control and experimental groups, and even the separation of the "treatment" into two stages. In both experimental schools the care card system was put in place. In one of these schools in the second year, children were involved by the nurse in the decision-making process as previously described. The schools involved served children from disadvantaged families. Approximately 38% of these families were on Aid to Dependent Children. There was a multi-ethnic student body: 38% of the children were Hispanic, 28% black, and 25% white.

School officials expressed considerable apprehension about the consequences of installing this system in these schools. However, the rate of "embargoing" or removing children's privileges to use the system because of gross abuse turned out to be only 3%. That figure was very similar to that recorded at the University Elementary School, where the majority of children were from upper-middle-class, highly educated, white families.

The results of this replication study have recently been summarized for publication (Lewis, Lewis, & Lorimer, 1982). The same patterns of use of services were observed. The same changes in health beliefs also were found as a result of giving children an opportunity to seek care on their own. There was one major difference, which we attributed to the differences in beliefs and expectations of the children involved. In the original study, children saw medicine and physicians in a *supporting* role, in terms of maintenance of their health. In the disadvantaged population, physicians and medicines were seen as the most important ways of maintaining health and of getting well when sick. Given these differences, it may not be surprising to find that children from disadvantaged families were much higher users of service. This may reflect a higher level of stress impinging on these children in the school, family, and community environments. They also demonstrated a higher rate of pretending to be ill, *i.e.*, using the sick role to escape from unpleasant circumstances.

While observational data indicate that children were offered options to be involved in the formulation of decisions about their own treatment, minority group children did *not* perceive this to be true. Among white children in the study there was a significant shift in their perceptions of "who decided" when they went to the nurse, from pretest to posttest interviews. This perception was not shared by black and Hispanic children. Perhaps for some groups in our society, opportunities for choices are so limited, especially for children, that the presentation of such opportunities may not be perceived as "real."

Teaching Decision Making to Children

As a result of observations made about problems with decision making by inappropriate utilizers at the University Elementary School, two steps were taken. First, we added a series of questions to our interview schedule for children that focused on their perceived scope of decision making in a variety of "activities of daily living in childhood." We also decided that the best "treatment" for these children would be to teach decision-making skills *per se* in the classroom as an overlay as part of a broader health education curriculum.

Data on scope of decision making in childhood were collected on the children from disadvantaged families in the replication study of child-initiated care. Children were asked about eight activities—watching television, choosing a playmate, selecting what clothes to wear, when to do homework, when to take a bath, when to go to bed, when to get a haircut, and what medicines to take. They were asked to indicate who decided about each of these. Choices offered were, "I do," "we do" (the child and some adult member of the family), or "they do." Children perceived themselves as the principle decisionmakers in only two of these activities: television watching and the choice of playmate. They also saw themselves as involved in very little joint decision making—decisions involving them and other individuals. Most of the decisions for these children were made by mothers, with fathers being involved significantly only in the choice of playmates and television watching.

Actions for Health

The development of the curriculum proceeded based upon the following guidelines:

1. The two "overlay" or process units—decision making and self-reliance—would be taught *separately* from health content *before* being applied to the two selected health-content units—body cues and balanced living. This was a somewhat innovative approach, in and of itself. The process of decision making and the skills of self-reliance had not been taught as such. In some curricula they are

mixed at random with various health-content areas (causing confusion so that neither process nor content are learned clearly). It is the basic educational assumption of this curriculum (supported by learning theory) that a new skill needs to be taught separately in a familiar context before being applied to a new content area. The two process units of the curriculum teach the component parts of decision making and self-reliance in a variety of everyday situations/ problems *first* to increase the probability of children being able to apply them to specific health situations/problems later.

2. Each of the four units would be developed so that it could be used alone. Thus, teachers could select the unit(s) of their choice in the order of their choice. An optimal sequence of the four units would be suggested to maximize learning. Decision making is the recommended starting point, followed by the self-reliance unit, and then either of the health application units. However, we felt it was important to *let teachers make decisions* about how they would like to use the curriculum, since it is, after all, concerned with decision making.

3. To further individualize or "tailor" the curriculum to each teacher's classroom needs, core and optional lessons would be provided from which each teacher could pick and choose as needed. Again, an "ideal" sequence or flow chart of each unit's lessons would be suggested to maximize learning.

4. The curriculum would be a series of lesson plans for the teacher and not another health textbook for children; in this way, the lessons could be designed to be active to motivate students at all levels of skills rather than dependent on passive reading skills.

5. Because most of the lessons would be active and not dependent on reading levels, the same basic lesson plans would be used for grades 1–6; however, in those lessons requiring application of the decision-making and self-reliance processes, both primary and upper grade plans would be provided to accomodate age-level/cognitive differences.

6. The lesson plans would be written in sufficient detail to be self-sufficient so that no further planning was required other than gathering common classroom materials. By providing step-by-step procedures, the lesson plan would be easy to implement after one reading. Simple variations for decreasing as well as increasing the level of difficulty would also be provided to help the teacher "adjust" the lesson to a particular group of students.

7. Many of the lessons would be designed to be integrated with other areas of the curriculum, both to minimize teaching time constraints and to maximize transfer of learning to other areas of the students' lives. For example, several of the decision-making lessons would be designed to be integrated with language arts or social studies, as indicated on the top of each lesson plan. This consideration proved to be an important one since many teachers who had no time in their busy schedules for "health" were able to fit in those lessons that integrated with other areas of curriculum.

8. Each unit and/or lesson would include related home tasks in order to promote transfer of health-related learnings in school to the family settings. A sample letter to go home at the beginning of each unit also would be provided to help keep parents informed and, hopefully, involved at the various stages of the curriculum.

9. The curriculum would not require elaborate equipment or materials. These often are expensive, easily damaged or lost, and difficult to replace. Common classroom materials would be used and samples of any special worksheets could be copied out of the teacher's guide.

The finished product was originally conceived of as a file box of teaching cards. It evolved to its present form as a perforated teacher's guidebook.

Some time during the process of development the curriculum was named *Actions for Health* (AFH) (de la Sota, Lewis, & Lewis, 1978). The title serves to emphasize two important aspects of the program: (1) it is designed to be an *action*-oriented educational program in which students participate actively at every level; and (2) it attempts to help students become more self-reliant (reflective) decision makers who will choose to act in ways that maintain their health. The subtitle, *Decision-Making and Self-Reliance Activities for Healthful Living, Grades 1–6*, was added after we had received consistent feedback telling us that it was the decision-making and self-reliance units that attracted teachers.

Development of Specific Lessons Unit by Unit

The Decision-Making Unit

Since this unit on decision-making skills provides the basis for the rest of the curriculum, it was the first to be developed. Several of the concepts of Janis and Mann are embedded in this set of lessons, including types of decisions and the decision–making balance sheet. (Janis & Mann, 1979) The latter has been translated into "decision-making tic-tac-toe," but there remains heavy emphasis on reviewing feelings and values associated with each option. A "Snap Decision" game is used to illustrate the differences between reflexive behavior (habits) and the reflective process of decision-making.

Other lessons deal with *types* of decision (I, We, or They decisions labeled as Types I, II, and III decisions). This is taught in "Stand Up and Be Counted," and the steps of decision making (from identifying the problem to evaluating a solution) are introduced concretely in Lesson 2, "What to Do About the Big Bad Wolf." They are then applied to real problems in Lesson 3a, "What to Do About a Bully," for primary grades, and in Lesson 3b, "Decision-Making Tic-Tac-Toe Grid," for upper graders.

The Self Reliance Unit

Specifically teaching decision-making skills represents a rather unique approach to health education. However, defining and teaching self-reliance skills represents a real innovation. Self-concept units abound in general education and self-care units are increasingly common in health education curricula. Focusing on self-reliance was a very different way to approach the teaching of self-concept and self-care skills to children. Consequently, there was no major consultant or classic work to use as in the development of the decision-making unit.

Our definition of self-reliance evolved from months of lesson design and piloting. Self-reliance is generally defined as depending on one's own abilities, efforts, and resources. However, in a health curriculum for children in the elementary grades, the term self-reliance required a two-part definition with equal emphasis on both parts: (1) solving a problem on one's own when appropriate and (2) seeking help when the problem is not appropriate for solving on one's own.

The importance of this new two-part definition, especially the second half, becomes evident when the self-reliance skills learned in this general process unit are transferred to self-care decisions in the Body Cues unit. Given a health problem, such as a head injury, it is as important to know when it is appropriate to take care of the problem on one's own as it is to know when it is necessary to seek adult help. Thus, the core lessons of the self-reliance unit are designed to help children begin to formulate criteria for determining when a self-reliant option is appropriate and when it is not.

The selected core and optional lessons in the self-reliance unit are easily integrated with a variety of other content areas in the general curriculum. The lessons provide children with many opportunities to practice appropriate self-reliant behaviors in both the school and home environments. They also provide teachers concrete ways to foster self-reliance. (We have found, incidentally, that this unit led to changes in teacher behavior, as well as changes in children's behavior.)

The Body Cues Unit

Once the children have learned basic/general decision-making and self-reliance skills, they can then be taught to apply these skills to specific health problems. Earlier research suggested that "health" was not a salient concept for children. Therefore, this health application unit focused on the 11 most common illnesses and injuries seen in the school nurse's office as identified in the study of child-initiated care.

The major portion of this unit is based on protocols or "Self-Care Guides" for each of the 11 common childhood illnesses and injuries. These guides are similar in concept to the decision charts used in a popular self-care book, *Take Care of Yourself: A Consumer's Guide to Medical Care* (Vickery & Fries, 1976). However, the format of these Self-Care Guides is not the usual flow chart, but a grid of decision alternatives patterned after the "Decision-Making Tic-Tac-Toe Grid" in the decision-making unit. Using a grid familiar to children from previous practice in decision making, the focus of this unit is applying that process to problems commonly faced by them.

To facilitate this transfer of previously learned skills, the Type I-II-III criteria for deciding when self-care is appropriate or not appropriate are built into the top of each Self-Care Guide. Once the children have used these criteria to make an initial decision about whether to seek adult help or apply self-care, they are directed to one of two areas of the Self-Care Guide.

If the criteria indicate that adult help is needed, a section of the guide tells the child what to expect at the nurse's or doctor's office—a type of "emotional innoculation" as suggested by Janis. If the criteria indicate self-care, however, the other section of the guide provides a decision-making tic-tac-toe grid of the various alternatives for self-care mapped out in a form familiar to the children. Each of the Self-Care Guides gives not only alternatives for self-care but also the positive and negative outcomes of each alternative to aid reflective decision making. Each guide, with medical alternatives and their outcomes, was developed and approved by a panel of pediatricians.

A major problem in this unit was how to motivate the use of these Self-Care Guides. To help personalize the eleven illnesses and injuries to be studied in this unit, "Body Maps" (large cartoon drawings) were developed along with small stickers containing cartoon symbols for each of the health complaints. In one lesson, children make individual and class body maps that serve to demonstrate the epidemiology of these 11 illnesses and injuries. The illustrated care symbols were also devised to be used in a variety of ways, such as a treatment lotto game, to show appropriate care of each health complaint.

The Balanced Living Unit

This unit was the last to be completed and was by far the most difficult to develop. It is designed for teachers who wish to extend the decision-making and self-reliance skills learned earlier to the promotion of preventive health behaviors. By taking a broad or total approach to health— physical, emotional, social, and intellectual—this final unit attempts to round out the curriculum by applying/transferring the children's self-reliant decision-making skills to such health content areas as: nutrition, exercise, hygiene, accident prevention, feelings (emotions), socialization, and intellectual needs.

The unit begins and ends with each child calculating their "NET" Score.

In this exercise children analyze the balance of their health habits ("NET" = N for Not Enough, E for Enough, and T for Too Much). Children next learn to balance a meal based on the four-food-group model. This model then is extended to become "A Balanced Life Wheel." The importance of balancing one's physical, emotional, social, and intellectual needs is emphasized. After these core lessons, teachers can use the optional lessons to help them create (or have the children create) learning centers which balance health needs within the classroom. In these centers children can take an exercise break, talk out a problem with a friend or group of peers, or push themselves to take on a challenging intellectual task.

With generous support from the Robert Wood Johnson Foundation, we have just completed a randomized clinical trial of this curriculum in six school districts throughout the United States. This study has involved over 200 classrooms and 5,000 students. The data are currently being analyzed, but several things are obvious at this stage. First, the extent to which decision making for self-care is taught depends upon the teachers' personal beliefs and values related to these concepts. If a teacher does not believe that children should be involved in decision making, or if the teacher is concerned about children providing self-care for their minor wounds and illnesses, then the lessons are taught with such a lack of enthusiasm that there is no evidence of impact. Second, when taught "well," there are consequences both for the teachers, who often realize the extent to which they are encouraging dependence or constricting children's personal opportunities for decision making, and for children's immediate application of these skills.

When Can/Should Children Decide?

There are no data in the literature that permit an answer to these questions. In fact, there are no published data on the scope of children's decision making in a variety of areas. That is not surprising, since we know very little about the social context of childhood.

Can or could implies concern with competency, including the ability to comprehend the consequences tomorrow of action taken today. Should expresses a value statement. While the two represent quite different domains, they are related. That is, competency derives from more than just pure cognitive developmental level. It also reflects social learning from opportunities provided by those who believe children should practice relevant skills. Which is worse, in terms of consequences to the child, to require/permit a child to make decisions that are beyond his or her capacity, or to refuse to permit them to exercise a capacity that (theoretically) exists?

In the case of children's decision making as consumers of health care (including the giving of informed consent), we have defined competency in terms of the specific issue. We have permitted children to practice deciding between several options in the treatment of an abrasion or a runny nose. We have allowed them to "screen" decisions related to participation in a vaccine trial, but made this a Type II (we) decision.

As a result, we have stimulated children to seek involvement (not control) in other decisions that may be surprising to a family. We have had mothers tell us of occasions when their child asked to talk directly to "their doctor" over the telephone.

It is important to distinguish between the unusual circumstances surrounding the types of "cases" of interest to the courts-psychiatry-law and the relation of these experiences to children's involvement in health-related decisions. In the former, the child-family relationship is often strained or nonexistent. The court sees those cases where a Type II (we) decision does not or cannot exist. The legal question is whether it should be a Type I (I, the child) or Type III (they) decision. Experiences within the courts may be useful in terms of subsequent similar "cases." However, data on the age of competency for consent for abortion (when *can* one decide) cannot be translated into a prescription as to when one *should* decide about this or other health-related actions.

Research

It seems appropriate, given the preceding question, to conclude by suggesting some research issues for future investigation. Proceeding from the basic to the applied:

1. What are the types or styles of decision making exhibited by children? Can one identify the Janis–Mann types of decisions; if so, at what age?
2. What are the determinants of competency in decision making? How important are self-esteem and self-concept?
3. How does the subject topic and social context influence performance?
4. What is the natural history of the scope of decision making in childhood as perceived by children and adult family members?
5. What is the impact of teaching decision making skills on performance and scope of decisions made?
6. What is the relative use of information and values in the decisions rendered by those concerned with children's decision making?

Our current research activities are related to questions 1, 4, and 5.

Summary

Our work over the past 10 years has provided us no experience with the processes of informed consent by children related to major problems of medical/legal or societal concern. We have had no experience with children who have been wards of the court. However, we have worked with several thousand children. We have been enormously impressed with their competence. In fact, our major conclusion is that children are far more competent in decision making than adults believe them to be. Children *can* learn decision making and, when given the opportunity, make remarkably responsible decisions.

Our experiences and the literature indicate that very little is known about the scope of decision making in childhood and the extent to which children are adequately prepared for their adult roles as responsible decision makers. It seems apparent that society does nothing to encourage the graded practicing of these skills.

Perhaps investigations of the kind that we have described are most useful in begging questions about the social context of childhood. They should cause us to ask why adults find it so difficult to permit children to practice, within defined limits, those skills which many of them perform so poorly.

References

Avnet, H. H. *Physicians' service patterns and illness rates.* New York: Group Health Insurance Company, 1967.

de la Sota, A., Lewis, C. E., & Lewis, M. A. *Actions for health.* Menlo Park, Calif.: Addision-Wesley, 1980.

Gellert, E. Reducing the emotional stresses of hospitalization for children. *American Journal of Occupational Therapy*, 1958, *12*, 125–129.

Hackett, T. P., Cassem, M. H., & Raker, J. W. Patient delay in cancer. *New England Journal of Medicine*, 1973, *289*, 14.

Janis, I. L., & Mann, L. *Decision Making.* New York: Free Press, 1977.

Lewis, C. E., Lewis, M. A., Lorimer, A., & Palmer, B. Child-initiates care: The use of school nursing services by children in an 'adult-free' system. *Pediatrics*, 1977, *60*, 499–507.

Lewis, C. E., Lewis, M. A., & Ifekwunigue, M. Informed consent by children and participation in an influenza vaccine trial. *American Journal of Public Health*, 1978, *68*, 1079–1082.

Lewis, C. E., Lewis, M. A., & Lorimer, A. *Children's use of school health services.* Report to a research project supported by the UCLA Health Services Research Center, 1982.

Marston, M. Compliance with medical regimes: A review of the literature. *Nursing Research Report*, 1970, *19*, 312.

Steckel, S. B., & Swain, M. A. Contracting with patients to improve compliance. *Hospitals*, 1977 *51*, 81–83.

Vickery, D. M., & Fries, J. F. *Take care of yourself: A consumer's guide to medical care.* Menlo Park, Calif.: Addison-Wesley, 1976.

CHAPTER 6

Informed Consent and Pediatric Care

MICHAEL A. GRODIN and JOEL J. ALPERT

The nature and scope of medical practice over the past century has expanded rapidly. The physician's ability to diagnose and to treat exceedingly complex diseases has brought a new set of ethical, psychosocial, legal, and economic dilemmas. Today's physician is in a cultural milieu with demands and expectations that far surpass those of his predecessors. These changes have affected the physician-patient relationship that has evolved from one with the patient dependent upon the physician to one that requires more interaction.

A growing literature, especially legal, has addressed issues of informed consent, children's rights, and medical research (Bergen, 1974). The legal system has made enormous strides toward accepting minors as competent clients. Social scientists have explored the changing nature of family structure and child care practices (Bronfenbrenner, 1977). Psychologists have provided new developmental information and clearer insights into cognitive competency (Grisso & Vierling, 1978). Physician behavior and practice have been affected by both legal decisions and the acquisition of new social and psychological data.

Much has been written about the need for informed consent in conducting research with children. These data require careful application to providing health services for children (Shaw, 1973). If the physician is to be concerned with the total health and well-being of the pediatric patient, then he or she

MICHAEL A. GRODIN and JOEL J. ALPERT ● Department of Pediatrics, Boston University School of Medicine and Boston City Hospital, Boston, Massachusetts 02118.

must learn to incorporate these changes into day-to-day practice. In this chapter we will explore the nature of pediatric consent issues as consent relates to medical treatment. We will present a careful analysis of the child, parent and physician interaction. Our discussion will include the characteristics of the pediatric setting, the vulnerability of the child within this setting, and the sources of that vulnerability. Key areas and how they affect the consent problem will be discussed in detail. These include the developmental level of the child, the medical condition being treated, and the nature of the physician, child, and family relationship. Finally, we will raise questions that may be addressed by further research and investigation.

Issues in the Pediatric Patient's Ability to Consent

Limited Information and Legal Requirements

Successful medical care and health care maintenance requires informed patients. Long-term health and well-being within the framework of a medical model can be successfully achieved only with the cooperation and active participation of both the pediatric patient and, where appropriate, the guardian or parent. An appropriate understanding and knowledge about disease, including natural history, prognosis, and therapeutic modalities, is necessary for active participation in decision making. Information and explanation then form the cornerstone for the child, family, and physician interaction. It is only after information has been provided in a supportive and sensitive physician–patient relationship that the obtaining of consent can be realistically approached.

From a legal viewpoint, the patient-physician contract is based upon and formally entered into only when there exists a mutual consent agreement (Vaccarino, 1978). If the patient is incompetent to consent, then a legal guardian is needed to accept that role and act in the patient's best interests. The minor's competence to consent to medical care cannot be evaluated without careful reference to appropriate legal concepts.

In recent years there have been legal trends toward allowing minors to consent for medical treatment if it can be demonstrated that they have sufficient maturity to understand the full significance of the contemplated therapy (Mnookin, 1978). Though the courts realize that age alone is not always an indicator of intelligence or maturity, they have tried to establish guidelines to lend uniformity to the legality of informed consent by minors. Statutory provisions have been adopted in at least 40 states to recognize as competent patients "certain categories of minors without parental consent for medical examination and treatment" (American Academy of Pediatrics, 1976). This judicial and legislative trend to free minors to seek medical help on their own and to allow physicians to treat minors without fear of possible litigation will undoubtedly continue.

Key Supreme Court cases involving children over the past 15 years suggest that the Court's assessment of minors' "maturity" in giving consent depends on a determination of the extent to which the minor may exercise rights accorded adults. Court rulings with respect to consent for abortion provide an interesting example. As constituted prior to the addition of Justice O'Connor, the Court has ruled that a "mature minor" must have access to an independent decisionmaker without the burden of parental notice. The term "mature" has not been adequately defined. In some decisions it seems to be equated with independence from parents in "domicile and livelihood" (*Bellotti v. Bair*),[1] while in others it seems to mean a capacity to, "appreciate its [an abortion's] nature and consequences" (*Planned Parenthood of Central Missouri v. Danforth*).[2] Unfortunately, courts have seldom offered much guidance to physicians with respect to how such maturity ought to be assessed.

Because of the diversity of statutory law and paucity of appellate decisions with regard to minors and consent, the American Academy of Pediatrics (AAP) Task Force has issued specific guidelines and recommendations to help the practicing pediatrician. Following a compilation and review of present state laws, the AAP proposed as a reasonable safeguard to the practicing pediatrician that "in all elective cases written consent to surgery or treatment should be obtained from any minor 13 years of age or older in addition to that of the parent" (American Academy of Pediatrics, 1976). It is further suggested that consent or assent to research procedures be obtained from children older than 7 years (often considered the "age of discretion" under common law). Procedures must be explained verbally to the child and the child's wishes to discontinue a research protocol must be respected (American Academy of Pediatrics, 1977).

The guidelines of 7 and 13 years of age are based on the child's supposed ability to comprehend the intent and full significance of the contemplated treatment. Each case must be reviewed individually by the physician who will attempt to assess competency to consent based on age, disease, severity, prognosis, risks, and proposed benefits of therapy. The pediatrician should also seek data concerning the patient's level of intelligence, reasoning ability, and emotional state from appropriately trained psychological or psychiatric consultants. Finally, the physician will draw on his/her past experiences in caring for the particular child and note the patient's past history of medical related decisions (Mnookin, 1978). For purposes of this chapter the AAP age criteria provide general guidelines for addressing the issues of the pediatric patient's competence to consent.

[1] Bellotti v. Baird, 443 U.S. 622 (1979).
[2] Planned Parenthood of Central Missouri v. Danforth, 428 U.S. 52 (1976).

Vulnerability of the Child

Children are in an especially vulnerable position with regard to providing consent for medical treatment. Much of this vulnerability comes from the pain and progression of the disease process. The desire to seek relief from physical and mental anguish is an exceedingly strong force. Children and adults are often frightened by illness and its disruption of their lives. They strive for a reestablishment of security and normality. Children also often lack a clear understanding of illness and the natural history of disease. A limited life experience with sickness and pain makes the experience all the more unpredictable and upsetting. Children frequently have a limited experience with physicians. Their only encounter with the medical team may have centered around painful experiences and direct invasions of their bodies. The separation from family and home inherent in hospitalization may compound an already heightened anxiety and feeling of helplessness. The child's ability to cope with these stresses is limited by levels of psychosocial development far less sophisticated than those available to the adult patient.

The child's perception of illness and bodily function will influence his capacity to consent (Bibace & Walsh, 1981). Young children (less than 6 or 7 years old) do not adapt easily to another person's viewpoint or reasoning. Children of this age group often utilize magical thinking when addressing real-life situations. Such thinking may stand in the way of logical reasoning. For example, a child who believes that death is reversible may not fully comprehend the meaning of life or death decisions (Koocher, 1977). The small child's difficulty with the concept of object constancy may interfere with fully understanding that his amputated leg will not regrow, that his diabetes will not resolve as his common cold did, or that his physical deformity will not somehow go away (Piaget, 1960). Clearly, such magical thinking in the small child will limit his/her capacity to give consent.

The older child (7 to 13 years of age) beyond the stage of magical thinking may view the world in concrete terms. While older children may comprehend the nature of their disease and current situation, they may have great difficulty anticipating what will be in the future. Such concrete thinking may also stand in the way of truly informed consent.

Finally, adolescents (13 years of age or older) are usually equipped with the cognitive capacity to understand the nature of their medical problem at least as well as are adults. Emotional conflicts related to individuation, separation, and independence are major tasks for adolescence (Erikson, 1968). Such conflicts with authority figures and peer pressure for acceptance may provoke the struggling adolescent to make consent decisions inconsistent with his/her best interests. In contrast, the adolescent (minor) with the cognitive and emotional ability to understand the full significance of medical treatment should be allowed to participate in those decisions.

Dependence appears to form the crucial context for the child's transition from the role of a minor and incompetent to that of the role of an adult with independence and self-control. The nature of that dependence lies in four major areas. The most basic level might be considered to be the biological. The infant and young child are intimately, almost exclusively, dependent on a caretaker or provider for nourishment, sustenance, and protection. With the acquisition of increasing ambulatory, physical, and communication skills, the child's basic biologic vulnerability is lessened. The second level in seeking independence might be deemed psychological or emotional. With the development of unique personality traits and emotional characteristics, the child progresses as an individual. Third, the ability to socialize and to interact within the family, school, and community adds additional depth to the process. Finally, a financial independence occasionally appears that enables a child or adolescent eventually to sustain him or herself completely and separate from the ties of caretaker dependency. It is clear that all four of these levels serve to change the nature, degree, and perception of vulnerability within which the child must cope.

The type of illness also contributes to the child's vulnerability. A disease that is acute and short-lived may have a limited disruptive impact on a child's life. A chronic disease, however, not only sets a child apart as different from his or her peers, but also has far reaching consequences on individual growth and development. Normal milestones may be delayed, disrupted, or never attained. The real and perceived need for constant medical attention may promote a dependence and vulnerability with enormous repercussions upon the child (Prugh, Staub, Sands, Kirschbaum, & Lenihan, 1952; Yancy, 1973).

Limited Cognitive and Social Development

The ability of a pediatric patient to consent to medical treatment must be based upon the child. The physician dealing with children should be aware of the dramatic developmental variability existing in the pediatric population (Skolnick, 1975). The pediatric patients referred to in this chapter may be infants, toddlers, school age, or adolescents. The developmental differences between a 3-year-old and an adolescent are obvious, but are often overlooked when the physician is not accustomed to dealing with children.

A clear understanding of child development is necessary to any discussion of how a child might participate in health care delivery. Whether one chooses to study Freud, Piaget, Gesell, or Erikson, most developmental models look at maturation essentially as a set of stages or tasks. These stages lead the child toward further autonomy and control of self and environment. The physician must understand and consider the stage of the patient's cognitive development in order to assure proper comprehension of medical information. Only then can the physician begin to assess the most appropriate level of involvement for a child in the consent process.

Even though children under 13 years of age may not be directly asked to consent to medical care, they must be informed as to what treatment will entail. Perhaps the most important role the pediatrician can play in interaction with a small child is to offer honest and clear explanations in language the child can comprehend. It would seem most appropriate to give the child a brief and substantive overview of the problems and then provide ample opportunity for the child to ask questions. With experience, the physician also learns when to supply information that a child may be too afraid to ask for himself. A statement such as: "Children often wonder about what a disease like yours is like and what will happen over a period of time," is a good place to start. The physician must then supply appropriate data that may be used constructively in explaining and offering treatment to the child.

The physician must learn to use terminology and examples with which the patient is familiar and which can be applied readily to the clinical situation. The art of medicine comes from the ability to know just how much information to supply and, perhaps more importantly, how, where, and when to supply it. It is important to understand not only what the child wants to know by his/her questions, but also why the child needs to know it. Often the question a child asks is misinterpreted as asking more than is meant. For example, when Johnny asks where he came from, he may expect a geographic, rather than a biologic explanation. Thus, one could plunge into a lengthy discussion of sex education that would be not only inappropriate, but also would not have met the needs of the child when a simple answer might have sufficed. The adolescent, on the other hand, may also need full information, but may not request it because issues of illicit drug use, sexuality, and peer relationships are too emotionally charged to be discussed easily with the physician.

One need not ask the young child's permission to carry out a necessary painful procedure such as blood drawing. If the physician does make such inquiry, the child will undoubtedly refuse what is deemed a necessary procedure. By proceeding further despite such refusal, the physician has reduced the likelihood of retaining a trusting relationship with the child. Instead, a warm and sensitive explanation of that procedure and its necessity ("I need to do a blood test. It will hurt, but. . .") may go a long way in terms of cooperation and allaying fear and anxiety. In stark contrast, the physician performing an initial pelvic examination for an 18-year-old adolescent will be in a situation where, not only must full information be given as to the reason and nature of the procedure, but also consent obtained, if the examination is to be a success.

For the child less than 13 years of age, limited participation in consent appears reasonable, and the majority of physician interactions should be on educational information and the answering of questions appropriate to the age and developmental level of the child. For many consent decisions, the older child (13 years or above) is developmentally competent to make reasonable judgments as well as conceptualize and analyze actions and consequences. Within the framework of a particular psychosocial situation, it would appear quite sufficient to utilize sole consent by minors for the initiation and carrying out of a therapeutic regimen. Competence to consent may be thought of as a developmental milestone. This suggests that the physician must temper the arbitrary age of 13 with knowledge of the individual child. The nature and timing of attaining competence to consent and its acquisition requires further investigation especially by developmental psychologists.

The Medical Setting and Changing Physician Relations

With the advent of specialized medical care and the ever-growing complexities of medical practice, the setting for health care delivery may be quite wide and varied. Since each setting will have its own stresses, demands, and policies, the setting further contributes to the child's vulnerable position. The child may have to cope with the emergency room, outpatient clinic, hospital ward, or private physicians' office. Each setting has its own norm of patient care practice. The state of interaction, explanation, orientation, and supportive care may vary widely. The patient load in each setting may differ greatly as may the goals of the particular medical practice. If a child is to successfully interact with these health care systems he or she will be expected to demonstrate an enormous flexibility in the face of limited experience.

The physician must be capable of altering his or her approach depending upon the child's development, age, the disease, and the setting. To use the same approach everywhere everytime would be inappropriate and unsuccessful. The physician does not ask whether an airway should be inserted when breathing is obstructed. Similarly, the child can take part in the decision whether one or two daily injections of insulin achieve the best diabetic control. There is no single model of approaching the patient, although differences in medical conditions will dictate some factors as noted below.

Obtaining Consent for Different Medical Conditions

Either the patient, if legally competent, or the parent or guardian will be involved in the consent decision. The medical condition and the disease process often dictate the need and extent of consent. The best method for obtaining consent requires the medical knowledge of diseases, prognosis, and the urgency of therapy. A typology of three levels of medical urgency can be established: the true emergency, the impending emergency, and the nonemergency.

The True Emergency

In the case of a true emergency, it seems obvious that treatment must be instituted without consent and, if the patient is unconscious, without information. In such circumstances, the nature of the medical condition is such that failure to initiate immediate care would lead to a serious consequence (i.e., the loss of life or limb). The nature of the emergency is such that the prognosis and natural history of the disease are clearly defined and the prognosis or natural history will be changed for the worse with the failure to initiate therapy. The urgency for critical care would be sufficient grounds medically and legally to bypass standard consent processes. Examples of such conditions involve potentially life threatening situations where specific therapies with specific goals exist. The efficacy of such therapy is established and failure to implement therapy under such conditions will have a negative effect on the disease course. Such emergency situations in the pediatric age group would include: major trauma, shock, serious burns, seizures, organ failure, respiratory obstruction or arrest, ingestion of poisons or foreign bodies, dehydration, bleeding, anaphylaxis, or drowning.

The Impending Emergency

In the case of an impending emergency the need for obtaining consent is evident. The patient in this category would have an illness where prolonged delay (hours) in treatment would likely result in serious consequence or change in prognosis. Within this category an attempt at obtaining consent must be initiated and a reasonable course to secure such consent be continued. The guardian might be reached by phone, telegram, or by sending police to escort the guardian to the medical facility. If consent cannot be obtained within a reasonable time, then therapy may be initiated without consent. Again, the relative urgency of the medical condition, the known therapeutic efficacy, and the untreated prognosis can lead to an established treatment protocol. Examples in this semi-emergency category would include less severe or early presentations of the illnesses found in the emergency classification. These might include a moderate asthmatic attack, moderate dehydration, a seizure that has ended, or bleeding that has stopped but requires suturing. These first two categories—that of emergency and semi-emergency—lend themselves to a relatively clear-cut and justifiable approach to the need for or lack of consent. This clarity stems from the medical knowledge of prognosis and indication for urgent therapy in the face of limited time to obtain informed consent. It would seem that these circumstances must stand alone for they involve the inherent waiving of tort rights. It is the physician who must accept the potential liability for the appropriateness of treatment decisions under these circumstances. In fact, where the physician has a long-term relationship with the child and family, the family's expectation could well be that treatment would be initiated.

Nonemergencies

It is the nonemergency category which causes the medical community the most difficulty with respect to minor's consent. Nonemergency conditions may be divided essentially into two types. The first might be a condition in which delay of therapy will have little or no effect on the prognosis, at least over the short term (days). The second category would be one in which a delay would not change the prognosis over the short term (days), but would over the patient's lifetime (years).

There are many minor conditions that affect children for which a delay of therapy or even a lack of therapy will have little consequence. In these instances therapy should not be instituted without express consent by either the competent minor or the legal guardian. The protection of individual liberty and privacy would outweigh the professed therapeutic benefit. Examples would include conditions that might be uncomfortable or even painful but not necessitating immediate attention, such as rashes, minor cuts, bruises, and self-limited infections.

The case of elective surgical procedures presents a particularly perplexing problem. Should a legal guardian's consent be sufficient to perform plastic surgery on a minor? It would seem reasonable to defer an elective procedure until the patient (child) is capable of active participation in the consent process. The physician must be guided by the nature of the proposed procedure, its risk, benefits, and the indications for its initiation, including data on outcomes with other children. The agreement of the child would be a valuable and desirable reinforcement for such decisions.

Perhaps the most ethically disturbing category of nonemergency care is one in which delay would not change the prognosis over the short term (days), but may have far-reaching consequence over the long term. A classic example would be childhood malignancy and, in particular, leukemia. Conflict occurs when addressing what is potentially a curable disease such as acute lymphocytic leukemia. The prognosis is clearly based on many factors, such as the age at diagnosis, type of leukemia, and time of discovery. Based on current statistical data, a reasonable prognosis can be anticipated. The state has a certain interest in protecting the rights of the incompetent child or minor. One might wish to question the competence of a guardian or presumed competent minor who might refuse such treatment. When conflicts of interest arise between child, guardian, physician, and state, they must be addressed within the judicial system.

Beginning with the case of Karen Quinlan in 1976 (*In re Quinlan*),[3] there have been a growing number of cases focusing on nontreatment or "passive euthanasia" issues. Courts have been willing to delegate consent authority to others in cases involving incompetent patients (*e.g., In re Eichner*[4]; *In re Quinlan*[5]; *In re Spring*[6]; *In re Storar*[7]). It is thus clear that the courts after deliberation may, when so addressed, authorize substituted judgments in difficult cases involving quality-of-life value decisions (*Saikewicz v. Superintendent of Belchertown State School*).[8] The ethical and moral dilemmas associated with nontreatment or termination of care decisions must be carefully explored before a democratic society can waive basic rights (Baron, 1978; Capron, 1976).

Chronic Diseases

Pediatric patients with chronic diseases form a substantial and unique population. Though these diseases are often not immediately life-threatening, their impact on growth, development, and overall well-being is substantial. Chronic disease may be insidious in onset and have a prolonged and relentless course. Thanks to advances in medical knowledge, many chronic diseases have a more favorable prognosis with the institution of adequate treatment. It often is possible to alter significantly the course of the disease from what would otherwise be a steadily deteriorating course. Even without changing the ultimate outcome, it is possible to alleviate pain and suffering and significantly improve the patient's life. Medical therapy may decrease the need for hospitalizations and inpatient procedures requiring time away from home and disruption of day-to-day activities. Through supportive medical care for chronic disease, these children's lives often approach the normal.

Consent for therapy of chronic disease must come from either a competent minor or legal guardian. It may not be legally binding to obtain consent from

[3] *In re* Quinlan, 335 A.2d 647 (N. J. 1976), *cert. denied,* 429 U. S. 922 (1976).
[4] *In re* Eichner, 423 N.Y.S.2d 580 (App. Div. 1980); Eichner v. Dillon, 426 N.Y.S.2d 517 (App. Div. 1980).
[5] *In re* Quinlan, *supra* note 3.
[6] *In re* Spring, 405 N.E.2d 115 (Mass. 1980).
[7] *In re* Storar, 433 N.Y.S.2d 388 (Monroe Co. Sup. Ct. 1980); 434 N.Y.S.2d 46 (app. Div. 1980).
[8] Saikewicz v. Superintendent of Belchertown State School, 370 N.E.2d 417 (Mass. 1977).

the older child in these cases. Such consent may be crucial to the ability to carry out a given treatment protocol. With the acquisition of further knowledge about the child's disease, the child learns to feel more in control of not only the therapy but also of his or her life as well. A more positive self-image often follows this sense of body control and this in turn leads to an increase in compliance. Juvenile diabetes provides an excellent example. The degree to which the diabetic child is informed and consents to insulin and diet therapy could determine the short-term effect of therapy and may delay long-term complications of the disease. Unfortunately, there are essentially no systematically collected data available to support this view.

We suggest that compliance stands as the key to effective medical therapy. In order to achieve maximum compliance, the patient must not only be actively involved, but also a participant in his or her own care. Participation will include discussions related to choice of therapy as well as what mode of administration such therapy might necessitate. This may be as simple as allowing the younger child to decide which of two medicines of equal efficacy taste better and thus which would be preferred. It has been observed that when elementary school children are allowed to initiate their own health care, they appear to have a decreased sense of vulnerability but no change in the manner of health service utilization (Lewis, Lewis, Lorimer, & Palmer, 1977). It also means participation by adolescents in decisions about chemotherapy versus radiotherapy where efficacy of the medical treatment is unclear. Such participation also means understanding on the part of the child as to why undesirable side effects are a reasonable risk because the alternative (*i.e.*, no treatment) is eventually life threatening. The physician can no longer be the mere administrator of treatments, but must become involved in a relationship marked by mutual respect and concern. Such a relationship must be both sensitive and understanding of the patient's needs.

Rodin and Janis (1979) have documented the importance of establishing patient trust in realistic preparation for potential discomforts and problems that may lie ahead. A strong trust relationship based on the physician's demonstrated caring and concern has been positively related to recovery rates following abdominal surgery, heart attack, or other acute illnesses (Rodin & Janis, 1979).

There may also be instances when judicial action must be sought in the face of denied parental consent. The classic example occurs in the face of the child of the Jehovah's Witness faith who requires a blood transfusion. Members of this faith believe that the Bible proscribes blood transfusions. While courts will routinely order such transfusions over parental objection to "save the life of a child," the decision is more difficult when the threat to life is not acute. The case of Ricky Ricardo Green (*In re Green*)[9] is instructive on this issue.

[9] *In re* Green, 448 Pa. 338, 292 A.2d 387 (1972).

Ricky had had two attacks of poliomyelitis, resulting in problems of obesity and paralytic scoliosis (94% curvature of the spine). At age 16 he was unable to stand or ambulate and a "spinal fusion" operation was recommended by his physicians. While there was no parental objection to the surgery *per se*, consent was refused on the basis of the mother's Jehovah's Witness faith because the operation would have necessitated blood transfusions. The court ordered the surgery, noting that the child's health was paramount and, although the immediate risk (without surgery) did not pose a "life or death" situation, the quality of Ricky's life as an adult was at stake. Thus, the court acted in an attempt to provide Ricky with a "semblance of a normal life which the vast majority of our society has come to enjoy and cherish."

In another recent case (*In re Philip B.*),[10] the parents of a moderately retarded child with Down's Syndrome and a congenital heart problem (ventricular septal defect) refused to authorize corrective surgery. Their child had been institutionalized since infancy and they claimed a desire that he should not outlive them and thereby not become a burden on his siblings or the victim of a "warehouse institution." Despite the fact that their refusal to authorize surgery sentenced Philip to a slow death from heart failure, courts refused to order surgery over parental objections and the Supreme Court refused to intervene against the parents' wishes. In a somewhat unusual legal move, local advocacy groups went to court seeking to have Philip's parents declared neglectful for not authorizing surgery. The court agreed, placing Philip's legal guardianship in the hands of a court-appointed surrogate, who then authorized the surgery.

The physician must be sensitive to the issue of conflict between the interest of the child and the interests of the parents, which are not invariably congruent. There are clearly instances when concepts alien to medicine (such as due process and privacy rights) may be evoked by the consent process. Often the court's judgment may turn on medical testimony regarding the certainty of prognosis with or without treatment. Those practicing medicine at the interface of such situations where significant conflict of interest precludes a morally relevant resolution might obtain legal consultation in those rare instances.

Other Conditions

There exist certain medical conditions that may have sufficient public health implications to warrant acceptance of sole consent by a minor for treatment. These conditions have a significant social context that affords them this

---

[10] *In re* Philip B., 156 Cal. Rptr. 48 (Ct. App. 1979), *cert. denied sub nom.* Bothman v. Warren B., 48 U.S.L.W. 3626 (3/24/80).

unique societal privilege. Allowing the minor to consent independently promotes not only ready access and availability to therapy, but also promotes society's wish to control these conditions without deterrents. Problems related to alcohol and drug abuse are prime examples. Requiring guardian consent to initiate therapy for these conditions would only serve to complicate and deter the use of available treatment facilities. There is invoked a value-laden interest that society is seeking to protect itself. Nonetheless, protection of established social policy may be encouraged by careful selection of conditions to waive established consent protocol. Other conditions such as veneral disease or selected contagious diseases such as hepatitis might also be treated in this manner.

The ability of a minor to consent to a blood transfusion poses yet another complexity. The court has made it clear that although a Jehovah's Witness may refuse transfusion for himself based on religious freedom, he may not deny such consent for the child (Frankel, Damme, & Eys, 1977). The courts have also struggled with consent issues about the availability of contraception and abortion. Societal values and ethics become entwined in the controversy over the need for guardian consent for the minor to use these services.

Mass screening programs form still another area of societal imposition with regard to the waiver of consent protocol. Pediatric patients may be screened without consent when lack of therapy might place them and society at sufficient risk because of the failure to obtain treatment. Examples include tuberculin testing and immunization programs in the school-age child and genetic disorder screening in the newborn nursery (see Mnookin, pp. 409–413). These programs are mandated by law and serve to protect society's members. Lack of therapy in a certain population might put others at significant risk. Once again, it must be understood that the waiver of such rights is based on very value-laden principles.

Physician–Child–Family Relationship

The final factor to be considered with respect to a consent model in the pediatric setting is the physician–child–family relationship. The powerful character of the physician–patient interaction has been extensively studied (Korsch, Gozzi, & Francis, 1968; Francis, Korsch, & Morris, 1969). The source of that power stems from the nature of the relationship itself. If used to advantage it can facilitate a successful journey from illness to recovery and health. If used for self-advantage the relationship can serve as a major obstacle to good health care.

The physician may serve many roles within the framework of the patient relationship and provide a crucial resource of information and explantaion. Through understanding and concern the professional helps to allay fear and anxiety and serves as the interface between the often unfamiliar and occasionally hostile elements of the health care system. Physicians may help with decision making, give advice where indicated, and continuously serve as a source of patient support. Follow-up care and concerns should serve to reinforce the physician's position as a caretaker. Pediatric concerns often extend to family adjustments, school problems, and the development of social skills. Within the context of such a relationship, the physician will become a more effective health care provider and counselor.

Just as we have explored the positive nature of the physician–patient interaction, so it may be a negative or nonexistent one. The physician may approach his patient with the sterility of a "shot" giver or the sympathy of a disinterested passerby. Interactions may even take on a negative character when the physician accepts his task as a burden, fails to supply adequate information, is unbending, or seeks his or her own interests rather than those of the patients. The destructive nature of such a relationship precludes in our minds the delivery of successful medical care.

One of the most important aspects of the doctor–patient relationship is that of continuity. This becomes particularly important as health care has become more and more complex. Even appropriate utilization of various expert consultants and health-care facilities is often disruptive. Continuity may be said to form the foundation or framework for effective interactions. Patient satisfaction increases with a positive relationship provided by a known and trusted primary health care provider (Becker, Drachman, & Kirscht, 1975). With increased satisfaction comes increased patient compliance which is the necessary link to effective therapy. The increase in satisfaction and compliance leads not only to a happier patient but also has a major effect on health care utilization as manifested by fewer operations and fewer and shorter hospitalizations. Patients with this newfound positive reinforcement tend to use the physician more often for prevention and health maintenance than merely as a source for the treatment of illness. Health care becomes not only more effective and humane, but the patient is much more accepting of what the doctor has to offer. This care is also less expensive (Alpert, Robertson, Kosa, Heagarty, & Haggerty, 1976).

Health care in the twentieth century has been influenced by the development of Western civilization and culture. Along with industrialization has come a concept of health that is quite different from the holistic approach of many Eastern traditions. Health in our society is viewed not only as a positive force, but also as a state in which patients are not plagued by disease or sickness (Engelhardt & Tristam, 1974). Such a philosophy is nurtured by an increasing complexity of medical therapeutics. Medical science has become so intricate that the patient finds a disease specialist rather than an all encompassing health specialist (Fox, 1976). The patient suddenly becomes entangled in a network of medical technology. This may in turn lead to a diminution of contact with the patient's primary-care physician. The disintegration of the patient–physician relationship and the positive interaction it has previously brought will take its toll in patient compliance and satisfaction unless current attempts to restore the elements of the holistic model are successful (Alpert, 1973).

It is our premise that it is the primary-care continuity model that provides the best setting for provision of care and the obtaining of informed consent. Part of the services of this model is the appropriate use of disease specialists. Such specialists provide new data in the changing prognosis of diseases and needed technical skills as well as help in furnishing carefully planned treatment protocols. It is the primary-care physician who should be involved with issues of consent, compliance, and prolonged health care. Because the primary-care physician not only knows the patient intimately, but also knows the patient's family and the patient's available support systems, he or she is in the optimal position to help differentiate various medical conditions. With the establishment of the continuity model, mutual participation and cooperation becomes the dominant model of communication rather than the model of an active and controlling physician and a passive and accepting patient (Szasz & Hollender, 1956).

The patient places trust in the physician by the nature of the continuity contract and not merely by its existence. The physician earns that trust by serving as a health provider who knows the patient and is available when needed. The informed primary-care physician knows what is appropriate and necessary to insure the proper care of the patient. The physician understands that some patients need details while others prefer concepts.

Finally, medical knowledge is changing rapidly within our society, and is continually being updated and expanded. The new morbidity of pediatric practice has seen learning disorders and accidents replace disease such as polio and measles. Diseases previously felt to be incurable, such as malignancy and leukemia, now may have an ever-growing possibility of long-term survival and even cure. Surgical advances have allowed the repair of congenital heart defects today when only palliative approaches existed previously. In addition, new or previously unrecognized diseases are being discovered and described. All of these advances require education, further training, and an open mind on the part of the health care providers. Physicians must have the combination of technical skills, current knowledge, and understanding about child and family issues. The physician of today and tomorrow must be prepared to supply the necessary information to insure that consent by patients is informed.

Research

Research is an essential part of addressing the many issues identified in this chapter. Experiments are required that will determine which medical interventions are effective and which are not. Although there is an important amount of acute disease that responds to an effective intervention (a patient with appendicitis is cured by appendectomy), the new morbidity, which includes behavioral disorders and chronic disease, requires careful evaluation through research. Our goal should be to replace anecdote and belief with systematically acquired knowledge.

A number of research questions need to be asked. What is the extent and nature of the medical setting as an independent variable in the obtaining of consent? How does the definition of emergency influence the consent process? In chronic diseases can the effect of providing information and the obtaining of consent be measured and can it be demonstrated to affect disease outcome? While continuity of medical care has been demonstrated to be of benefit to patients, can this measured benefit be extended to include the consent process? Can consent increase compliance? Are there measurable negative consequences where continuity interferes with the obtaining of consent? Can the physician dealing with the episode of illness obtain an informed consent and impact upon disease outcome without involving other members of the medical team? How will the simplification and demystification of medical disease in a holistic model affect the physician-patient interaction? What are the long-term effects on utilization of medical services if consent is sought? What is the effect of giving elementary school children choice in their medical therapies, not only upon the outcome of the immediate illness, but also in the long-term outcome?

The controlled clinical trial remains the most effective design for measuring differences. However, it is unlikely that large trials with complete randomization can be ethically carried out, especially in the area of consent. These and other research-consent problems are discussed in detail in Dr. Keith-Spiegel's chapter in this volume (see Chapter 10).

Conclusion

In conclusion, addressing the issues of informed consent in children requires more than legalistic logical or developmental reasoning. Within the health care setting, the physician remains the dominant figure both for provision of information and for the obtaining of consent. It is only after physicians have mastered their art and learned to approach patients by providing information and seeking consent with dignity, humanity, and understanding that they will be able to serve the needs of the pediatric generations to come.

References

Alpert, J. J., & Charney, E. The education of physicians for primary care. *DHEW Publication (HRA)*, 1973, *74*, 3113.

Alpert, J. J., Robertson, L. S., Kosa, J., Heagarty, M. C., & Haggerty, R. J. Delivery of health care for children: Report of an experiment. *Pediatrics*, 1976, *57*, 917–930.

American Academy of Pediatrics (Task Force). Consent. *Pediatrics*, 1976, *57*, 414–416.

American Academy of Pediatrics (Committee on Drugs). Guidelines for the ethical conduct of studies to evaluate drugs in pediatric populations. *Pediatrics*, 1977, *60*, 91–101.

Baron, C. Assuring detached but passionate investigation and decisions: The role of guardians ad litem in *Saikewicz*-type cases. *American Journal of Law and Medicine*, 1978, *4*, 111–130.

Becker, M. H., Drachman, R. H., & Kirscht, P. Continuity of pediatrics. *Journal of Pediatrics*, 1975, *84*, 599–605.

Bergen, R. The confusing law of informed consent. *Journal of the American Medical Association*, 1974, *229*, 325.

Bibace, R., & Walsh, M. *Children's conceptions of illness and bodily functions.* San Francisco: Jossey-Bass, 1981.

Bronfenbrenner, U. Toward an experimental ecology of human development. *American Psychologist*, 1977, *32*, 513–531.

Brown, R. Consent: Report of the Task Force on Pediatric Research, Informed Consent, and Medical Ethics. *Pediatrics*, 1976, *57*, 414–416.

Capron, A. M. The *Quinlan* decision: Shifting the burden of decision making. *The Hastings Center Report*, 1976, *6*, 17–19.

Charney, E. Patient–doctor communication. *Pediatric Clinics of North America*, 1970, *19*, 263–279.

Curran, W., & Beecher, H. Experimentation in children: A reexamination of legal ethical principles. *Journal of the American Medical Association*, 1969, *210*, 77–82.

Engelhardt, H. T., Jr. The concepts of health and disease. In H. T. Engelhardt, Jr., & S. Spicker (Eds.), *Philosophy and medicine.* Dordecht, Holland: D. Reidel, 1974.

Erickson, E. H. *Childhood and society.* New York: Norton, 1950. Erickson, E. H. *Identity, youth, and crisis.* New York: Norton, 1968.

Fox, R. Advanced medical technology: Social and ethical implications. In I. Alex (Ed.), *Annual review of sociology.* Palo Alto, Calif.: Annual Reviews, 1976.

Francis, V., Korsch, B., & Morris, M. Gaps in doctor–patient communication: Patient's response to medical advice. *New England Journal of Medicine*, 1969, *280*, 535–540.

Frankel, L., Damme, C., & Eys, J. V. Childhood cancer and the Jehovah's Witness faith. *Pediatrics*, 1977, *60*, 916–921.

Grisso, T., & Vierling, L. Minors' consent to treatment: A developmental perspective. *Professional Psychology*, 1978, *9*, 412–427.

Koocher, G. P. Childhood, death, and cognitive development. *Developmental Psychology*, 1973, *9*, 369–375.

Korsch, B., Gozzi, E., & Francis, V. Gaps in doctor–patient communication. *Pediatrics*, 1968, *42*, 855–871.

Lewis, C. E., Lewis, M. A., Lorrimer, A., & Palmer, B. B. Child initiated care: The use of school nursing services in an "adult-free" system. *Pediatrics*, 1977, *60*, 499–507.

Mnookin, R. *Child, family, and state: Problems and materials on children and the law.* Boston: Little, Brown, 1978.

National Commission for the Protection of Human Subjects of Biomedical and Behavioral Research. *Research involving children.* Washington, D. C.: U. S. Government Printing Officer, 1977.

Piaget, J. *The child's conception of the world.* Totowa, N. J.: Littlefield, Adams, 1972.

Prugh, D., Staub, E., Sands, H., Kirschbaum, R., & Lenihan, E. A study of the emotional reactions

of children and families to hospitalization and illness. *American Journal of Orthopsychiatry*, 1952,
    23, 70–106.
Rodin, J., & Janis, I. L. The social power of health care practitioners as agents of change. *Journal of
    Social Issues*, 1979, *35*(1), 60–81.
Shaw, A. Dilemmas of informed consent in children. *New England Journal of Medicine*, 1973, *289*,
    885–890.
Skolnick, A. The limits of childhood: Conceptions of child development and social context. *Law and
    Contemporary Problems*, 1975, *39*, 38–77.
Szasz, T. S., & Hollender, M. H. A contribution to the philosophy of medicine. *Archives of Internal
    Medicine*, 1956, *97*, 585–592.
Vaccarino, J. Consent: Informed consent form. *New England Journal of Medicine*, 1978, *298*, 455.
Yancy, W. S. Approaches to emotional management of the child with a chronic illness. *Clinical
    Pediatrics*, 1973, *232*, 64–67.

Chapter 7

Competence to Consent

Psychotherapy

GERALD P. KOOCHER

There are probably as many definitions of psychotherapy as there are people who write about it. One review paper cites 48 different definitions (Weiner, 1976) and goes on to complicate matters by distinguishing psychotherapy from activities and events that may have psychotherapeutic value *per se*. While goals, strategies, tactics, and theoretical underpinnings vary widely, most psychotherapists would assert that their work with clients is intended to enhance emotional growth, foster maturity, and promote general adaptive functioning. Others would claim only that they strive to help clients develop an "understanding of their own behavior." There is also a substantial body of literature, typified by the writings of Eysenck (1965, 1966), that challenges the value and effectiveness of psychotherapy or cites potential harmful effects of so-called psychotherapeutic interventions. Such claims have been effectively rebutted (Weiner, 1976), but the existing literature is replete with controversy.

As one reads the work of different theoreticians, it is difficult to find uniform agreement on the nature of "therapy" or even "therapeutic" activity. Because of these disagreements and potential confusions, I wish to state three underlying assumptions for the purposes of this chapter. First, I shall assume that psychotherapy (in the context that I apply it) is being provided by a competent, well-trained professional who has a genuine concern for the children being treated. Second, I assume that psychotherapy with children is intended to bring about some change in behavior as a means of facilitating

GERALD P. KOOCHER ● Department of Psychiatry, Children's Hospital Medical Center (Boston) and Harvard Medical School, Boston, Massachusetts 02115.

adaptation. Finally, I shall assume that the values, needs, desires, and so-called best interests of parents and their children are not necessarily congruent. In fact, I expect that the best interests of parents and their children will often be different or even contradictory. It is quite normal in any segment of society for the needs of individual members or subgroups to vary, resulting in the subordination of some interests and promotion of others. This poses interesting questions with respect to the nature and goals of psychotherapy when the identified client (Simmonds, 1976) is a member of a family.

Mental health professionals cannot rely solely on the courts for guidance when the issue of a child's "best interests" is at hand. In some instances there have been clear rulings that when parents' and child's interests conflict the child's interests are of paramount concern.[1] In other instances of substantive conflict courts have even been willing to terminate parental rights.[2] The rights of adolescents in the mental health system, however, are complex and at times contradictory (Wilson, 1978). Recent decisions of the Supreme Court have implied an almost naive assertion of the "parents know best" philosophy (Rothman & Rothman, 1980). The law is an evolving social system, and these issues are at the cutting edge. Psychotherapists should clearly not wait to be guided by definitive legal precedent with respect to children's consent to treatment.

Enrolling in Psychotherapy

Socialization in Childhood

In the case of child clients initiation of psychotherapy is most often the idea of some adults, rather than of the child. Referral for such treatment often represents an agreement among a group of adults (*i.e.*, parents, teachers, court officers, psychologists, etc.) that some need to facilitate behavior change exists and that the child is identified as the person who should change. In this respect psychotherapy may be regarded as a tool of the socialization process. The development of competence to consent becomes important as one considers the level of the child's involvement in the treatment process, as well as the evolving capacity to comprehend what treatment is all about.

Children are not socialized to think in terms of their own rights. Generally, they are unlikely to perceive themselves as having decision-making authority,

---

[1] *See, e.g., In re* Pernishek, 268 Pa. Super. 447, 408 A. 2d 872 (1979); Matter of Male R., 102 Misc. 2d 1, 422 N.Y.S. 819 (Kings Co. Fam. Ct. 1979); Doe v. Doe, 119 N. H. 773, 408 A.2d 785 (1979).

[2] *See, e.g.*, Nebraska v. Wedige, 205 Neb. 687, 289 N.W. 2d 538 (1980); *In re* C.M.S., —Mont.—, 609 P. 2d 240 (1979); Jewish Child Care Ass'n v. Elaine S.Y., 73 A.D. 2d 154, 425 N.Y.S 2d 336 (1980).

regardless of the "objective reality" of their legal status (Melton, 1980 a, b). Children are taught that they should obey parents, and just about anyone else bigger than they are (Keith-Spiegel, 1976). The usual childhood experience also includes punishment for noncompliance, and this process is likely to render children somewhat suspicious or disbelieving of gestures designed to increase their autonomy. Societal entitlements also play a critical role in the understanding children have of their discretionary decisions. Lower-class children, for example, may still conceptualize "rights" as those tangibles one may have or activities one can engage in without being punished much later in their development than upper-midde-class children (Melton, 1980a).

The socialization experiences of children will clearly influence how they, their families, and their psychotherapists work together. Issues of determining a child's "best interests," involvement of children in setting goals for treatment, the extent and nature of confidentiality, use of involuntary or aversive treatments, and the child as an "incompetent client" are all a part of enrolling in psychotherapy. In considering them one must remain cognizant of the major background variable: socialization.

Best Interests

Many statutes and professional standards exhort judges, policymakers, and clinicians to act in the best interest of children they deal with. Law generally presumes that parents are free to determine what is "best" for their children considering their own beliefs, preferences, and life-styles (Goldstein, Freud, & Solnit, 1979). Although these presumptions have often been debated and discussed in terms of child custody and medical treatment decisions (see, for example, Goldstein Freud, & Solnit, 1973, 1979; Shore, 1979; Starr, 1979), they have only occasionally been raised as issues in referrals for psychotherapy (Koocher, 1976a, 1978). Although adults are presumed competent (in the legal sense) unless proven incompetent, children are presumed incompetent for purposes of legal consent. This principle and related case law is well detailed elsewhere in this volume. The questions requiring a closer look in this chapter revolve about the relative validity of parental and children's own judgements of what is "best interest" with respect to psychotherapy.

One potential means of assessing children's judgments about entering psychotherapy grew out of enactment in Virginia of a statute permitting minors the right to consent as adults to outpatient psychotherapy. In a survey conducted some nine months following implementation of the statute, Melton (1981b) found that there had been virtually no change in the frequency of minors' treatment seeking sans parental consent. There are numerous possible explanations for this situation. Many of the community mental health centers surveyed had not attempted to inform youngsters in their catchment areas of service availability. Even if all children in the state had been informed of their new entitlement, however, one must wonder whether the basic inertia with respect to assertiveness as taught through the socialization process would have kept self-referrals by children low. One Virginia mental health center serving serving several rural counties did make an effort to inform adolescents in their catchment area about the change in state law. The clinic reported a caseload increase of only 3%, or approximately 10 minors seeking treatment independently each month, despite the outreach effort (Melton, 1981b).

Role of the Child-Client

The decision to actually enroll in psychotherapy or not is only the initial step within which there may be incongruities between what is "best" from the parents' standpoint vis-a-vis the child's concerns. The matters of focus and goal-setting in the planning of psychotherapy are also points at which the best interests of family members may diverge. Children's understanding of psychotherapy will be discussed later in this chapter. But it is evident from the outset that evolving cognitive, social, and emotional concepts will play a critical role in the child's ability to participate actively in planning the course of psychotherapy.

From the cognitive standpoint it is clear that the ability to conceptualize one's own behavior as changeable or even as different from other people's behavior will vary developmentally. For example, the ability to discuss one's own motivations, often called "insight" by some psychotherapists, would not be expected to evolve prior to the onset of what Piaget has called "concrete operations." Until this level of cognitive development is attained at about age seven, the child is not able to explore his or her motivation from the standpoint of another person (Phillips, 1975). Abstract concepts such as "unconscious" motivations or the ability to consider long-term consequences of behavior will also be dependent on developing cognitive functioning.

Social and self-help skills are also critical in determining the role a child is able to play in his or her own psychotherapy. Interpersonal skills, communication abilities, or simply the independent mobility functions needed to find one's way to the therapist's office all influence the potential to exercise competent judgement in psychotherapy. The degree of social individuation from one's parent and family is also obviously a significant factor in determining ability to set individual priorities and plans.

Emotional factors are clearly at the heart of anyone's psychotherapy, but it is important to recognize differences in emotional factors across developmental lines. Emotional individuation, the ability to reflect on feelings, and the relationship of guilt or anxiety to interpersonal functioning are all examples of factors that vary dramatically over relatively short time periods in childhood. What a child feels or conceptualizes or is able to accomplish socially will largely determine the extent to which direction of the psychotherapeutic process is possible. The most client-guided of therapists is limited by client capabilities in efforts to engage that client in treatment planning.

These principles are explicitly recognized in the most recent revision of the American Psychological Association's (1981) *Ethical Principles*:

> When working with minors or other persons who are unable to give voluntary, informed consent, psychologists take special care to protect the minors' best interests. Within this context, even in states which clearly allow minors to seek treatment independently, the clinician probably has an ethical duty to determine the actual competence of the client to consent. (Melton, 1981a)

Confidentiality

The principle of confidentiality in psychotherapeutic interviews has been well established and widely accepted. In some jurisdictions legal privilege is granted to interactions between psychotherapist and client. When the client is a child, however, exercise of such privilege is generally assigned to some adult acting on behalf of the child. The ethical principle of confidentiality, as opposed to any specific statutory requirements, generally leaves interpretation of proper behavior to the clinician's judgment. In the days when the "child guidance center" model was a widely used paradigm, children and their parents were seen by separate therapists, making a degree of enhanced confidentiality possible by insulating the child's therapist from frequent direct contact with the child's parents (Koocher, 1976a). The more usual scenario in recent years is for a single therapist to interview the child and also consult with parents or other family members (Koocher & Pedulla, 1977). There have also been increasing demands over the past decade for child psychotherapists to communicate with a variety of institutions and individuals about their clients. Parents want to know what is going on in treatment sessions. Schools want information to use in educational planning for children with special needs.[3] Insurance companies, as well as other "third party payers," want quality assurance or utilization review data including treatment plans, diagnoses, and other such confidential material.

The purpose of confidentiality to begin with is to facilitate a trusting therapeutic relationship (Ross, 1966). Treating children with truthfulness, personal respect, serious consideration, and involvement in goal setting is probably far more important in establishing a trusting relationship with a child client

[3] As mandated under Pub. L. 94–142.

than is any promise of absolute confidentiality *per se* (Koocher, 1976a). Creation of a therapeutic climate of this sort is the clinician's primary goal, and within that context it is also possible to discuss with the child the extent and nature of material to be shared with others. For example, one might tell a child, "This is what I want to talk to your parents about, and here are the reasons why. . . . Is that okay with you? Are there any parts we should keep just between the two of us?" The same type of conversation could take place prior to a school conference or similar session.

The therapist must of course make judgments regarding disclosures that have subtle implications not salient to the child or even the parents. For example, will a diagnostic label on an insurance company form or in a school report create problems for a child client years later or lead to tracking and stigmatization in the near term (Hobbs, 1975)? If a history of psychiatric care could cost Senator Thomas Eagleton a vice-presidential nomination, who is to say that a childhood diagnosis of a "conduct" or "identity" disorder could not have a similar haunting effect years from now on today's child clients? How does one attempt to explain these risks to a child for whom "next month" seems like forever. Can a child who views parents as omnipotent and omniscient conceive of another adult's witholding any information from them? Can an angry adolescent work therapeutically with a clinician who seems too willing to communicate with parents and teachers? Clearly there is an important role for the exercise of professional judgment and consideration of individual case factors in making such decisions.

Although a psychotherapist need not always seek permission of a child client to disclose confidential data in a legal sense, it is ethically mandatory to attempt getting such permission. This implies recognition of the child's cognitive, social, and emotional developmental levels with appropriate allowances. It also implies a recognition of the child's special vulnerabilities vis-à-vis adults, and the resulting relative levels of protection confidentiality affords. In most states, for example, a clinician would be required to report to authorities a parent who revealed continuing acts of child abuse during otherwise confidential communications. There may also be times when a psychotherapist is obligated to violate a confidence to prevent imminent danger from resulting in personal harm.[4] The general trend from the legal arena has been to lower the age at which a client must be asked for written consent prior to record disclosure. In some instances written consent must legally be obtained from children as young as age 12 (Foster, 1980).

---

[4] *See* Tarasoff v. Regents of University of California, 17 Cal. 3d 425, 551 P. 2d 334, 131 Cal. Rptr. 14 (1976); Mc Intosh v. Milano, 168 N. J. Super. 466, 403 A.2d 500 (1979).

Involuntary or Restrictive Treatment

If children's special status warrants extra consideration with respect to involvement in psychotherapy in general, the matter of involuntary, restrictive, or aversive psychotherapies takes on particular significance. These issues include the matter of institutionalization or inpatient hospitalization, the question of refusing treatment, and the involvement of children in choosing the least restrictive of available therapeutic alternatives. The use of aversive techniques including seclusion, restraint, and pain or startle-inducing techniques also falls in this category. Enrolling the child-client for these types of treatment requires special consideration of the consent problem.

The case of *Parham v. J. L. and J. R.*[5] provides a good example of why the matter of children's rights and competence to consent is such a complicated and oft times disputed issue. The facts of this Georgia case are complicated (Rothman & Rothman, 1980), but focus on the matter of due process and procedural safeguards to insure that parents and hospital admissions officers do not use their powers to indefinitely hospitalize children for "psychotherapeutic care" in an arbitrary manner. Beyer and Wilson (1976) described this as the problem of the "reluctant volunteer," when minors are "voluntarily" committed to psychiatric facilities by their parents or guardians. The United States Supreme Court rendered a decision that seems to approach the concept of the family from a romantic and sentimental frame of reference. The decision runs contrary to my own assertion that the interest of the child is not identical to the interest of the parent, and the Court assumes that the parent will inevitably act so as to promote the child's welfare.

Writing for the Court in *Parham*, Chief Justice Warren Burger notes: "Although we acknowledge the fallibility of medical and psychiatric diagnosis, we do not accept the notion that the shortcomings of specialists can always be avoided by shifting the decision . . . to an untrained judge."[6] The court assumes that the hospital's admitting officer will in some fashion serve as a neutral third party to sort out the appropriateness of the parental judgement when hospitalization for a child is sought. While this may often be the case, the growing number of proprietary hospitals and the socialization problems discussed earlier raise potential conflicts. It seems somewhat ironic that the "untrained judge" presumes that the family will generally exercise best interest from the child's standpoint, while routinely assessing potential conflicts of interest in probate law, jury selection, and similar matters.

Another type of problem situation accompanies the use of noxious stimuli for psychotheraeutic purpose. The use of so-called aversive conditioning proce-

[5] Parham v. J. R., 442 U.S. 584 (1979).
[6] Parham v. J. R., 442 U.S. 584 (1979).

dures is occasionally advocated as a treatment of choice "in efforts to overcome recalcitrant problems" (Davidson & Stuart, 1975, p. 756). Examples might include the work of Lovaas and Simmons (1969) who used electric shocks to the extremities as part of a treatment program aimed at terminating self-multilation behaviors of some autistic and retarded children. The general paradigm applied in such situations often includes an unfortunate focus on specific behaviors to the exclusion of the child as a whole person with a multiplicity of needs, abilities, and sensitivities. The child-client most often regarded as a candidate for such treatment is usually the least socially or intellectually able to make a decision about therapy.

Due process demands that therapy plans of this sort require review by qualified professionals functioning independently of the family, institution, or therapist proposing use of such techniques. Without such a professional review plans to administer any noxious stimulation to a child in an attempt to alter behavior would be inconsistent with ethical practice. In many reported cases, it is not always easy to discern whether the treatment goal justifies the means. Even though there is reasonable evidence to suggest that in some limited circumstances this sort of conditioning, coupled with reinforcement or reward of alternative behaviors, may produce adaptive changes, few meaningful ethical guidelines exist for its application (Koocher, 1976b).

It also seems reasonable to insist that whenever any person whose capacity to give full, unpressured, informed consent, is a candidate for such conditioning procedure, an outside advocate is necessary. Such an advocate, who is not associated with or financially linked to the family, institution, or therapists involved would be in the best position to resolve the issue of what is necessary treatment and what is in the child's best interest.

The right to resist or refuse treatment is also a pressing concern to psychotherapists. Virtually all of the current controversy on this topic has focused on the adult institutionalized patient's right to refuse forcible medication use.[7] The law in these cases has generally maintained the need for impartial decisionmakers or a hearing, except in emergency situations, so far as adults are concerned. Although child clients have not been the focus of cases, the attitude toward children implied by the courts suggests that the impartial decisionmaker may be an institutional employee, if one is even needed given the role of the family upheld in *Parham*.[8]

In this context it is highly unlikely that the courts would support any challenge to a parental authority to enroll a child in outpatient psychotherapy.

---

[7] *See, e.g.*, Davis v. Hubbard, 506 F. Supp. 915 (N.D. Ohio 1980); Rennie v. Klein, 476 F. Supp. 1294 (D.N.J. 1979); Rogers v. Okin, 478 F. Supp. 1342 (D. Mass. 1979); *In re* K.K.B., 609 P. 2d 747 Oki. 1980).

[8] For detailed discussion, *see 4 Mental Disability L. Rptr.* 396–398.

I do not suggest that such challenges are warranted, but simply that the psychotherapist who treats children bears a heavy social responsibility. Glenn (1980) suggests that such professionals should be advocates, information providers, social-political-legal change agents, and researchers all rolled into one. This combination also seems highly unlikely.

The Doubly Incompetent

Many children referred for psychotherapeutic care might be considered "doubly incompetent." Such children are first incompetent in the legal sense by virtue of being minors. They may have additional handicaps further diminishing their psychological competence (*e.g.*, mental retardation, autism, or childhood psychosis). Some of these children might be candidates for aversive therapies as discussed above, and others could be enrolled in or kept from treatment programs by relatives or surrogates with questionable reasoning.

The case of Phillip Becker[9] provides a recent example which has attracted national attention (Annas, 1979). Philip is an adolescent with Down's Syndrome and a congenital heart defect. He has lived in state care since shortly after birth and is moderately mentally retarded. His parents, who refused adoption offers years ago and who visit him only a few times per year, have refused to authorize surgical correction. With each passing day the potential for surgical success declines and an uncomfortable death from cardiac insufficiency draws closer for Phillip. It seems that his parents believe that Phillip's best interest is not to survive them, so they are withholding treatment with the potential to extend a normal life span to Phillip. The same Supreme Court that supported family values in *Parham*[10] refused to review the lower court decision in support of the parents' views. This refusal would have been unlikely were Phillip not retarded.

The decision to provide or withhold psychotherapeutic care is not often a life or death judgment. The implications of such care for a child's quality of life, however, can be of critical importance. The day-to-day decisions will not be made in public courts, but in private consulting rooms and it is there that professional judgment must be sensibly applied.

Children's Understanding of Psychotherapy

A variety of research areas touch on developmental aspects of children's

[9] *In re* Phillip B., 94 Cal. App. 3d 796, 156 Cal. Rptr. 48 (1st Ct. App. 1979).
[10] Parham v. J.R., 442 U.S. 584 (1979).

understanding of psychotherapy providers and activities, as well as the preparation of children for psychotherapy, and children's perceptions of deviance and disorder. All of these are relevant to assessment of children's consent capacities.

Dollinger and Thelen (1978) surveyed 1,314 children in grades 5 through 12 and discovered that 42% knew someone who had gone to see a psychologist. Among boys being a psychologist ranked ahead of being a farmer, dentist, or teacher, but below a pilot, athlete, lawyer, or truck driver on a job preference hierarchy. For girls the occupation of psychologist was preferable to being a fire fighter, lawyer, or dentist, but not as good as being a teacher, actor, or athlete. Both sexes expressed the viewpoint that being a psychologist was preferable to being President. When asked what psychologists do, 10% gave derogatory responses such as "shrink heads" or "fix weirdos," while 8% gave answers suggesting misunderstanding such as, "check your eyes" or "fix broken bones." When asked whether a psychologist needs a couch for work, 50% of elementary, 24% of junior high school, and 11% of high school students responded in the affirmative. Dollinger and Thelen also noted that psychologists often misidentify themselves as "play doctors," people who want to "play some games" with children, or in other ways that misinform children, and may increase rather than reduce suspicions.

Several groups of researchers have investigated children's reactions and social judgements concerning emotionally disturbed peers (Mass et al., 1978 Marsden et al., 1977; Novak, 1974). Coie and Pennington (1976) focused on developmental differences shown by children in grades 1, 4, 7, and 11. They noted an increasing emphasis on social definitions as a function of development, and found that adult rule violations were a focus of special attention. Essentially, they provided empirical documentation of how a social consensus model of perceiving deviance evolves. Dollinger and his colleagues (1980) elaborated on these findings with a study of 818 children in grades 5 through 12. They found that children primarily conceptualize psychological prolems as being social in nature. For boys this trend increased with age, and both sexes showed an increased tendency with age to conceptualize problems as "internal to the person" (i.e., involving emotions and cognitions). Some use of terms or labels seemed to change as a possible function of development and intelligence. With age, for example, girls seemed to increase the use of the term "tension" and decrease use of the term "nerves."

A study by Kister and Patterson (1980) suggests still another relevant dimension. They explored children's concepts of illness and accidents with special attention to questions of causality, contagion, and the use of immanent justice. They note that pediatric patients often develop feelings of guilt about their illnesses and go on to document developmental trends in conceptions of causality and contagion in illness. Immanent justice (i.e., belief that an accident or illness may result from some perceived transgression) was also seen as causal by some children, but predictably this trend decreased with age. It seems that the decline of immanent justice thinking results from growing awareness of actual causes of illness. The critical point here is the importance of helping the child to understand the nature of the illness (or psychological problem) as a strategy to alleviate some of the fear and guilt that might accompany the onset of an illness or symptom cluster. These results and the need to provide children with information are clearly generalizable to the context of psychotherapy.

If children do not know why they are being referred for psychotherapy, one could reasonably expect some degree of guilt, embarrassment, and even resistance. Given the concepts evidenced in the studies cited above, especially Dollinger and Thelen's (1978), some unfortunate fantasies or assumptions on the child's part are clearly possible. The significance of the problem is well illustrated by Holmes and Urie's (1975) study of the effects of preparing children for psychotherapy. In their project 88 children participated in either a "therapy preparation" or a "social history" interview prior to beginning treatment. In the preparation interview the 6- to 12- year-olds were generally told what to expect and what therapy was all about. Specifically, they were told why people go into therapy and why they were referred. They were told what might go on in the sessions and what they should do (e.g., talk about their worries). The results showed that the prepared children were less likely than their unprepared peers to terminate treatment prematurely. The prepared children also had a better understanding of therapy and were regarded by therapists as less disturbed than the unprepared children.

Many therapists clearly understand these principles and act responsibly to provide a context within that psychotherapy may be used effectively. On the other hand, it is clear that considerable effort would be needed to provide an appropriate measure of information to many child-clients. In an empirical sense this extra effort to provide children with a degree of information seems well worth it and implies that some measure of informed consent is indeed possible with children as young as 6 years old. It is not the same sort of consent one would obtain from an adult who sought out therapy, but it is no less appropriate.

Minors' Competence in General Treatment

As noted earlier in this chapter, adults are presumed legally competent while minors are presumed incompetent. A model developed by Grisso and Vierling (1978) provides a useful basis for conceptualizing general treatment issues both legally and developmentally. They highlight three general types of consent by minors. First is the matter of minors' consenting to treatment independent of their parents' knowledge or consent. Some jurisdicions permit this by specific authorizations, as in the case of treatment for venereal disease or drug dependency and at least one state also permits minors to seek psychotherapy independently (Melton, 1981b). The second type involves the power to dissent, when parents have consented. This is generally not recognized, although some jurisdictions may provide for a special hearing or other mediation. One example might be a 15- or 16-year-old who wished to challenge "voluntary commitment" to a psychiatric hospital by his or her parents (Beyer & Wilson, 1976). The third general consent paradigm involves the child's right to know and/or participate in treatment decisions without veto power. While this is often espoused as a worthy ideal, it is not always easily implemented in practice (Melton, 1981a). Many developmental aspects of ability to process data must be considered as essential to competent decision making. Salience of the issue in question is one such ability. If the child does not have the ability to attend to the task or conceptualize the salient issues, meaningful participation in the decision is not possible. Similarly, the child must have the capacity to discriminate or differentiate among alternatives in order to voice a preference. In some instances it will also be highly desirable for the child to have potential for cost/benefit analysis. That is to say, the ability to consider and weigh abstract or hypothetical risks would often be desirable. The issues are clearly not simple ones, especially when there is incongruity between the views or best interests of different family members (see Chapter 2). Some would argue that such incongruity is often the case when a child is referred for psychotherapy (Koocher, 1976a; Simmonds, 1976).

Case Examples

Perhaps the best means of examining children's ability to consent for psychotherapy is through case examples. These composite cases are not intended to cover the full range of issues, but rather to illustrate some not uncommon problems.

Paula, age 9, is an active, attractive, physically healthy youngster with a two-year-old sibling. Her parents are both college graduates. Father is a computer programmer, and mother divides her time between the traditional role of housewife/mother and a part-time job as a bookkeeper. Both parents have relatively rigid personality styles, belong to a fundamentalist religious sect, and consider themselves "pillars of the community." They have brought Paula for a psychological evaluation and psychotherapy because they regard her as "overactive," and hope that medication and/or psychotherapy can help her. Specifically, they note she gnerally prefers to wear pants rather than dresses, has begun to contradict them in conversations at home, cannot seem to sit still in church, and has been associating with some "very nasty children" in the neighborhood from whom she is learning "foul language." They hope that she will soon be restored to the "little lady" she was just a year ago. School reports suggest good academic progress and no particular behavior problems, but the parents regard that information with some skepticism, noting their low regard for the standards of Paula's teacher who is divorced. A professional evaluation reveals an essentialy normal youngster whose social development is reasonably appropriate to her age level, although clearly in conflict with parental values.

Kevin is one of four children in a home with many problems. His mother is followed in outpatient psychotherapy a local mental health clinic where she is regarded as having a "borderline psychotic personality disturbance." There has been much marital strain and family fatigue with intermittent separations over the past few years. At present all of the children reside with the mother, the parents have been separated for the last time, and a divorce is on the horizon. Kevin's behavior, which was never especially laudable, has worsened since his recent 15th birthday. This is manifest chiefly in acting-out behaviors, such as being disobedient, staying out late at night, occasionally becoming intoxicated, fighting with his siblings, and generally being beyond the control of his mother. In the face of her own difficulties, the mother decided to seek residential treatment for Kevin and takes him to the child psychiatry unit of a local hospital. Since Kevin is a minor she signs him into the hospital as a "voluntary admission" so that he may be treated. Kevin is angry and unwilling to be hospitalized, asserting, "I'm not crazy . . . you have no right to put me here." He demands to see a lawyer. Ultimately he is released and a class-action suit forces changes in state law which assure a hearing for such youngsters, but not before he is turned down for at least one job opening because of his "history of psychiatric hospitalization."

Max, age 12, is an angry youngster brought for psychological evaluation by his parents who found detailed designs for bombs and a "sister-killing machine" in his room. He is depressed, angry, and jealous of his sibling and his perception of parental favoritism toward her. The drawings are private expressions of the anger he is unable to express directly, but he is not likely to act out against anyone in the family. The parents are concerned and express a wilingness to work toward resolving the difficulty in whatever ways they can, but Max is resistant. He says, "I don't need any help, I don't want any help, and I can take care of myself." His parents are prepared to compel his participation in psychotherapy, if it is recommended.

Case Commentaries

Paula: It is highly likely that this well-socialized youngster could be engaged in a psychotherapeutic relationship, especially if her parents were supportive of it, but how should such therapy be conceptualized? Is it aceptable for Paula to become the identified patient, with potential implications for her self-esteem as a person in need of psychotherapeutic help for behaving as a reasonaby normal nine-year-old? One alternative course could be for the therapist to attempt to remake Paula in the image her parents wish. At the opposite end of the continuum, one could inform the parents that they are the ones with the problem and that the child needs no psychotherapy *per se*. The former strategy is doomed to fail because it presumes a potential for inordinate readjustment by Paula. The latter approach could also fail by alienating the parents, who will either shop for a therapist who agrees with them or be too threatened to consult another mental health professional. Another strategy might be to accept Paula in psychotherapy with the goal of helping her to adapt to her neurotic parents. Still another strategy could include a family-oriented approach to treatment aimed at exploring the needs of all parties in a facilitative atmosphere. It is unlikely that Paula will fully be able to conceptualize these issues and make informed choices. In part this is true because of relatively immature cognitive capabilities (assuming normal development), but it also stems from her role in a continuing family organization where she received support as well as stress and depends on her parents to meet her basic needs. Still, it should be possible to provide her with the potential to participate in any therapeutic scheme without additional injury to her self-esteem.

Kevin: Such concepts as the "right to treatment in the least restrictive setting" come to mind immediately in this case, but what would Kevin have chosen for himself? Presumably, less restrictive measures (*i.e.*, outpatient psychotherapy) had failed or were refused by him. Remaining in the overtaxed home might have contributed more harm than benefit. In the end he returned home, following an angry hospitalization. It is difficult to say whether the hospitalization accomplished any more than a "time out" for both Kevin and his mother, except that his history of "psychiatric hospitalization" did cause him difficulty in finding employment later. If his mother had thrown him out of the house, would he have fared better? Would he have been involuntarily hospitalized under current standards? Would he be permitted to sign himself into the hospital voluntarily today, without his mother's consent if he had been the one to say he need help?

Max: This boy could probably be helped through psychotherapeutic intervention, although he does not believe it at the moment. If he were six years older he could refuse with impunity. If his parents compel his participation, he could offer resistance in many ways. If he is intellectually capable of hearing and understanding what happens (or is proposed) in psychotherapy, but is emotionally opposed to participating, should he have the right to veto intervention of this sort? Does a child have the right to choose discomfort over a potentialy helpful treatment? If Max were refusing a tetanus immunization following a puncture wound his protests would certainly be overridden, but psychotherapy is not as predictably effective. Perhaps if he is left alone as he wishes he will be cured via maturation.

Realistic Alternatives

As the case examples and commentaries illustrate, there are many routes that may be traveled in attempting to engage the child as a consenting client in psychotherapy. Glenn's (1980) conceptualization of the child psychotherapist as "advocate, information provider, social/political/legal change agent, and researcher" seems a bit overly ambitious. It is clear, however, that attention to several foci can insure the best goals of consent-getting while actually facilitating the process of psychotherapy.

First among these would be a definition of the child's psychotherapist as a sensitive mediator between parties with different interests. There may often be times when all concerned have common goals and interests, but the therapist must be especially sensitive to conflicts of interest and endeavor to facilitate mutual accommodation. It will seldom be in the child's best interest to avoid incorporating his or her viewpoint in treatment planning and the therapist may have to take the lead here.

Second, incorporation of the child's input in treatment planning may also be considered apart from the therapist's role as a mediator. Children in therapy should be given information about how they are perceived and routinely be involved in discussion of the course of therapy. The degree to which this is possible will certainly vary with the child's cognitive and social abilities, but it should be possible to some degree with almost every child-client.

A third focus would involve recognition of the legitimate developmental competencies of children to express their own desires and best interests. It would be just as foolhardy to assert the validity of the legal fiction that minors are incapable of making a decision in their own best interests as it would be to assert that adults do not make bad decisions from time to time. The input of any child should be given appropriate weight in any decision-making process. What is "appropriate" may depend on the child's cognitive, social, and emotional status, but should not be determined by age *per se*. It would be wiser to approach the child in quest of competence, rather than by presuming incompetence.

Finally, it is important that the psychotherapist recognize the special vulnerabilities of the child-client with respect to consent issues and work to reduce potential untoward results. Children may be physically, socially, and psychologically more vulnerable than adults both because of their legal status because of their relative developmental disadvantage. Children are more susceptible than adults to disruption in developmental trajectories that may have substantial long-term consequences.

Researchable Questions

It should be evident that there are a number of potentially researchable questions that could provide meaningful answers to some of the questions that remain with respect to children's consent for psychotherapy. Perhaps the most prominent would involve the role of intelligence and verbal facility as mediating variables in children's conceptions of human behavior (Dollinger *et al.*, 1980). This would also offer an approach to clarifying the meaning that terms such as *emotional problems* or *mental problems* have for children of different ages. If psychotherapists knew what types of problems children associate with various labels, we would be better able to address their personal experiences in treatment. Other related areas that have been underexplored include children's perceptions of causation with respect to emotional disturbance and their understanding of defense mechanisms.

Melton's (1981b) preliminary report on children who may seek out psychotherapy without their parents' knowledge or consent opens the door to another potential realm of inquiry. Frequency studies of this phenomenon in states where it is allowed would be most interesting. As Melton notes, however, the matter of public information and socialization issues may keep the numbers of such children low. A parallel issue might involve a study of children's willingness to become "voluntary" inpatients in psychotherapeutic settings, despite legal incompetence. That is to say, how frequently and under what circumstances would the child "volunteer" actually be reluctant (Beyer and Wilson, 1976)? Such studies might provide directions for reducing parent child conflicts on this issue, if indeed such conflicts often exist.

Another realm of inquiry that could prove quite fruitful would be an assessment of children's attitudes prior to entering psychotherapy and after several sessions. Similarly, a comparison of reasons for referral and therapeutic goals for congruence (or incongruity) between parent and child assessments would be quite interesting. One might predict that satisfaction with psychotherapeutic outcome would be positively correlated with congruity of goals for both parents and children. It could also be anticipated that children will feel more favorably engaged and hence more motivated in psychotherapy when their attitudes and input are sought.

In the final analysis, data may actually reveal that efforts to engage children in consent-granting procedures have a positive psychotherapeutic benefit. The actual practice of successful psychotherapists who work with children has long reflected such behavior, although it would not have been fashionable to refer to this as consent getting. Instead it might have been termed listening to the child or fostering self-respect.

References

Amerian Psychological Associatin. Latest changes in ethics code. *APA Monitor*, 1979, *10*(10), 16–17.

Annas, G. J. Denying the rights of the retarded: The Philip Becker case. *Hastings Center Report*, 1979, *9*(6), 18–20.

Beyer, H. A., & Wilson, J. P. The reluctant volunteer: A child's right to resist commitment. In G. P. Koocher (Ed.), *Children's rights and the mental health professions*. New York: Wiley, 1976.

Coie, J. D., & Pennington, B. F. Children's perceptions of deviance and disorder. *Child Development*, 1976, *47*(2), 407–413.

Davidson, G.C. & Stuart, R.B. Behavior therapy and civil liberties. *American Psychologist*, 1975, *30*, 755–763.

Dollinger, S. J., & Thelen, M. H. Children's perceptions of psychology. *Professional Psychology*, 1978, *9*(1), 117–126.

Dollinger, S. J., Thelen, M. H. & Walsh, M. L. Children's conceptions of psychological problems. *Journal of Clinical Child Psychology*, 1980, *9*(3), 191–194.

Eysenck, H. J. The effects of psychotherapy. *International Journal of Psychiatry*, 1965, *1*, 97–178.

Eysenck, H. J. *The effects of psychotherapy*. New York: International Science Press, 1966.

Foster, L. M. State confidentiality laws. *American Journal of Orthopsychiatry*, 1980, *50*(4), 659–665.

Glenn, C. M. Ethical issues in the practice of child psychotherapy. *Professional Psychology*, 1980, *11*(4), 613–619.

Goldstein, J., Freud, A., & Solnit, A. J. *Beyond the best interests of the child*. New York: Free Press, 1973.

Goldstein, J., Freud, A., Solnit, A. J. *Before the best interests of the child*. New York: Free Press, 1979.

Grisso, T., & Vierling, L. Minors' consent to treatment: A developmental perspective. *Professional Psychology*, 1978, *9*(3), 412–427.

Hobbs, M. (Ed.). *Issues in the classification of children*. San Francisco: Jossey-Bass, 1975.

Holmes, D. S., & Urie, R. G. Effects of preparing children for psychotherapy. *Journal of Consulting and Clinical Psychology*, 1975, *43*(3), 311–318.

Keith-Spiegel, P. Children's rights as participants in research. In G. P. Koocher (Ed.), *Children's rights and the mental health professions*. New York: Wiley, 1976.

Kister, M. C. & Patterson, C. J. Children's conceptions of the causes of illness: Understanding of contagion and use of immanent justice. *Child Development*, 1980, *51*, 839–846.

Koocher, G. P. A bill of rights for children in psychotherapy. In G. P. Koocher (Ed.), *Children's rights and the mental health professions*. New York: Wiley, 1976. (a)

Koocher, G. P. Civil liberties and aversive conditioning for children. *American Psychologist*, 1976, *31*(1), 94–95. (b)

Koocher, G. P. Child advocacy and mental health professionals. In P. A. Vardin & I. N. Brody (Eds.), *Children's rights: Contemporary perspectives* New York: Columbia University Teacher's College Press, 1978.

Koocher, G. P. & Pedulla, B. M. Current practices in child psychotherapy. *Professional Psychology*, 1977, *8*, 275,287.

Lovaas, O. I. & Simmons, J. Q. Manipulation of self-destruction in three retarded children. *Journal of Applied Behavior Analysis*, 1969, *2*, 143–157.

Maas, E., Marecek, J., & Travers, J. R. Children's conceptions of disordered behavior. *Child Development*, 1978, *49* 146–154.

Marsden, G., Kalter, N. M., Plunkett, J. W. & Barr-Grossman, T. Children's social judgements concerning emotionally disturbed peers. *Journal of Consulting and Clinical Psychology*, 1977, *45*, 948.

Melton, G. B. Children's concepts of their rights. *Journal of Clinical Child Psychology*, 1980, *9*(3), 186–190. (a)

Melton, G. B. Psychological effects of increased autonomy on children. *Educational Perspectives*, 1980, *19*(4), 10–14. (b)

Melton, G. B. Children's participation in treatment planning: Psychological and legal issues. *Professional Psychology*, 1981, *12*, 246–252. (a)

Melton, G. B. Effects of a state law permitting minors to consent to psychotherapy. *Professional Psychology*, 1981, *12*, 647–654. (b)

Novak, D. W. Children's reactions to emotional disturbance in imaginary peers. *Journal of Consulting and Clinical Psychology*, 1974, *42*, 462.

Phillips, J. L. *The origins of intellect: Piaget's theory*. San Francisco: W. H. Freeman, 1975.

Ross, A. O. Confidentiality in child therapy: A re-evaluation. *Mental Hygiene*, 1966, *50*, 360–366.

Rothman, D. J., and Rothman, S. M. The conflict over children's rights. *The Hastings Center Report*, 1980, *10*(3), 7–10.

Shore, M. F. Legislation, advocacy, and the rights of children and youth. *American Psychologist*, 1979, *34*(10), 1017–1019.

Simmonds, D. W. Children's rights and family dysfunction. In G. P. Koocher (Ed.), *Children's rights and the mental health professions*. New York: Wiley, 1976.

Starr, R. H. Child abuse. *American Psychologist*, 1979, *34*(10), 872–878.

Weiner, I. B. Individual psychotherapy. In I. B. Weiner (Ed.), *Clinical methods in psychology*. New York: Wiley, 1976.

Wilson, J. P. *The rights of Adolescents in the mental health system*. Lexington, Mass.: D. C. Heath, 1978.

Part III

Children's Consent in Nonmedical Areas

CHAPTER 8

Juveniles' Consent in Delinquency Proceedings

THOMAS GRISSO

The Fifth and Sixth Amendment rights—the rights to silence and to the benefit of legal counsel—are extended to persons in legal proceedings that might lead to their conviction of criminal offenses. *In re Gault*[1] and subsequent cases extended these rights to minors. Whenever police or court officers wish to question a minor about alleged involvement in a delinquent act, the minor must first have waived the rights to silence and counsel: that is, must have consented to questioning in the absence of legal counsel. Waiver of rights must have been made knowingly, intelligently, and voluntarily in order for the products of the waiver (*e.g.*, confession) to be validly obtained and admissable as evidence in proceedings against the suspect. These circumstances raise a critical question: to what extent can the waiver of the rights to silence and legal counsel by minors be made competently—that is, knowingly, intelligently, and voluntarily?

In this chapter, we will review legal theory and precedent that are essential to consider when developing empirical research to address questions of juveniles' consent and decisions about rights in delinquency proceedings. Then we will discuss three areas of research related to the questions of juveniles' competence to waive rights: (a) research on the legal system and legal processes related to rights waiver; (b) research on juveniles' capacities to waive rights; and (c) research on juveniles' capacities to make use of legal advocacy in the

---

[1] *In re* Gault, 387 U.S. 1 (1967).

THOMAS GRISSO • Department of Psychology, St. Louis University, St. Louis, Missouri 63103.

process of making decisions about rights. In each of these three areas, we will examine the relevant research questions and progress that has already been made in addressing them, then provide directions for future research, and finally suggest (where possible) certain directions for policy and practice in delinquency proceedings based on existing research results.

Legal Background[2]

Miranda v. Arizona[3] established the constitutional requirement that persons accused of crimes must be informed of their absolute rights to legal counsel and to avoid self-incrimination. Information subsequently obtained from the person is admissable as evidence in legal proceedings against the person only if preceded by a knowing, intelligent, and voluntary waiver of these rights. In *In re Gault*,[4] the U.S. Supreme Court extended this requirement to apply to delinquency proceedings involving juveniles. While *Gault* focused on the rights in the adjudicatory process alone, subsequent courts have established the applicability of *Miranda* and *Gault* at almost all stages of the legal process once the juvenile has been taken into custody by police.

There are many points in the juvenile justice process at which a juvenile's rights to silence and legal counsel might be critical: *e.g.*, at the time of interrogation subsequent to arrest, at detention hearings, intake interviews with court caseworkers, preliminary hearings, the adjudicatory hearing, and disposition hearings. Yet the great majority of appellate court interpretations of juveniles' waiver of rights have arisen in relation to waiver preliminary to police interrogation shortly after the juvenile has been taken into custody.

It is at this time, after having been informed of his or her rights in accordance with *Miranda*, that a juvenile's waiver of the rights and subsequent confession may have the greatest impact upon later court decisions about the juvenile's life. Often a juvenile's confession will be the primary evidence upon which a delinquency adjudication is based. Courts have long recognized that frightened juveniles might confess to offenses they have not committed.[5] The consequences of a confession can be serious, of course, as when a juvenile is required to spend several years in a training school as a result of a delinquency finding. Yet even less severe dispositions have their negative consequences; a frightened juvenile's confession to some minor offense that he in fact did not commit adds

[2] For a more detailed review of the legal background in this area of juvenile law, *see* Grisso, 1980; Grisso, 1981; Piersma *et al.*, 1977.
[3] Miranda v. Arizona, 348 U.S. 436 (1966).
[4] *In re* Gault, 387 U.S. 1 (1967).
[5] *Id.*, at 45 and 48–55.

one more event to a court record which may result in harsher treatment at some later contact.

The legal question of the competency of waiver of rights has been raised in relation to juveniles more often than to adults. This is primarily because juveniles' greater immaturity has been seen as increasing the likelihood that they cannot understand the rights or the implications of their waiver or that they are more likely to be intimidated by even routine, benign police procedures.[6]

It is important to understand that the issue of the validity (or competence) of a juvenile's waiver of rights is a matter of procedure as well as a matter of the juvenile's capacities. The law's view of the validity of waiver, just as in questions of the effectiveness of a classroom teaching method or a form of psychotherapy, takes into account both the manner in which the procedure occurs (*e.g.*, how the juvenile was informed of the rights, in what environmental and interpersonal context) and the characteristics of the juvenile (*e.g.*, the cognitive and interpersonal capacities of the individual).[7]

The law has employed two approaches to dealing with these complexities when deciding on the validity of juveniles' waiver of rights in interrogation: the totality of circumstances approach and the *per se* exclusionary approach.

The totality of circumstances approach requires that when the question of the validity of a juvenile's waiver is raised, judges must weigh all of the circumstances in a case in deciding whether a juvenile's waiver of rights was valid. This approach has been predominant since *People v. Lara*,[8] in which the California Supreme Court stated that the mere fact of age (or of any other single variable) was not to be viewed as critical in determining whether a juvenile's waiver was valid. The U.S. Supreme Court's 1979 decision in *Fare v. Michael C.*[9] reinforced the totality of circumstances approach. The rationale for supporting a totality approach has been that this discretionary method provides the flexibility that is needed to protect those juveniles who by reason of their incapacities or certain police procedures are in need of protection greater than that

[6] Gault comports with earlier recognition of this point in Haley v. Ohio, 332 U.S. 596, 599–600 (1948) and Gallegos v. Colorado, 370 U.S. 49, 54–55 (1962).

[7] West v. United States, 399 F.2d 467 (5th Cir. 1968), *Cert. denied*, 393 U.S. 1102 (1969), and State v. White, 494 S.W. 687, 690 (Mo. Ct. App. 1973), among others, generally suggest these two types of factors to be weighed when deciding issues of the validity of juveniles' waivers. In West, two personal characteristics (age, education) and seven procedural considerations were enumerated. White and Fare v. Michael C., 442 U.S. at 725 (1979) provided more extensive guidelines concerning specific personal characteristics (*e.g.*, "age, experience, background, and intelligence," *Id.*).

[8] People v. Lara, 432 P.2d 202 (Cal., 1967) formally established the totality of circumstances approach, which had been in general use in earlier juvenile cases, notably Gallegos v. Colorado, 370 U.S. 49 (1962).

[9] Fare v. Michael C., 442 U.S. 707 (1979).

provided to most adult suspects, while at the same time avoiding interference with police investigations of juveniles who are more sophisticated.[10] Supporters of the totality approach have assumed that courts are capable of evaluating all of the necessary circumstances just as in other cases.[11]

In contrast, the *per se* exclusionary approach automatically rules invalid the waiver of rights by certain classes of juveniles or under certain procedural circumstances.[12] It does not leave the question open to discretionary error or abuse which potentially can occur with the totality of circumstances approach. For example, some states now require the presence of a parent, guardian, or attorney at the time of a rights waiver in order for it to be valid.[13] Three states, by statute or precedent, specifically require the presence of legal counsel before a juvenile may validly waive the right to silence or counsel.[14] In essence, they presume that juveniles as a class do not have the capacity to make a meaningful waiver of rights unassisted, given the usual police or court procedures for obtaining rights waiver.[15]

A review of relevant appellate cases[16] employing the totality of circumstances approach indicated that in addition to several procedural variables, courts have considered a number of variables potentially related to juveniles' capacities to understand and appreciate the significance of the rights of which they are informed by police. These variables include the juvenile's age, education, intelligence, amount of prior experience with police and courts, and physical condition.[17] Consistent with the totality approach, however, courts generally

---

[10] *Id.*, at 725.

[11] *E.g.*, Commonwealth v. Roane, 329 A.2d 286, 289–90 (1974) (Eagen, J., dissenting); Fare v. Michael C., 442 U.S. at 725 (1979). Yet Fare resulted in a 5–4 decision; the majority's conclusions about the juvenile's understanding of his rights (at 726) were dramatically different from Justice Powell's (dissenting) conclusions concerning the youth's lack of understanding (at 733), even though the disparate conclusions were based on the same evidence (*i.e.*, the age, demeanor, education, and other characteristics of Michael C.).

[12] Miranda itself has the effect of a *per se* requirement for the validity of waivers. The question in the present instance has been whether or not additional *per se* requirements should be recognized in juvenile cases.

[13] *See, e.g.*, Colo. Rev. Stat. Ann. § 19–2–102(3) (c) (I) (1978); Conn. Gen. Stat. Ann. § 466–137(a) (Supp. 1979); N.M. Stat. Ann. § 32–1–27(A) (1978). *See also*, Lewis v. State, 288 N.E.2d 138 (Ind., 1972); *In re* K.W.B., 500 S.W.2d 275 (Mo., 1973); People v. Burton, 491 P.2d 793 (Cal., 1971); Commonwealth v. Markle, 380 A.2d 346 (Pa., 1977).

[14] Ala. Code § 12–15–67 (1975); Tex. Fam. Code Ann. § 51;09 (Supp. 1980); Ezell v. State, 489 P.2d 781 (Okla., 1971).

[15] But it is arguable, too, that requiring the presence of parents does not assure adequate protection for juveniles during rights waiver and interrogation. For a summary of legal commentary concerning the dubious value of parents' presence, *see* Grisso (1981), p. 166–168, and an empirically based rejection of the value of parents' presence at p. 168–190.

[16] Specific citation of this sizable body of case law has been omitted in the interest of brevity; it can be examined in Grisso (1980, 1981).

[17] The review noted in 16, *supra*, revealed that ages 13–15 represent a range below which juveniles'

have affirmed that no single variable among these is critical, and that no particular value of any of these variables (*e.g.*, a particular IQ range or specific number of prior arrests) should be used as sole criterion for decisions about the validity of waiver. Thus judges are provided few guidelines to assist in application of the totality test.

In summary, empirical research on juveniles' consent, or waiver of rights, in delinquency proceedings should focus on juveniles' capacities and on the effects of various procedural circumstances upon juveniles' abilities to provide knowing, intelligent, and voluntary waiver of rights. Empirical information would be useful to those in law who seek adequate procedural rules, as well as to those who support a case-by-case totality of circumstances approach to deciding about the validity of juveniles' waiver of rights.

The remainder of this chapter examines three types of empirical research that could meet this objective: examination of the social context of rights waiver, juveniles' abilities to understand the rights to silence and legal counsel, and their perceptions of the attorneys who might supplement their abilities to decide about their rights.

The Social Context of Rights Waiver

Review

Questions of the validity of juveniles' waiver of rights require an understanding of the social contexts in which juveniles make waiver decisions. This is consistent with the legal view that both circumstantial variables and juveniles' characteristics must be weighed in order to decide on the validity of waiver. It is also consistent with recent perspectives in psychological assessment that view competence as not merely a person's capacities in the abstract, but as one's functioning in the context of specific situational demands.

As noted earlier, the point in the legal process at which rights waiver is most critical is in the course of police officers' preparation of a suspect for questioning immediately following arrest. Although in-custody questioning often may occur on the street, many states require that if police wish to obtain information that can validly be used in court to establish the juvenile's delinquency, they must first take the juvenile to a police station or a court facility (*e.g.*, detention center) prior to any further action, and some states require the

---

unassisted waivers are most often rejected, and above which there is a strong tendency to accept them as valid. Most cases in which requisite comprehension of Miranda was considered by courts to be lacking involved juveniles with IQ scores below 75, although this IQ level was far from determinative.

presence of a court officer (*e.g.*, probation officer) or parent before any questions may be asked by police. Many juveniles will be informed of their rights at the site of the arrest and again just prior to interrogation attempts after the aforementioned procedural requirements have been met (Grisso, 1981).

Although there have been studies of variables influencing police arrests of juveniles (*e.g.*, Piliavin & Briar, 1964), very little is known empirically about the sequence of events preceding juveniles' waiver of rights in relation to interrogation or about the relationship between these events and juveniles' decisions about their rights. In the only study of this type to date, Grisso and Pomicter (1977) examined archival data regarding the arrests of 491 juveniles suspected of felonies. The study provided data on procedures in one jurisdiction during a year in which procedural requirements were relatively lax, and during two subsequent years following a legislated change to more stringent and protective procedures. Among the findings was the observation that police interrogation occurred in about 75% of the cases involving felony charges. Parents were present in one-half of the cases in the first year but in almost all cases following the new legislation. Presence of a court representative, to act as monitor of the rights waiver, increased from about 10% of the cases in the first year to nearly three-quarters of the cases in the last year. It was found that over 90% of the juveniles waived rights to silence and counsel. Interestingly, this rate was consistent across all years and therefore was unrelated to the various degrees of protection represented by different procedures during the three years studied.

More studies of this type are needed in order to provide a view of the range of circumstances across jurisdictions. Yet such studies leave many critical questions unanswered. Most notably, the study provided no information on the social dynamics of the process by which juveniles were informed of the rights and prepared by police for the decision about the rights.

There have been no systematic studies of the words or form used in communicating the rights to juveniles, of the style of presentation by police or court officers, of social cues that might augment or attenuate the status difference between police and the juvenile suspect, or of other procedural variables that conceptually could be related to knowing, intelligent, and voluntary waiver. All that is known about this process is based on anecdote, occasional case studies (Barthel, 1977), police interrogation manuals (Inbau & Reid, 1967), and descriptions of case facts in appellate judges' case opinions. Together these sources suggest that coercion by brute force is relatively rare and that procedures and tactics vary widely from one jurisdiction to another as well as from one police officer to another. Presentation of the rights themselves most often includes a "boiler-plate" reading of the rights approximately as worded in *Miranda v. Arizona*. Other communications may range from overt verbal threats to police officers' reliance on nonverbal messages communicating their authority. Interrogation manuals (Inbau & Reid, 1967) describe some elaborate but subtle "psychological" methods for the manipulation of suspects. Driver (1968) has pointed out that even well-meaning benevolence on the part of the police may be coercive, potentially playing upon the fright and uncertainty experienced by many juveniles. Yet we have no direct observational data with which to clarify these processes. Our social psychological principles regarding acquiescence, conformity, or assertiveness might be relevant in explaining the social circumstances of rights waiver; yet they are of little use without the factual data to which to apply them.

Some states require the presence of parents at the time of rights waiver to provide juveniles with the counsel and support they might need. Many commentators have been dubious, however, about parents' abilities to provide such assistance (Paulsen & Whitebread, 1974; McMillian & McMurtry, 1969–70). In fact, Grisso and Ring's (1979) study of parents' attitudes toward children's rights suggested that 75% of parents did not believe children ought to have a right to silence at all. In another study of parents' behavior at the time of their children's rights waiver (Grisso, 1981), more than two-thirds of them gave no advice and, indeed, said nothing at all to their children throughout the preinterrogation waiver process. Whether there are other procedural variables that might afford more meaningful protection to juveniles has not been studied.

Research Recommendations

It is apparent from the foregoing review that research is needed on the legal contexts in which juveniles are informed of Fifth and Sixth Amendment rights and are asked to waive them: when, by whom, in what environmental and interpersonal circumstances, and in what words. Archival data when available will be helpful, but there can be no substitute for direct observation of these processes. Observation should occur in different selected jurisdictions—e.g., urban and rural courts, more or less "due process oriented" courts—in order to establish the generalizability or idiosyncracy of various observations. Little else can be done to examine the impact of interrogation upon various types of children until we have reliable data on these specific methods and circumstances of police questioning.

When these procedural circumstances are known, then it may be possible to examine in more detail the responses of children to police requests for rights waiver, either *in vivo* or in situations which benignly simulate some of the circumstances set forth by the former, descriptive studies. Children's responses (*e.g.*, frequency of rights waiver, reasoning they employ in making waiver decisions) could be analyzed according to demographic or developmental characteristics of children. In that way we might better be able to describe to courts the conditions under which children of various types are or are not likely to be able to deal meaningfully with decisions about rights during police questioning. Studies of this type would be most helpful if they are structured by our social psychological knowledge of interpersonal variables that are critical for explaining behavior in interpersonal situations. For example, there are data from basic research on children's acquiesence and conformity (Costanza & Shaw, 1966; Kagan & Kogan, 1970; Landsbaum & Willis, 1971), role-taking in children (*e.g.*, Flavell, 1970), and children's social problem-solving (Spivack, Platt, & Shure, 1976) that suggest that certain contextual variables may be especially important in determining the quality and types of responses of children to social situations. (See also the review by Driver, 1968, and by Grisso & Vierling, 1978).

Applied Recommendations

While we await more definitive research in this area, it would be fortunate if we could glean from existing studies what procedural safeguards would appear to be most appropriate when police are dealing with juveniles' waiver of rights. Yet existing research offers nothing in this regard, apart from skepticism regarding certain procedures now in use that have been intended as safeguards. Specifically, requiring the presence of parents would seem to offer no satisfactory remedy to the possibility that juveniles might have difficulty deciding on the waiver question unassisted. Apart from this, it is simply premature to be recommending particular procedures regarding the conduct of law enforcement officers or the social context in which the waiver decision should be made when we know little about either conduct or social context in this area. As we proceed to the next two areas of research, however, we will have occasion to return to the question of recommendations for certain procedural elements that do not specifically involve either police conduct or the social psychology of police interrogation.

Juveniles' Capacities to Understand Their Rights

Review

The ability of juveniles to waive rights knowingly, intelligently, and voluntarily will depend not only upon variations in procedures for informing them of their rights, but also upon variations in juveniles' capacities to understand and appreciate the rights that they are asked to waive. Some research has been directed toward characterizing the cognitive capacities of various classes of juveniles to deal meaningfully with rights waiver.

One line of research related to this objective has employed concepts from Piagetian developmental theory to structure the study of juveniles' conceptualizations of rights in general. Drawing upon Tapp and Kohlberg's (1971) adaptation of Piagetian stages of cognitive development, Melton (1979) has found that conceptualizations of rights develop from a view of rights as allowances by authority to a grasp of rights as transcending control by authority. This line of research has several strengths. It contributes to the larger body of empirical and theoretical knowledge regarding cognitive development in children, and the principles derived from it may be relevant in approaching a wide range of situations in which children's independent consent is of concern.

Yet the results are difficult to use in addressing practical, legal concerns regarding the validity of juveniles' waiver of rights to silence and legal counsel. One reason is that developmental stage concepts are difficult for judges or lawmakers to employ in making practical judgments about juveniles' waiver of rights. In addition, juveniles understanding of the specific content and concepts embodied in the rights to silence and legal counsel is not addressed by research that was designed to demonstrate more general principles in cognitive development.

A second approach has been to evaluate juveniles' understanding of the specific content and concepts related to the rights to silence and legal counsel, as these are explained to juveniles in the standard *Miranda* warnings which are used in most jurisdictions.[18] Although this approach offers less to general developmental theory, it can provide courts with information about juveniles' capacities that is more specific to their concerns.

Grisso (1980, 1981; Grisso & Manoogian, 1980) has completed a series of studies of this type, assessing the abilities of over 600 juvenile court wards and both offender and nonoffender adults to understand the *Miranda* warnings and their implications. Several experimental measures of "*Miranda* comprehension" were developed, using the concensus of legal professionals to develop criteria employed in the objective scoring of responses. Multiple measures allowed for assessment of juveniles' understanding through several response modes, thus minimizing error associated with assessments that rely too heavily upon verbal expressive abilities. In these studies, juveniles and adults were examined in research situations within detention or offender residential settings, but the circumstances bore no relation to or consequences for their present involvement with police or courts. Thus they were examined under relatively nonstressful conditions compared to actual interrogation circumstances.

---

[18] Most jurisdictions require that suspects be informed of their rights using words similar to the following: "You do not have to make a statement and have the right to remain silent. Anything you say can and will be used against you in a court of law. You have the right to consult an attorney prior to interrogation and to have an attorney present at the time of any interrogation. If you cannot afford an attorney, one will be appointed for you free of charge."

A complete description of the methods and results of the studies can be found elsewhere (Grisso, 1981). Based on empirical results of the full range of studies in this project, Grisso concluded that:

1. The vast majority of juveniles ages 14 and younger do not grasp the meaning of the *Miranda* warnings and their implications sufficiently to provide a meaningful waiver of rights. As a class, juveniles at these ages failed to meet an absolute standard for adequate comprehension of the rights and their significance and demonstrated significantly poorer comprehension than did the adult samples.

2. Juveniles who were 15 or 16 years of age and had intelligence test scores of 80 or below performed similarly on measures of *Miranda* comprehension to juveniles who were age 14 or younger. As a class, however, 15 and 16-year-olds demonstrated a level of comprehension not significantly different from that of the adults.

3. At least one-quarter of the adults failed to meet an absolute standard for legally adequate understanding of the *Miranda* warnings and their implications.

4. Among juveniles, understanding of the rights was not significantly related to amount of prior experience with courts or police, nor to race or socioeconomic status (except insofar as these covaried with intelligence test scores).

These results may be useful in addressing several questions faced by courts and legislatures concerned with legal due process for juveniles. Yet they do not address the question of juveniles' *potential* to understand the meaning of rights to silence and counsel, since these studies focused upon juveniles' understanding based only on a presentation of the standard *Miranda* warnings and whatever knowledge the juveniles themselves brought to the situation. It is conceivable that many juveniles, even in the younger age groups, have the potential to understand the rights if provided different explanations. One study (Manoogian, 1977), however, found no improvement in *Miranda* comprehension when juveniles were provided with simply worded explanations of the rights to silence and counsel.

Research Recommendations

There is little need for further studies of juveniles' capacities to understand specifically the standard *Miranda* warnings or their significance, except insofar as others might wish to replicate Grisso's findings with juveniles with population characteristics specific to a particular jurisdiction. A more fruitful direction for research in this area is the examination of circumstances that will improve juveniles' understanding of their rights to silence and counsel. There are two avenues of this type to pursue, one of which is highly recommended in contrast to the other, which I would discourage.

Concerning the more commendable approach, it may be possible to improve our early socialization of children to the concept of a right, and to better educate them regarding the meaning and implication of specific rights that apply in their potential interactions with police and courts. Levine and Tapp (1977) have made steps in this direction. Basic developmental theory on conceptualizations of law, rule, and rights can guide us here, and certain results from the forementioned project that assessed juveniles' comprehension of the *Miranda* rights provide guidelines for specific content which could be incorporated into educational attempts.

On the other hand, I would not encourage research designed to improve the manner in which police or court personnel explain to juveniles the rights to silence and counsel at the time of rights waiver and police questioning. Even if such a method were found, its potential for enhancing the protection of juveniles in such legal proceedings would be very questionable. The validity of a juvenile's waiver depends not only upon the individual's understanding of the rights, but also upon the voluntariness with which the waiver is made, a matter that probably rests as much with the social atmosphere of the proceeding as with the clarity with which the rights were explained to the juvenile. The implementation of an empirically-supported way of clearly explaining the rights does not address the issue of social dynamics of the situation, and indeed it might provide legal authorities with a false sense of having satisfied the increased needs of juveniles for care and protection in the waiver process.

Applied Recommendations

The results of the series of studies on comprehension of the *Miranda* warnings now provides psychologists involved in juvenile and adult criminal cases with an empirical base for rendering opinions to courts. That is, by referring to Grisso's (1981) reports, a psychologist or lawyer may use a juvenile's age, IQ, and other characteristics to provide an estimate of his or her degree of understanding of the *Miranda* rights. Unfortunately, though, the experimental measures of comprehension themselves cannot be unequivocally recommended as "diagnostic" instruments. They are too lengthy and their scoring is too complex to serve as routine screening instruments prior to interrogations. Further, they offer no safeguard against "self-serving" wrong answers by juveniles who might attempt to simulate poor comprehension when the instruments are administered in the context of actual police or court proceedings.

The results of the range of studies in the project referred to earlier suggest the need for extraordinary safeguards against uninformed or involuntary waivers by juveniles of ages 14 or younger, and by juveniles of 15 or 16 with relatively low IQ scores. As noted earlier, there is reason to be dubious about the value of parents' advice as a safeguard, and existing research does not encourage attempts to develop "simplified *Miranda* warnings." Better education or socialization to rights would be helpful, but does not address the need for more immediate remedies.

One possible remedy would be to make legal counsel automatic for all or some classes of juveniles. That is, these juveniles would not be allowed to waive rights to silence or legal counsel unassisted; legal counsel would routinely be provided to help them decide the matter. A variety of objections to this recommendation can and have been raised by law enforcement officials who fear that lawyers will hinder investigations, and these have been discussed elsewhere (Grisso, 1980). But even apart from those arguments, the value of automatic provision of legal counsel is likely to depend in part on juveniles' capacities or willingness to receive whatever counsel a lawyer might be able to provide. Therefore, let us examine the study of juveniles' perceptions of lawyers and juveniles' participation in the lawyer-client relationship.

Juveniles' Responses to Legal Advocates

Review

Juveniles' attitudes and expectancies regarding lawyers should be a major focus of research attention. Whether juveniles are left to decide about the need for legal counsel or instead are automatically provided counsel in legal proceedings, their attitudes and expectancies about legal assistance may critically influence the degree to which they avail themselves of the protections and advice that legal advocates may be capable of providing.

This area of inquiry has implications for settings and circumstances other than delinquency proceedings. With increasing frequency, children are represented by lawyers as a third party in neglect and custody proceedings or other circumstances in which the child's interests may be independent of the interests of the child's parents (Frederick, 1977). In addition, advocate lawyers and children are beginning to meet more frequently in institutional settings—*e..g.*, medical and mental hospitals, correctional facilities, and schools—where the lawyer acts to assist the juvenile in making independent treatment decisions or claims against institutions and other parties regarding rights or due procedures.

These new opportunities for attorney and child-client interaction have raised critical questions about the capacities and propensities of children to request or to accept the assistance of lawyers, as well as questions about the abilities of lawyers to adjust their procedures to the needs and intellectual capacities of children (Wald, 1976; Bersoff, 1976–77).

In a project described earlier, Grisso (1981) found that by age 12, almost all juveniles in a detention sample were able to identify the word *attorney* as synonymous with *lawyer*, and that a lawyer is someone who "knows the law" or helps others in legal proceedings. About two-thirds of juveniles at this age mentioned both of these elements. In a related study (Grisso, 1981), 85–90% of juveniles in a detention center (and a similar percentage of adults) said that: (1) the defense lawyer's main job was to help or protect the client; (2) that the client was expected to trust or cooperate with the lawyer; (3) that a lawyer and client would be likely to discuss how the client should respond in legal proceedings; and (4) that the lawyer should try to argue effectively for the client's side.

These results suggest that most adolescents have some basic notion of the intended role of defense counsel. In the same study, however, about one-third of the juveniles (compared to less than 10% of the adults) expressed the belief that a defense lawyer's advocacy ceases if the client admits his or her guilt to the attorney. They believed that the lawyer in such circumstances would refuse to represent the client or would be required to report the client's confession to the court.

The results of these studies, then, suggest that while juveniles often understand many basic functions of a lawyer, a substantial number may perceive serious limitations to the advocacy potential of legal counsel, especially with regard to client confidentiality. Similar findings have arisen in other exploratory work (Catton & Erickson, 1975), in which many juveniles seen soon after their court hearings believed that the lawyer's job was to "work for the court" or to collect facts for the judge.

Whatever juveniles do or do not know about lawyers' functions, there is some evidence that they have generally negative attitudes and expectancies about lawyers (Rafkey & Sealey, 1975), specifically about lawyers in juvenile court proceedings (Catton & Erickson, 1975; Connor, 1972; Walker, 1971). While none of these studies were definitive, all of them have produced exploratory evidence that juveniles generally do not expect lawyers to be helpful. If the findings are valid, then we cannot rely on juveniles to avail themselves of the opportunity to consult with a lawyer, nor to give careful consideration to the advice or assistance a lawyer might attempt to provide.

If juveniles tend to be skeptical about the helpfulness of lawyers, this attitude may simply reflect the actions of lawyers in defending juveniles or the ways in which defense lawyers have presented themselves to juveniles. There is considerable disagreement within the juvenile justice system regarding the role of defense counsel in delinquency proceedings (Kay & Segal, 1972–73; Landsman & Minow, 1978). Many writers advocate a role that provides juveniles with a vigorous defense appropriate for an adversarial system of justice

(McMillian & McMurtry, 1969; IJA-ABA, 1977; Piersma *et al.*, 1977). But Stapleton and Teitelbaum (1972) have documented the more prevalent view of the defense attorney as an agent of the court who shares the court's benevolent interest in the child. Similarly, Ferster, Courtless, and Snethen (1970) found that many defense attorneys claimed that they would report to the court any admission of guilt by their juvenile clients even if the admission were made in the context of confidential communications.

Juveniles who have experienced the latter style of lawyering might be expected to develop a dim view of the advocacy potential in the attorney-client relationship. This effect might be compounded by lawyers' frequent lack of skill in developing rapport with juveniles, in explaining their functions in way juveniles can understand, in perceiving situations as juveniles perceive them, and in being sensitive to juveniles' needs and concerns (Genden, 1976; Landsman & Minow, 1978; Catton & Erickson, 1975). This explanation of juveniles' negative perceptions of lawyers is also supported by a program described by Clendenen, Cullen, and Goldberg (1977). In that project, the attitudes of institutionalized juveniles toward ombudsman and civil legal assistance were quite positive, apparently because of the great care with which the lawyers explained their functions and patiently developed rapport.

Research Recommendations

First, existing data on juveniles' attitudes toward and perceptions of lawyers are intriguing, but they have been acquired primarily through indirect evidence and exploratory or pilot studies. At a very basic level, then, we need more careful, large-scale, descriptive research on how juveniles perceive legal advocacy.

Second, it would seem possible (though I will not attempt it here) to use developmental theories to construct hypotheses regarding children's and adults' perspectives of legal advocacy. Drawing from the works of Piaget, Kohlberg, and Tapp, one could hypothesize that perceptions of legal advocacy are organized according to preconventional, conventional, and postconventional views of law and legal authority, and that the way in which people assess the value of legal advocacy might be systematically different at each stage.

Third, we need much more systematic field studies of lawyering in juvenile courts. This research should focus not only on lawyers' perceptions of child clients and behaviors in their interactions with them, but also upon the attitudes, expectancies, and practical demands of the legal system within which lawyers work and receive their interpersonal and financial support. The broadening scope of legal advocacy for children requires that this research should be done in a variety of settings—juvenile courts, child mental health settings, and hospitals. With such information, it might then be possible to go further in examining the appropriateness of different types of legal advocacy for juveniles at various levels of psychological development. The interested reader may wish to examine Leon's (1978) hypotheses regarding the matching of advocacy roles with children of varying developmental capacities.

Applied Recommendations

The present research allows us to do little more than recommend that one cannot take for granted that juveniles understand an advocate lawyer's roles and functions. Asking juveniles to decide whether or not to waive counsel may often be a meaningless procedure, and automatically providing counsel does not assure that juveniles will benefit. Our knowledge is nowhere close to allowing us to suggest what may be done about these problems, except to make vague recommendations regarding the education of both children and lawyers. The types of research recommended earlier hopefully will provide us with a stronger base in the future for recommending interventions to improve the quality of legal advocacy and juveniles' capacities to benefit from it.

What's the Use?

The directions for research described in this chapter have all focused on addressing issues in current legal procedure in juvenile courts: the social situation of interrogation procedures, the adequacy of procedures for informing juveniles of their rights given the nature of juveniles' capacities, and examining the adequacy of legal counsel as a procedural protection for juveniles. In areas of research having such applied implications, the researcher must sometimes step back from matters of research design to consider broader, more "political" questions.

Current trends in juvenile law and policy do not bode well for the refinement of procedural protections for juvenile defendants, and I have wondered at times whether the aforementioned areas of research are really worth the effort. Let me recount a recent experience, while making no claim either to predicting the future or to answering unequivocally the question I raise.

As I sit to write this final section of the chapter, I have just returned from a trip to Tennessee to visit a juvenile court about which I had heard good comments. On the flight out, my newspaper tells of Chief Justice Burger's recent speech to the American Bar Association meeting in Houston. He advocates a reduction in the procedural rights of defendants. Rules and procedures designed to protect suspects from abuse in police searches and confessions or in trials only hamper the police, he says, or they provide unwarranted opportunities for appeals which delay swift and certain judgment. Such consequences, says the Chief Justice, are certainly the cause of an increasing crime rate. In his speech, he comments derisively about providing legal counsel to indigent defendants at public expense.

This is more than controversial rhetoric. Two years ago in *Fare v. Michael C.*, Chief Justice Burger was with the majority in the U.S. Supreme Court's decision that the admissibility of a juvenile's confession rests on a consideration of the total circumstances of each individual case, not on whether police adhered to a particular procedure or whether the juvenile is above or below a particular age or IQ. Reading this, the social scientist might well be discouraged from research intended to address questions of procedural protections that might be suggested by juveniles' needs or capacities.

I have two comments to the skeptical researcher. First, research of the type noted earlier can address questions of substantial justice just as surely as it would matters of procedural rule. Were we to abolish tomorrow all of the procedural rules for obtaining juveniles' confessions, this would not reduce the need for empirical data about juveniles with which to weigh potential irrationality in judges' case-by-case decisions concerning the substantive fairness of interrogation processes with juveniles.

My second comment arises from my visit to that court in Tennessee. The town is small enough not to have a separate juvenile court , and the two General Sessions judges hear both adult and juvenile cases. Considerable attention is given to due process in juvenile cases, yet the manner in which the court's Youth Service staff (two young men) deals with juveniles and their families is sensitive and attentive to individualized needs. I asked one of these young men how he handles the matter of informing juveniles of their rights prior to a hearing. He showed me a special eight-point rights form he had prepared. He explained that he reads each point aloud to both the juvenile and the parents, stopping after each point to explain it. Then he gently quizzes the juvenile on each one. Any that the juvenile does not answer well are reviewed again even if it takes precious time.

"And then you have him sign if he wishes to waive counsel," I said. "Oh, no", replied the young man,

> they sign merely to show that they understand. Then, if they are indigent, I give them the name of one of our private defense-oriented attorneys in town—who we'll pay, of course—and I tell them they can't decide about whether to waive counsel until they've talked to the attorney. When they bring the form back, I won't accept their waiver unless the attorney has signed saying they actually consulted him.

I commented that Tennessee law doesn't even come close to requiring this much. His reply: "We think it's fair."

The point is that policy is not always made in Washington. Whatever our highest court's eventual decisions concerning what minimally is required, there will always be some juvenile courts, large or inconspicuous, who will perceive children as deserving of more and greater protections if substantive justice is to be achieved. Empirical data about children can assist states or individual courts having these concerns. The impact would not be national in scope, but potentially some juveniles in some communities would receive fairer judgments as a result. For the researcher with a conscience, that should be enough.

References

Barthel, J. *A death in Canaan.* New York: Dell, 1977.

Bersoff, D. Representation for children in custody decisions: All that glitters is not *Gault. Journal of Family Law,* 1976–77, *15,* 17.

Catton, K., & Erickson, P. *The juvenile's perception of the role of defense counsel in juvenile court.* Center for Criminology, University of Toronto, Canada. Unpublished manuscript, 1975.

Clendenon, R., Cullen, J., & Goldberg, M. Legal assistance to delinquents. *Federal Probation,* 1977, *41,* 8–15.

Connor, N. *The juvenile court: Its impact on children adjudged to be delinquent.* Center for Criminology, University of Toronto, Canada. Unpublished master's thesis, 1972.

Costanza, P., & Shaw, M. Conformity as a function of age level. *Child Development,* 1966, *37,* 967–975.

Driver, E. Confessions and the social psychology of coercion. *Harvard Law Review,* 1968, *82,* 42–61.

Ferster, E., Courtless, T., & Snethen, E. The juvenile justice system: In search of the role of counsel. *Fordham Law Review,* 1970–71, *39,* 375–412.

Flavell, J. Concept development. In P. Mossen (Ed.), *Charmichael's manual of child psychology* (3rd ed.). New York: Wiley, 1970.

Fredericks, M. Custody battles: Mental health professionals in the courtroom. In G. Koocher (Ed.), *Children's rights and the mental health professions.* New York: Wiley, 1976.

Genden, J. Separate legal representation for children: Protecting the rights and interests of minors in judicial proceedings. *Harvard Civil Rights–Civil Liberties Law Review,* 1976, *11,* 565–595.

Grisso, T. Juveniles' capacities to waive *Miranda* rights: An empirical analysis. *California Law Review,* 1980, *68,* 1134–1166.

Grisso, T. *Juveniles' waiver of rights: Legal and psychological competence.* New York: Plenum Press, 1981.

Grisso, T., & Manoogian, S. Juveniles' comprehension of Miranda warnings. In P. Lipsitt & B. D. Sales (Eds.), *New directions in psycholegal research.* New York: Van Nostrand Reinhold, 1980.

Grisso, T., & Pomicter, C. Interrogation of juveniles: An empirical study of procedures, safeguards, and rights waiver. *Law and Human Behavior,* 1977, *1,* 321–342.

Grisso, T., & Ring, M. Parents' attitudes toward juveniles' rights in interrogation. *Criminal Justice and Behavior,* 1979, *6,* 221–226.

Grisso, T., & Vierling, L. Minors' consent to treatment: A developmental perspective. *Professional Psychology,* 1978, *9,* 412–427.

Inbau, F., & Reid, J. *Criminal interrogation and confessions.* Baltimore: Williams & Wilkins, 1967.

Institute of Judicial Administration–American Bar Association. *Juvenile justice standards project: Standards relating to pretrial court proceedings.* Cambridge, Mass.: Ballinger, 1977.

Kagan, J., & Kogan, N. Individual variation in cognitive process. In P. Mossen (Ed.), *Charmichael's manual of child psychology* (3rd. ed.). New York: Wiley, 1970.

Kay, R., & Segal, D. The role of the attorney in juvenile court proceedings: A non-polar approach. *Georgetown Law Journal*, 1972–73, *61*, 1401–1424.

Landsman, K., & Minow, M. Lawyering for the child: Principles of representation in custody and visitation disputes arising from divorce. *Yale Law Journal*, 1978, *87*, 1125–1190.

Leon, J. Recent developments in legal representation of children: A growing concern with the concept of competence. *Canadian Journal of Family Law*, 1978, *1*, 375–434.

Levine, F., & Tapp, J. The dialectic of legal socialization in community and school. In J. Tapp & F. Levine (Eds.), *Law, justice, and the individual in society*. New York: Holt, Rinehart & Winston, 1977.

Manoogian, S. *Factors affecting juveniles' comprehension of Miranda rights*. Unpublished doctoral dissertation, St. Louis University, 1978.

McMillian, T., & McMurtry, D. The role of the defense lawyer in the juvenile court: Advocate or social worker? *St. Louis University Law Review*, 1969–70, *14*, 561–603.

Melton, G. Children's rights: Children's own concepts and attitudes. Paper presented at meeting of the American Psychological Association, New York, September 1979.

Paulsen, M., & Whitebread, C. *Juvenile law and procedure*. Reno, Nev.: National Council of Juvenile Court Judges, 1974.

Piersma, P., Ganousis, J., Volenik, A., Swanger, H., & Connell, P. *Law and tactics in juvenile cases*. Philadelphia: American Law Institute–American Bar Association, 1977.

Piliavin, I., & Briar, S. Police encounters with juveniles. *American Journal of Sociology*, 1964, *70*, 206–214.

Rafkey, D., & Sealey, R. The adolescent and the law: A survey. *Crime and Delinquency*, 1975, *21*, 131–138.

Spirack, G., Platt, J., & Shure, M. *The problem-solving approach to adjustment*. San Francisco: Jossey–Bass, 1976.

Stapleton, W., & Teitelbaum, L. *In defense of youth*. New York: Russell Sage, 1972.

Tapp, J., & Kohlberg, L. Developing senses of law and legal justice. *Journal of Social Issues*, 1971, *27*, 65–91.

Wald, M. Legal policies affecting children: A lawyer's request for aid. *Child Development*, 1976, *47*, 1–5.

Walker, S. The lawyer–child relationship: A statistical analysis. *Duquesne Law Review*, 1971, *9*, 627–650.

CHAPTER 9

Children as Participants in Psychoeducational Assessment

DONALD N. BERSOFF

It has been estimated that more than 250 million standardized tests of academic ability, perceptual and motor skills, emotional and social characteristics, and vocational interests and talent are administered by school systems each year (Brim, Glass, Neulinger, Firestone, & Lerner, 1969; Holman & Docter, 1972). Tests are used in conjunction with almost every major educational practice, *e.g.*, screening, placement, program planning, program evaluation, and assessment of individual progress. Because they have such a significant impact on children's futures and have been criticized as discriminatory tools, denying full realization of the rights of minorities and the handicapped, and as devices fostering impermissible intrusion by the government into the private lives of its citizens tests have come under increasing legal scrutiny (Bersoff, 1979; 1982). Nevertheless, due to the perception and presumption that children are developmentally restricted in their ability to comprehend and respond meaningfully, they are generally precluded from deciding for themselves whether they should become a participant in assessment endeavors. Instead, they are enrolled as test takers by proxies, usually parents, who consent for them.

This chapter aims to explore the legal and ethical issues related to children's participation in assessment. It begins with a brief exploration of the concepts of consent and competency, reviews the federal government's rules

DONALD N. BERSOFF • Ennis, Friedman, Bersoff and Ewing, Washington, D.C. 20036; Joint Program in Law and Psychology, University of Maryland School of Law and the Johns Hopkins University, Baltimore, Maryland 21201.

regarding psychoeducational evaluation and the one judicial opinion on the issue, analyzes recent legal decisions concerning the rights of children that may affect attempts to secure greater involvement of children in decision making, and concludes with suggestions for behavioral scientists and practitioners who may wish aid in that process.

Consent and Competency

It is now universally agreed, though not always honored in practice, that human beings must give their informed consent prior to any significant intrusion of their person or privacy. The underlying legal and philosophical premise of the informed consent doctrine is the notion of "thoroughgoing self-determination" (*Natanson v. Kline*).[1] This doctrine emerged in the early part of the twentieth century as a rule of law in the context of physician-patient malpractice suits, but there was no reason for it to be limited to treatment relationships. The insensitivity of physicians to their patients has been matched in the past by psychologists and the school systems they served. On the basis of psychoeducational evaluations that were neither consented to by parents or children, many children, particularly minorities, were permanently tracked in poorly funded and inadequately taught ability groups while others were placed in segregated self-contained classrooms for the handicapped or excluded from school altogether. Disclosures of these practices led, as we shall see, to government regulation of the informed consent process. Consent, therefore, is crucial to much of what is to follow. While there is considerable dispute as to its meaning, it is generally accepted that the doctrine of informed consent comprises three basic characteristics:

1. *Knowledge.* The person seeking consent must disclose sufficient information in a manner that can be understood by the person from whom the consent is sought. But, the duty to disclose is tempered by what may be called the materiality rule, *i.e.*, testers need only disclose those risks that a reasonable person would need to know to make an informed decision to accept or reject being tested.

2. *Voluntariness.* Consent must be obtained in the absence of coercion, duress, misrepresentation, or undue inducement. Voluntariness implies that decisions are made without unacceptable influence or interference by the tester.

3. *Capacity.* Persons must be legally competent to give consent. While all adults are considered capable of making legally binding decisions (unless they have been adjudicated incompetent in a formal proceeding), children are not. With children, given their purported cognitive and affective immaturity and

[1] 186 Kan. 393, 406, 350 P.2d 1093 (1960).

the law's presumption of incompetency, the component of informed consent perceived as least satisfied is capacity.

Standards for determining competency change with the context in which it is considered. For example, the legal system has developed somewhat dissimilar rules for determining competency of adults to stand trial, to plead guilty, to make enforceable contracts, or to execute a will. The same is true of children. While children cannot vote, marry, or become independent plaintiffs to a lawsuit, they are deemed, in some cases, competent to secure an abortion, psychiatric counselling, or treatment for venereal disease.

How one defines competency assumes great significance. A judgment that a person is incompetent permits others to exercise the right of informed consent that would otherwise be left to the individual. "Neglecting to seek informed consent . . . indicates a . . . failure to recognize autonomy and hence, the humanity of the subject" (Macklin & Sherwin, 1975, p. 443). While the Supreme Court has never explicitly granted autonomy the predominant place in the hierarchy of human values that some scholars would like (*e.g.*, Richards, 1980), it has recognized the principle in two correlative strands of cases—one upholding the individual's right to self-determination and the other protecting against assaults on bodily integrity. The ultimate question, then, is not whether there is a right to autonomy but the extent to which its exercise will be enforced. As we will see, with regard to educational and psychological evaluations, children's right to autonomy is practically nonexistent.

Legal Regulation of Consent to Psychoeducational Assessment

The Federal Government's Perspective

The primary vehicle for federal regulation of the consent process in educational assessment is through the Education for All Handicapped Children Act, 20 U.S.C. §§ 1401–1461, more popularly known as Pub. L. 94–142. The consent regulations implementing the Act (DHEW, 1977, pp. 42, 494–42, 495) have the intent of increasing parent involvement in educational decision making. They do so by requiring that school systems inform parents before they take certain actions and that they obtain affirmative permission before they engage in other, more intrusive, actions.

At a minimum, the school musty notify parents when it wishes to identify, evaluate, or place a handicapped child in a special education program. It must also notify parents after they request these services and the school system refuses to perform them. Notice in these instances must be given to parents within a "reasonable time."

There are greater constraints when school systems propose to conduct a preplacement examination (or place a child in a special education program for the first time). While § 615(b) (1) (C) of Pub. L. 94–142 merely requires that schools give "written prior notice to the parents . . . when . . . it proposes to initiate . . . the evaluation or educational placement of the child," the implementing regulations require affirmative, written consent at those times. Therefore, while the Act apparently does not mandate that schools secure approval for testing or placement, the implementing regulations do. This disparity has not yet been seriously challenged by school systems and they appear to be abiding, in theory at least, by the regulations. Thus, when a particular child becomes the focus of an assessment whose effect or intent will be to recommend placement in a special education program for the first time, parental consent must be secured for all procedures involved in the psychoeducational assessment, including testing, interviewing, and observation. (See note added in proof, p. 175.)

In earlier drafts of the regulations, parents possessed an absolute veto both as to a proposed initial evaluation and to placement. Without their consent, neither could occur. But those drafts failed to take into account that there may be adverse interests between a parent and a child in need of special education and related services. It would have been possible under the proposed rules for parents to have denied their children access to psychological services and subsequent remedial intervention by special educators for arbitrary or unreasonable grounds.

Although probably not constitutionally required given recent Supreme Court decisions (see next major section), the final regulations that now control are most cognizant of children's independent interests and provide for an alternative mechanism permitting schools to act as child advocates and to challenge parental refusal to consent. Depending on the nature of the laws prevailing in each of the states, school systems have two means for overriding a parent veto. Where state law requires consent prior to a preplacement evaluation, state procedures govern the school system's attempt to override parental refusal to consent *e.g.*, neglect laws. Where no such state law exists, the school system may use the procedural safeguards delineated in Pub. L. 94–142. Under the Act, if an impartial hearing officer decides that the psychological evaluation may proceed, the school system may conduct the assessment even though the parents refuse to give their permission.

The implementing regulations define in both general and specific terms what parental consent entails. Generally, consent means that "the parent has been fully informed of all information relevant to the activity for which consent is sought, in his or her negative language, or other mode of communication" (34 C.F.R. § 300.500). More particularly, the consent letter must include "a description of the action proposed . . . by the agency, an explanation of why the agency proposes . . . to take the action, and a description of any options the agency considered and the reasons why those options were rejected." In addition, the school system must describe each evaluation procedure or test it proposes to use in the assessment (34 C.F.R. § 300.500). According to the Office of Special Education, when the school does not know in advance what particular tests will be administered, it may exercise the alternative of describing the kinds of tests that will be used. But, the regulations and implementing policy determinations emphasize that simply listing the names of tests without at least some minimal narrative explaining their nature does not meet the intent of the law.

As the rendering of Pub. L. 94–142 makes clear, minor children do not participate in the consent process at all. While the interests of parents and school systems are given direct expression, handicapped children are represented only though either one of these putative benefactors. In fact, while Pub. L. 94–142 is called the Education for All Handicapped Children Act, children themselves have little or no voice in its implementation. The only place within Pub. L. 94–142 where children may have an opportunity to relate their concerns is in those sections pertaining to the drafting of individual education programs (IEP). The Act requires a representative of the local school system, the child's current (or future) teacher, and one of the child's parents attend the IEP meeting. In addition, at the discretion of either the parents or the school system, other individuals may be invited. Finally, the law states that one of the participants may be "The child, where appropriate" (34 C.F.R. § 300.344). However, it offers no guidance at all as to what criteria are to be used in defining appropriateness or who is to make the decision to invite the child. However, in January, 1981, the Department of Education issued policy interpretations of the IEP requirement. In that document, the department indicated that it is the parent who decides if the child attends although it encourages the parent and the school system to discuss the decision together and to make some effort to persuade older handicapped children to participate (ED, 1981). But, at bottom, under the federal scheme, handicapped children have no right to consent, assent, or object to proposed psychoeducational evaluations. And, as far as I am able to discern, there are no federal laws permitting handicapped children to consent to educational assessments.

One Judicial Perspective

There is only one discoverable case in which the issue of children's consent to evaluation by public schools was clearly in issue, *Merriken v. Cressman.*[2] Although it was decided in a federal district court and does not have the far-reaching effect of an appellate or Supreme Court opinion, because it appears to be the only case of its kind it has received remarkably wide coverage in the

[2] 364 F. Supp. 913 (E.D. Pa. 1973).

legal literature (Moskowitz, 1975; Note, 1974; Recent Case, 1974; Recent Development, 1973–74; see also Bersoff, 1975, 1981).

The case had its origins in 1970 when a survey ordered by the Commissioners of Montgomery Country, Pennsylvania, and conducted by a company called Scientific Resources revealed that many children in the county were using drugs. Most of the children who used drugs, the study claimed, possessed some common characteristics. For example, 80% of the identified drug abusers indicated that they felt estranged from their families. On the basis of such data Scientific Resources proposed to the Montgomery County Drug Commission that they sponsor a drug prevention research and treatment program that was later to be labeled CPI, for the Critical Period of Intervention. All three of the county school districts agreed to participate in the program.

There were two phases to the study: identification and remediation. In the first phase, questionnaires were to be given to eighth-grade students and their teachers so that certain students, deemed potential drug abusers, could become part of the remediation program. The teachers were asked to identify pupils who most and least fit eight descriptions of antisocial behavior, *e.g.*, "This pupil makes unusual or inappropriate responses during normal school activity." The student form was to be somewhat lengthier. First, students would be asked to assess their own behavior, *e.g.*, to state which of the following descriptions was most like themselves: (1) someone who will probably be a success in life; (2) one who gets upset when faced with a difficult school problem; (3) someone who has lots of self confidence; (4) a student who has more problems than other students. In the next part of the questionnaire they would be asked questions about their relationships with their parents, *e.g.*, to indicate whether one or both parents "tell me how much they love me," "make me feel unloved," or "seem to regret that I am growing up and spending more time away from home." Finally, the students would select from their classmates those who fit certain descriptive statements similar in kind to the ones given the teachers.

The second phase of the study was intervention. When the CPI staff had analyzed all the results, they would compile a list of children who would have significant potential for becoming drug abusers. This list would then be given to the school superintendent who would organize a joint effort among guidance counselors, teachers, school psychologists, and others to provide group therapeutic experiences. One of these experiences was called the Guided Group Interaction, a program to which the identified students would be involuntarily assigned. One of its stated purposes was to use the peer groups as "a leveller or equalizer insuring that its members do not stray too far from its ranks."

When the program was first developed, the school system did not intend to obtain the affirmative consent of the parents for their children to participate. The administration did plan to send a letter home to each parent as follows:

Dear Parent:

This letter is to inform you that, this fall, we are initiating a Drug Program called "Critical Period of Intervention" (CPI). The aim of this program is to identify children who may be susceptible to drug abuse and to intervene with concrete measures to help these children. Diagnostic testing will be part of this program and will provide data enabling the prevention program to be specific and positive. . . .

We ask your support and cooperation in this program and assure you of the confidentiality of these studies. If you wish to examine or receive further information regarding the program, please feel free to contact the principal in your school. If you do not wish to participate in this program, please notify your principal of this decision. We will assume your cooperation unless otherwise notified by you. (*Merriken*, p. 917)

Also, as originally proposed, the study contained no provision for student consent.

Sylvia Merriken, the mother of one of the intended participants in the study, who happened to be a therapist in a drug and alcohol rehabilitation center, complained to the principal of the school where her son was enrolled and to the school board. The American Civil Liberties Union (ACLU) then announced it would represent Mrs. Merriken in an attempt to permanently enjoin the school from carrying out its plans. The ACLU began by filing a complaint in the appropriate federal district court claiming that the program would violate the constitutional rights of both Mrs. Merriken and her son. It quickly obtained a temporary injunction prohibiting the county from implementing its proposal until the litigation was completed. At that point, two of the three schools in Montgomery County decided to discontinue their participation but the Norristown system, which Mrs. Merriken's son attended, persisted, although it honored the temporary injunction.

When the suit began in earnest the school system offered to change the format of their letter so that affirmative written parental consent to participate would be required. In another attempt at compromise, the school modified the test so that students who did not want to be included could return an uncompleted protocol. But the proposal contained no provision for student consent and no data were to be provided whereby students could make an informed choice about participating.

Of the many constitutional challenges Mrs. Merriken made, the court entertained only one of them seriously—the right of privacy. The court found that the highly personal nature of the assessment instrument disrupted family associations and interfered with the right of the mother to rear her child. It said, "There is probably no more private a relationship, excepting marriage, which the Constitution safeguards than that between parent and child. This Court can look upon any invasion of that relationship as a direct violation of one's Constitutional right to privacy" (p. 918). Although there was no precedent to the effect in the Supreme Court, the district court declared that privacy was entitled to as much constitutional protection as free speech. But who possessed this right—the student, the parents, or both? The court seemed ready to answer that question when it declared that "the fact that students are juveniles does not in any way invalidate their right to assert their Constitutional right to privacy" (p. 918). However, the court had not yet reached the essential question of whether the lack of consent by children to the invasion of their privacy would be sufficient to invalidate the program. Apparently reluctant to provide a definite answer it found a means to avoid doing so:

> In the case at Bar, the children are never given the opportunity to consent to invasion of their privacy; only the opportunity to refuse to consent by returning a blank questionnaire. Whether this procedure is Constitutional is questionable, but the Court does not have to face that issue because the facts presented show that the parents could not have been properly informed about the CPI Program and as a result could not have given informed consent for their children to take the CPI Test. (p. 919)

In essence, the court evaded two important issues: whether the failure to secure the child's consent was independently sufficient to constitutionally discredit the procedure and, second, whether parents as guardians can waive their children's constitutional rights by consenting for them. Rather, the court concentrated on Mrs. Merriken's own right of privacy and found that she was unable to give genuinely informed consent to the invasion of her personal life because the parental permission letter was so inadequate. The court deridingly compared the letter to a Book-of-the-Month Club solicitation in which parents' silence would be construed as acquiescence. The letter was also criticized as a selling device in which parents were convinced to allow children to participate. It was not, as it properly should be, an objective document telling parents of the potentially negative features and dangerous aspects of the program. The court then proceeded to lecture school officials:

> The parents are not aware of the consequences [of participating] and there is no substitute for candor and honesty in fact, particularly by the school board who, as the ultimate decision maker as far as the education of our children is concerned, should give our citizenry a more forthright approach. The attempt to make the letter requesting consent similar to a promotional inducement to buy, lacks the necessary substance to give a parent the opportunity to give knowing, intelligent, and aware consent. (p. 920)

It has been immutable constitutional doctrine for the past four decades that waivers of constitutional rights must be voluntary, knowing, intellegent, and done with sufficient awareness of the relevant circumstances and likely consequences. It was in this respect that the request for permission was legally invalid. Mrs. Merriken had the right to waive her right of privacy by consenting to her child's participation. But because the request was little more than huckstering, it lacked the necessary substance to afford her the opportunity to meaningfully consent to the exploration of her personal life.

There were more infirmities to the program than those apparent in the information-gathering phase. There were also deficiencies, if not misrepresentation, in its dissemination aspect. Recall that the promotional letter promised confidentiality. But the program itself contemplated the development of a "massive data bank" (to use its own terms) and dissemination of data relating to specific, identifiable students to school superintendents, principals, guidance counselors, coaches, social workers, PTA members, and those on the school board. And, even if the school system had been more circumspect and had constructed means by which the data were less widely distributed (or not distributed at all), no promise of confidentiality can supersede a subpoena compelling the disclosure of the material to law enforcement officials. Thus, as the court warned,

> [T]here is no assurance that should an enterprising district attorney convene a special grand jury to investigate the drug problem in Montgomery County, the records of the CPI Program would remain inviolate from subpoenas and that he could not determine the identity of children who have been labelled by the CPI Program as potential drug abusers. (p. 916)

Parents were not at all informed of this possibility.

Compounding the problem was that the identification instruments did not possess enough psychometric soundness to overcome the hazards that may have flowed from their use. Not only could there have been considerable harm done to children correctly identified (*e.g.*, the self-fulfilling prophecy, scapegoating by peers, loyalty conflicts between parents and children if the latter wanted to participate and were thus forced to reveal personal family information to do so), but equally vulnerable, if not more so, were those children incorrectly identified. The latter possibility greatly concerned the court: "When a program talks about labeling someone as a particular type and such a label could remain with him for the remainder of his life, the margin of error must be almost nil" (p. 920).

Was there no justification at all for the school system's attempt to identify and treat potential drug abusers? Certainly one could mount a persuasive argument that a program designed to learn about and prevent drug abuse serves an important social end. Courts, when faced with the problem of the infringement of individuals' important or fundamental constitutional rights, often consider the competing interests claimed by the public at large and will balance the interests of the individual against the interests of the state or society. In *Merriken*, the court acknowledged that if the program had demonstrated adequate public need and had restricted itself to a minimal invasion of privacy, it might have passed constitutional muster. But, after studying all of the evidence, the court struck the balance in favor of the individual:

> [T]he reasons for this are that the test itself and the surrounding results of that test are not sufficiently presented to both the child and the parents, as well as the Court, as to its authenticity and credibility in fighting the drug problem in this country. There is too much of a chance that the wrong people for the wrong reasons will be singled out and counselled in the wrong manner. (p. 921)

While the outcome of this case appears sound, it must be reiterated that the person whose interests were protected was Mrs. Merriken, not her son. It is unclear as to what the court would have decided had the mother agreed to her son's participation but had he voiced strong objection to doing so.

The Developing Law of Children's Right to Independent Decision Making[3]

One legal scholar (Kleinfeld, 1970, 1971) has distinguished between the right of persons to make various choices and the right of persons to be protected from the choices or initiatives of others. For the most part, the child advocacy movement has secured advances falling within the latter category. Children remain, like Ralph Ellison's hero, Invisible Persons whose views are infrequently evoked and whose wishes are rarely controlling. The concern of Congress, the administrative agencies, and the courts that children's interests be protected represents advocacy only of the second kind. Everyone is asked to serve children's best interests even if that means over-riding their refusal to participate in educational assessments when adults believe children will benefit from them. Children's right to choose "is not viewed as presently existing . . . but as maturing in the future" (Hirshberg, 1980, p. 225).

Those who simply advocate greater representation for children fail to acknowledge the complexity of the concept. To "represent" is not to engage in a unidemensional activity. Parents as custodians, the state as protector, and advocates who seek to act in what they perceive to be in the best interests of children, represent only in the sense of taking care of another. They may be said to act merely "*in* behalf of," that is, in the interest of or for the benefit of another. Those who act "in behalf of" are under no obligation to consult with those they take care of or abide by their wishes. They do what they think best in the light of their trust obligations. Such a role is different from acting "*on* behalf of," which connotes that the advocate is acting on the part of, in the name of another, or as the one represented might act (Pitkin 1967). If we are genuinely

---

[3] This section is a revised version of one appearing in Bersoff (1981).

to urge the expanded rights of children such advocacy must include the right of children to full-fledged participation in the decision-making process when their significant interests and future hang in the balance.

But, whether children will ever exercise the independent right to consent to psychological testing depends a great deal on how the courts allocate power among parents, children, and various arms of federal and state government. That issue has received considered attention from legal scholars (*e.g.*, Bersoff, 1981; Developments in the Law, 1980; Hirshberg, 1980; Kleinfeld, 1970 1971; Mnookin, 1978; Richards, 1980; M. Wald, 1979; P. Wald, 1974) and from the courts. It is to an analysis of that issue that we now turn.

Historically, both parents and the state have exerted inordinate control over children. Under ancient Roman law, fathers had the power of life and death over their offspring and infanticide was not uncommon (especially if children were female or deformed). Before the Norman Conquest English fathers were able to murder newborns and sell children under 7 years of age into slavery. It was not uncommon during the beginning of this century for parents to place children in jails without trials. The modern manifestation of this control is the right of parents to commit their sons and daughters to mental hospitals. The Supreme Court, in *Parham v. J.R.*,[4] a case I shall discuss more fully, has recently upheld this "volunteering of children" (Ellis, 1974) with only minor protections to reduce erroneous classification or unnecessary institutionalization.

The legal systems' solicitude for the family unit and the primacy of parental control does not mean, of course, that children are at the mercy of their mothers and fathers. "Parents may be free to become martyrs themselves. But it does not follow they are free . . . to make martyrs of their children"(*Prince v. Massachusetts*).[5] Courts will override parental prerogatives when parents are unable or refuse to care for their children's physical, medical, or emotional needs, when there is an abuse of parental authority, or when protectable property interests of children (*e.g.*, inheritances) conflict with those of their parents. The most clear-cut example of state interference in family life is the passage of child abuse laws in all 50 of the United States (see Katz, Howe, & McGrath, 1975). The perceived consequences of all this benevolent intrusion by parents and the state in behalf of children has been summarized by one commentator:

> In this continuing struggle, the child has always been the pawn. Neither philosophically nor legally has he been recognized as having a right to *do* anything about the vicissitudes of his life, but only to await the action of others in his behalf or in his best interests. He is in a state of powerlessness, and for that reason, the institution of slavery. It has been called the "last legal relic of feudalism." (P. Wald, 1974, p. 15)

---

[4] 442 U.S. 584 (1979).
[5] 321 U.S. 158, 177 (1944).

As the more egregious and cruder forms of discrimination against minorities have been ameliorated in the past two decades, attention has turned to the plight of other groups who have not been afforded the full and equal protection of the laws. Those who have sought to enhance the status of children and broaden their rights under the Constitution and federal and state laws have done so within what has been called a child advocacy movement. The results of their activity has been a significant alteration of the balance of power in child-populated, adult-dominated institutions. Most conspicuously, in juvenile courts, research settings, and schools, older persons have found it more difficult to make unilateral decisions when those decisions directly involve important and often fundamental interests of children.

The burgeoning of concern and litigation with regard to children's rights in the last decade can be traced to 15-year-old Gerald Gault's obscene phone call to an Arizona woman in the mid-1960s. As a result of his conduct Gault was brought before the juvenile court. Because at that time proceedings before such courts were considered rehabilitative and noncriminal, no records were kept, no charges specified, there was no protection against self-incrimination, and counsel was not provided. Under those conditions, Gault was sentenced to a youth detention center until his 21st birthday, a sentence of six years for a crime that would have cost an adult two months imprisonment and a $50 fine. The case, formally known as *In re Gault*,[6] ultimately was brought to the United States Supreme Court, which reversed the conviction and held that children in juvenile court proceedings were constitutionally entitled to certain due process guarantees previously limited to adults in criminal prosecutions. The case tolled the death knell of the doctrine of *parens patriae*—the state's parentalistic authority to protect or promote the welfare of certain classes of persons who are considered to lack the capacity to act in their own best interest—at least with regard to juvenile court proceedings (see Bersoff, 1976–77 and references therein). The Supreme Court concluded in *Gault* that the state was neither the sole nor proper representative even when the state sought to further what it judged to be children's interests. Perhaps more importantly, while earlier cases had held that children were entitled to constitutional protection, "*Gault* was the first case squarely to hold that children had constitutional rights" (Developments in the Law, 1980, p. 1228).

The broader impact of *Gault* was reinforced two years later when the Supreme Court explicitly declared in *Tinker v. Des Moines Independent Community School District*[7] that children were *persons* under the Constitution and possessed fundamental rights that the state was required to respect, even when those rights were exercised in the relatively controlled environment of the public

[6] 387 U.S. 1 (1967).
[7] 393 U.S. 503 (1969).

schools. *Tinker*, thus, is important on at least three levels. First, it may be said to have ended educators' untrammelled immunity from judicial scrutiny. Second, by declaring children as persons it placed them directly within the protections of the Fourteenth Amendment's due process clause which shields only those entities denominated as persons against arbitrary deprivations of life, liberty, or property by the state. Lastly, the Court intimated that at least some rights were evenly distributed among children and adults: "First Amendment rights are available to teachers and students. It can hardly be argued that either students or teachers shed their constitutional rights to freedom of speech or expression at the schoolhouse gate" (*Tinker*, p. 506). However, the Supreme Court has also made it clear that children do not share equally in all provisions of the Constitution. *In re Gault* only afforded children in juvenile court proceedings some, but not the entire range, of due process protections granted adult criminals. In *Ginsburg v. New York*[8] the Supreme Court said that it was rational for the state legislature to prohibit the sale of sexually related material to minors even though it would not be allowed to do so with regard to the sale of the same material to adults. And, while it violates the Eighth Amendment's cruel and inhuman punishment clause to physically discipline adult prisoners, the Court ruled that corporal punishment of school children was constitutionally permissible (*Ingraham v. Wright*).[9]

The Supreme Court's recent abortion-related decisions indicate that in some facets of personal life, certain children possess privacy rights that will be allowed expression even though to do so may conflict with parental wishes. In 1976 the Court declared unconstitutional a state statute requiring parental consent before a pregnant minor could obtain an abortion, saying "Constitutional rights do not mature and come into being magically only when one attains the state-defined age of majority. Minors, as well as adults, are protected by the Constitution and possess constitutional rights" (*Planned Parenthood of Central Missouri v. Danforth*).[10] Thus it refused to uphold a blanket provision requiring the consent of a parent as a condition for all unmarried minors to obtain an abortion during the first trimester of pregnancy. A year later the Court was faced with a challenge to the constitutionality of a statute prohibiting the sale or distribution of contraceptives to children under 16. Given that it had previously concluded that minors could secure abortions without consent it felt that an absolute ban against access to contraceptives was even more violative of children's independent rights to privacy. "The State's interests in protection of the mental and physical health of the pregnant minor, and in protection of potential life are clearly more implicated by the abortion decision than by

---

[8] 390 U.S. 629 (1968).
[9] 430 U.S. 651 (1977).
[10] 428 U.S. 52, 74 (1976).

the decision to use a nonhazardous contraceptive" (*Carey v. Population Services International Inc.*).[11] Finally, the Court had the occasion in 1979 to once again rule on a minor's unencumbered right to abortion. In the light of the Supreme Court's decision in *Danforth*, Massachusetts amended its law so as to require parental consent for abortion but at the same time afford the child access to court if one or both parents refused to consent. But judges would have the discretion to prohibit the abortion if they found the youngster insufficiently mature to make a decision or if the abortion were not in her best interests. The Court ultimately found that even this new legislation unduly burdened minors' rights to an abortion (*Bellotti v. Baird*).[12] Justice Powell, speaking for a four-member plurality, said that the state could not require parental consent or even consultation if the pregnant minor could show an impartial adjudicator that she was able to make an intelligent decision concerning abortion on her own. If the adjudicator finds she does not meet this standard of competency the young woman is still entitled to an abortion if it is determined that it would be in her best interests.

These decisions should not lead the reader to think that children have been granted broad independent decision-making powers. Although the Court has extended to children the privacy rights previously granted to adults in earlier abortion cases, matters of procreation have received special treatment by the Court:

> The abortion decision differs in important ways from other decisions that may be made during minority. The need to preserve the constitutional right and the unique nature of the abortion decision, especially when made by a minor, require a State to act with particular sensitivity when it legislates to foster parental involvement in this matter. (*Bellotti v. Baird*, 1979, p. 642)

Thus, there is no reason to believe that the independent rights of children will be honored in other domains where their interests may also be at stake or even in abortion cases where the young woman is determined to be too immature to make decisions without parental consultation or court approval.

The validity of this hypothesis has been borne out in the Supreme Court's most recent abortion-related decision, *H.L. v. Matheson*,[13] and in *Parham v. J.L.*, a most important decision rendered during the same 1979 term that the Court issued *Bellotti*. At issue in *Matheson* was a 1974 Utah statute requiring physicians to "notify, if possible, the parents or guardian of the woman upon whom the abortion is to be performed, if she is a minor." Doctors who violated that mandate would be subjected to criminal misdemeanor penalties of imprisonment up to one year or a $1,000 fine. A 15-year-old unmarried pregnant girl

---

[11] 431 U.S. 678, 694 (1977).
[12] 443 U.S. 622 (1979).
[13] 450 U.S. 398 (1981).

living at home with her parents challenged the statute as an infringement on her federal constitutional right to an abortion. However, a five-man majority of the Court, distinguishing prior cases, held that a law "setting out a 'mere requirement of parental notice' does not violate the constitutional rights of an immature, dependent minor" (Matheson, p. 409). The statute, it said, gave neither parents nor judges a veto over a young woman's abortion decision and because it served the important interests of family integrity and the protection of adolescents, "[t]he Utah statute is reasonably calculated to protect minors in [H.L.]'s class by enhancing the potential for parental consultation concerning a decision that has potentially traumatic and permanent consequences" (p. 412). The Court did go to great lengths to restrict its decision to minors living at home, dependent on their parents, who made no claim or showing as to their maturity, their immersion in hostile home environments or their status as emancipated minors. While the Court's decision is limited to this relatively narrow class of adolescents, it is the first time since 1965 that it has ruled in favor of the state rather than the individual in the area of sexual freedom and self-determination.

In *Parham*, the Court was called on to decide the constitutionality of a statute permitting parents to admit their children to mental institutions. When the state seeks to commit adults involuntarily they are afforded a number of procedural safeguards, including a hearing before an impartial decisionmaker and representation by an attorney. But, in almost all states, when parents seek to place their children in mental hospitals it is considered a voluntary admission and children have no due process rights. In *Parham*, child advocates claimed that such admissions were voluntary in name only, that there were dangers of parents acting adversely to the interests of their children and that, as a result, children should be given procedural protections similar to those of adults.

In considering these claims the Chief Justice, writing for a five-member majority, balanced the children's interests, the state's interest, and the parents' interest. Justice Burger acknowledged that children have a substantial liberty interest in not being confined unnecessarily for medical treatment and in not being labeled erroneously by institutional authorities. The state had an interest in restricting use of costly mental health facilities to cases of genuine need. On the other hand, it also had an interest in not imposing unnecessary procedural obstacles which would discourage mentally ill children and their families from seeking psychiatric assistance. What the Court disparagingly called "time-consuming minuets" (what others would call an impartial due process hearing) not only would interfere with the treatment activities of professionals but would prove too onerous, too embarrassing, or too contentious for parents. In the end, the Court found the interests of the parents paramount. It reiterated its traditional concern for the family unit and of the primacy of the family over the

State. While noting the incidence of child neglect and abuse, it relied on what it called the "pages of human experience" to undergird its conclusion that "parents generally do act in the child's best interest" (*Parham*, pp. 602–603).

Most importantly for our purposes, the Court renewed its belief that children are incompetent to make decisions. It said, "The law's concept of the family rests on the presumption that parents possess what a child lacks in maturity, experience, and capacity for judgment required to making life's difficult decisions" (p. 602) and concluded that "most children, even in adolescence, simply are not able to make sound judgments concerning many decisions, including their need for medical care or treatment" (p. 603). "Parents," it declared, "can and must make those judgments" (p. 603). The overall result of this tripartite interest analysis was to simply hold that a "neutral factfinder," *i.e.*, a staff physician at the admitting hospital, should review all available sources of information to determine that parental requests for institutionalization were not in error.

These sentiments were repeated by the Court in *Bellotti* a few weeks after *Parham*. Justice Powell, announcing the judgment of the Court, made it clear that "States may validly limit the freedom of children to choose for themselves in the making of important, affirmative choices with potentially serious consequences" (*Bellotti*, p. 635). That power, he said, was "grounded in the recognition that, during the formative years of childhood and adolescence, minors often lack the experience, perspective, and judgment to recognize and avoid choices that could be detrimental to them" (p. 635). While acknowledging that children have constitutional rights that cannot be easily abridged, Justice Powell asserted that "the State is entitled to adjust its legal system to account for children's vulnerability and their needs for 'concern, . . . sympathy, and . . . paternal attention'" (p. 635). In addition to its assumption that children are unable to "make critical decisions in an informed, mature manner" (p. 634), the Court felt justified in limiting children's rights to make independent decisions because of the "guiding role of parents in the upbringing of their children" (p. 637). "Legal restrictions on minors," Powell stated, "especially those supportive of the parental role, may be important to the child's chances for the full growth and maturity that make eventual participation in a free society meaningful and rewarding" (pp. 638–39). Chief Justice Burger echoed those thoughts in his majority opinion in *Matheson*. In upholding the Utah's parental notification statute, he reemphasized "parents' claim to authority . . . to direct the rearing of their children" (Matheson, p. 410), and the importance of protecting immature pregnant adolescents whose decisions to abort may have serious medical, emotional, and psychological consequences. "There is no logical relationship," the Chief Justice remarked, "between the capacity to become pregnant and the capacity for mature judgment concerning the wisdom of an abortion" (p. 408).

Parenthetically, it cannot go unnoticed that on the same day in June 1979 that the Court decided *Parham*, holding that the Constitution did not require hearings for children before they were involuntarily placed in mental hospitals, it decided *Fare v. Michael C.*[14] In that case the Court held that a 16-year-old whose request for his probation officer was refused by the police who were questioning him and then made incriminating statements, waived his right under the fifth and fourteenth amendments to remain silent. Despite the fact that there was evidence that Michael was crying during the interrogation and that he had relatively little schooling, the Court asserted that he waived his constitutional rights knowingly and intelligently. Obviously, to a majority of the present Supreme Court, when children commit crimes they magically assume the decision-making ability of adults; when they are about to be placed in a mental hospital, they are but children who must rely on their parents' judgment of their best interests.

Involving Children in Consent to Psychoeducational Assessment

It is hoped that this lengthy litany of recent Supreme Court law gives readers some reference points to evaluate the current status and future possibilities for children's participation as independent decisionmakers in assessment. In the main, the law considers children generally incapable of knowing what is best for themselves. In their salutary goal to protect families from unreasonable state interference and in a more questionable desire to protect children from immature and potentially harmful autonomous decisions, the courts have presumed that parents, as preferred caregivers, are competent to represent their children's interests. Only when this presumption is rebutted by evidence of significant injury to the child do courts replace parents—either permanently or for limited purposes—with alternative decisionmakers. But, although the right of parents to control the upbringing of their children has strong foundations in tradition and in the Constitution's preference for minimal state interference in family life, "that right is nevertheless unusual among constitutional rights in that it protects the ability to control another person. Ordinarily, constitutional rights do not protect an individual's power to control someone else" (Developments in the Law, 1980, p. 1353).

However, if parental prerogatives are also founded on the premise that children are incapable of making informed decisions it may be possible to rebut that premise also, making it permissible not only to shift decisions from parent to state but from parent to child. As we have seen, this has occurred in instances

[14] 442 U.S. 707 (1979).

where a particular class of rights, *e.g.*, child-bearing and contraception, have been considered so fundamental that parental control and intervention are judged to be unconstitutionally burdensome. Similarly, statutory and case law is presently affording adolescents greater freedom to seek medical and psychological help without parental permission, a change advocated by many writers and legal scholars in recent years (Bersoff, 1976–77; Bricker, 1979; Foster & Freed, 1972; Holt, 1974; Kleinfeld, 1970, 1971; Richards, 1980; P. Wald, 1974). Many states now have statutes permitting minors to give valid consent to treatment for veneral disease and other sex-related problems (Note, 1975). One state permits those 16 years of age or over to consent to treatment for emotional disorders from psychiatrists (Note, 1971). A joint commission of the Institute of Judicial Administration and the American Bar Association (IJA/ ABA, 1977), while upholding the general principle of parental consent to medical care, has issued a set of recommendations that, if adopted, would significantly expand certain children's right to treatment without third party consent. For the treatment of chemical dependency, veneral disease, contraception, and pregnancy, the commission would only require the physician to obtain the minor's permission to notify (but not secure the consent of) parents to such treatment. Minors' objection to notification would be binding unless the physician judged that failure to inform would seriously jeopardize the health of the minor. Children over 14 who sought treatment for mental or emotional difficulties from psychotherapists or counselors would be permitted to do so for three sessions before notification would be required. However, for mature minors, *i.e.*, those over 16, and for emancipated minors, *i.e.*, those living separate and apart from parents and who are managing their own financial affairs, the commission would permit autonomous decision making without parental notification.

But despite these developments, the right of children to seek aid (or reject it) by giving valid consent is far from universal. In the light of the Supreme Court's overriding preference for parental control and its distrust of minor's ability to make mature judgments, it is unlikely that children will be granted the right to decide for themselves whether they wish to be the subjects of psychoeducational evaluation. The majority view of the Supreme Court fails

> to recognize the single most important factor in the analysis of a child's right to [choose]. It is the child who is at the center of this dilemma and it is his rights which should be accorded at least equal, if not greater, weight than those of the parents or the state. (Hirschberg, p. 225)

If prior cases are a guide, the courts will more likely employ the analysis used in *Wisconsin v. Yoder*[15] In this case the Supreme Court upheld the right of Amish parents to violate state compulsory education laws and to keep their

---

[15] 406 U.S. 205 (1971).

children at home once they completed eight grades. The exemption, the Court felt, was necessary to the free exercise of religion. In its positive light, the decision may be seen as allowing at least a limited class of parents the right to make decisions concerning family life even though it may interfere with a long acknowledged state interest, in this case compulsory education. On the other hand, it may be seen as another instance of adults generally failing to afford children the opportunity to articulate their own interests or to develop autonomy. Chief Justice Burger, who wrote the majority opinion, saw the case as involving only the "fundamental interests of the parents, as contrasted with that of the State" (p. 232). Justice Douglas, dissenting in part, was the only member of the Court to recognize that the critical interests at stake were those of the children:

> On this important and vital matter of education, I think the children should be entitled to be heard. While the parents . . . normally speak for the entire family, the education of the child is a matter on which the child will often have decided views. . . .
> It is the future of the student, not the future of the parents, that is imperiled in today's decision. . . . It is the student's judgment, not his parents', that is essential if we are to give full meaning to what we have said about the Bill of Rights and of the right of students to be masters of their own destiny. (pp. 244–245)

It is probably true that the decision to take a test is not quite so vital as that of total exclusion from schooling. But there is little argument that participation in many assessment programs also imperils the future lives of children. Testing may determine whether a child is placed in academically or vocationally oriented tracks in secondary school (*e.g., Hobson v. Hansen*)[16]; relegated to elementary school classes for the educably retarded that have been described by at least one court as "dead-end, isolating, stigmatizing, educational anachronisms" (*Larry P. v. Riles*)[17]; diagnosed as emotionally disturbed and separated from peers in institutions or segregated educational facilities (*e.g., Parham v. J.R.; Lora v. Board of Education of City of New York*)[18]; or permitted to graduate from high school as minimally competent (*e.g., Debra P. v. Turlington*).[19] See generally Bersoff (1979). And yet the tests upon which these decisions are based are of questionable validity for the specific purposes for which they are used (Bersoff, 1973a; Note, 1979). In that light it does not appear justifiable to fail to permit children to at least share in the decision to become the subject of an educational assessment.

One does not want to create more responsibilities for an already overburdened school system but it may be possible to construct schools so that

[16] 269 F.Supp. 401 (D.D.C. 1967) *aff'd sub nom.*, Smuck v. Hobson, 408 F.2d 175 (D.C.Cir. 1969).

[17] 495 F.Supp 926 (N.D.Cal. 1979) *appeal docketed*, No. 80–4027 (9th Cir., Jan. 17, 1980).

[18] 456 F.Supp. 1211 (E.D.N.Y. 1979) *vacated and remanded on other grounds*, 623 F.2d 248 (2d Cir. 1980).

[19] 474 F.Supp. 244 (M.D.Fla. 1979) *aff'd*, 644 F.2d 397 (5th Cir. 1981).

they will routinely and systematically include children in decisions that affect their lives. Elsewhere (Bersoff, 1973b; see also Fischer, 1978), I have suggested one method for doing so in the context of psychoeducational assessment. I paraphrase that suggestion here. The approach has three steps:

1. *Coadvisement.* Coadvisement is an expansion of the principle of informed consent. The evaluator tells the child and his or her parents how he or she functions; informs them of the person who referred the child and the reasons for the referral; describes the nature of the assessment devices to be used as well as their merits and limitations; and relates what kinds of information will eventually be put into a report and who might eventually read the report. The evaluator then asks the child to tell how he or she perceives the purposes of the assessment (thus increasing the accuracy of subsequent interpretation of test behavior) and what he or she feels the consequences of such an assessment might be. The evaluator then secures written consent from the parents and child, if possible, to proceed with the assessment.

2. *Sharing Impressions.* Immediately after each evaluation session, the evaluator, the child, and the parents engage in a discussion in which the evaluator gives his or her interpretations of the child's test, interview, or classroom behavior as the evaluator has just experienced it. By conferring with the child, the evaluator attempts to extrapolate from the assessment situation to real-life situations. This kind of discussion provides immediate information to the child about how others perceive his or her behavior and enables the assessor to verify hypotheses about how equivalent the observed test behavior, for example, is to actual classroom behavior. It also gives the child a chance to disagree with the evaluator's initial interpretations and to offer perceptions of his or her own behavior. For example, a psychologist may note that on the block design subtest of the Wechsler Intelligence Scale for Children-Revised (WISC-R), a timed subtest where the child is asked to put multicolored wooden or plastic blocks together to match a design on a printed card, the child very neatly arranges the blocks for the first three test items but becomes increasingly sloppy and careless. After the WISC-R has been completed, the psychologist then might say: "I noticed that you did the blocks very carefully at first but then didn't do them as neatly after a while. Is that how things go in school? Do you start your work with a lot of good intentions to begin with but soon give up and become careless?" The child could agree with this interpretation, thus yielding important information about the causes of the child's academic difficulties and possible modes of educational intervention. Or, the child could disagree and say that he or she worked fast at the end because he or she was tired, wanted to go out to play because the test was given during the normal recess period, or had to go to the bathroom (and so on). Thus, rather than assuming that behavior observed in the testing situation, interview, or one classroom session can be extrapolated to all other situations, the evaluator has an opportunity to discover the situa-

tions or contexts in which the behavior does occur. This method prevents the child from being mislabeled and interpretations of his or her behavior from being overgeneralized. The outcome should lead to few challenges to the school's evaluation, diagnosis, and proposed class placement.

3. *Critique of the Written Evaluation.* After the assessment is complete and the evaluator has prepared the report, he or she shows the parents and the child, if possible, a copy of the written evaluation. This insures that the report will be recorded so that it is understandable to all concerned. In addition, knowing that the parent is going to read the report, the evaluator will strive all the more to be true to the child, to capture his or her world as well as words allow, and to avoid overstatements, unintended implications, and loose descriptions. Then, the child and the parents are given the opportunity to clarify the points made, to add further material and, if there is a disagreement between the evaluator and the parents or child, an opportunity to provide a dissenting view, in writing if warranted. Finally, the evaluator receives permission to disseminate the report to relevant school personnel.

This process would permit school people to model more equal relationships, increase mutual disclosure, and most importantly, directly involve the child in the consent, assessment, and interpretation process. In general, the role of the school would be expanded so that it would develop decision-making skills. It would teach how to make choices and encourage children to do so.

Guidelines and Goals for Future Research

As this chapter has discussed, children, by and large, are not trusted with the right to make independent decisions because it is assumed that they are unable to give knowing, voluntary, and competent consent. Courts and legislatures have thus far ignored or are not (or have not been made) aware of the literature that does exist to the contrary. While they can be faulted for neglecting the data, I must admit that they may be right in doing so at this time. The available evidence is only tangentially relevant to the issue. In psychologists' terms, the data are not situation specific. Applied psychologists have an unparalleled opportunity to contribute to the judicial and legislative expansion of the right of children to be directly involved in decisions that significantly affect their lives. There have been some attempts by lawyers and psychologists to join forces to gather information that may ultimately permit them to do so (see especially Grisso, 1980; Grisso & Vierling, 1978; Keasey & Sales, 1977; Tapp, 1976), but it is probably indisputable that by and large:

> [M]ost developmental research has little to say about children and their daily lives. . . . American developmental psychology . . . has tended to emphasize laboratory studies in which the child performs an unfamiliar task in a strange situation

with a strange adult. It has tended to neglect the study of social settings in which children live and the persons who are central to them emotionally. (Skolnick, 1975, pp. 52–53)

It is in response to this criticism that psychologists who produce applied research have the greatest potential for contribution to judicial decision making. For those who want to engage in this process, it may be more helpful for psychologists to gather data directly relevant to legal issues than to devote themselves to "abstracted empiricism" (Skolnick, 1975). It may be possible to rebut the judicial and statutory presumption that children are not able to give legally sufficient consent by gathering data in specific, appropriate situations. The successful accomplishment of this task is perhaps best performed by psychologists who possess research skills and familiarity with the relevant settings (*e.g.*, homes, schools). Data gleaned in these situations and specifically related to a matter of judicial concern may be far more persuasive than statistics gathered in an isolated research setting and not readily applicable to the legal issue in question.

I personally believe that we should reverse our current presumptions. Rather than assume that children are too young emotionally, experientially, and cognitively to make "appropriate" decisions, we can alternatively presume that children are capable of making those decisions no more disastrously than adults. Only if there is a significant risk of irreversible damage or clear and convincing empirical evidence that at particular ages children do not have sufficiently developed skills to exercise discretion should parents and the state have the right to make unilateral decisions that meaningfully affect children. The burden would fall on those wishing to deny the right of children to choose; it would not fall to children and their advocates to show that children are capable. Such a proposal is in keeping with the legal doctrine that rights can be deprived only after a showing of incompetency, as is true when those called mentally ill are no longer allowed to control their finances or when parents are required to relinquish custody of their children.

As I have stated throughout, the major barrier to anything more than incremental change in the status of children's claims to autonomy is the presumption that they are incompetent to make decisions. However, the notion of competency is a variable one. In most cases, whether a person will be permitted to act independently depends upon a judgment concerning rationality. Like competency, there are several possible meanings to the term. It can be viewed as the distinguishing feature that separates humans from all other entities; it can denote the capacity of persons to use their reason to maximize chosen or accepted ends; or it may refer to the ends themselves. In this latter meaning, chosen means are not the criterion; it is the ends themselves that confer rationality (Macklin & Sherwin, 1975). How courts and legislatures view rationality may determine whether children will be capable of consenting for themselves. Friedman (1975) has provided a helpful analysis in this regard:

1. Some courts define competency as the capacity to reach a decision based on rational reasons. Here the judge determines whether the person has the ability to understand the nature of the procedure, to weigh its risks and benefits, and to come to a reasonable determination. In essence, the court expresses a value preference for a particular mode of thinking.

2. Other courts define competency as reaching a reasonable result. This approach requires the judge to decide whether the result of the person's decision is one that a reasonably competent person might have made. Thus, when persons, who as a consequence of mental illness, retardation, brain dysfunction, or immaturity are likely to make decisions that result in substantial damage to their mental or physical well-being, the court employing this standard will consider the person incompetent.

3. Finally, a minority of courts define competency as the capacity to make a decision. This approach avoids the difficulties inherent in evaluating whether a person's thinking is rational or irrational but would preclude the apparent consent of those clearly out of touch with reality. The judge under this standard would merely decide whether the person has sufficient understanding of the nature of the procedures, its risks and benefits, and possible alternatives. If so, any decision, provided there is a decision, will be honored.

Some legal commentators have offered the more radical proposal that standards concerning competency either be abolished or established at a very low threshold. For example, Friedman (1975) describes a rule in which there would be no concern at all about the individual's ability to understand (see also Goldstein, 1977). Rather, the inquiry would simply focus on whether persons were able to hear the question and were able to answer the questions concerning their willingness to consent affirmatively or negatively. As long as these conditions existed, all answers would be honored, despite the fact that they might have been evoked by reality distortions or stated in a perseverative manner, e.g., "No, no, no," to any and all questions.

No court has adopted the more liberal of these definitions, although a recent decision by the New Jersey Supreme Court may have come close. In *State in the Interest of R.R.*,[20] the court ruled that a 4-year-old child was competent to testify as a witness in a delinquency adjudication against an adolescent who had allegedly subjected him to sodomous acts. The court refused to rule that age *per se* rendered any proposed witness incompetent. Rather, the court

[20] 79 N.J. 97, 398 A.2d 76 (1979).

looked at two narrow factors—whether the child consciously recognized the duty to tell the truth and whether he had the ability to understand questions and to frame an intelligent answer. Despite the fact that the child sometimes responded in gestures and needed his mother's help to interpret his verbal answers, he was deemed to have met these two tests and the court upheld the admission of his testimony.

The ability to express oneself does not qualify a child to accept or reject participation as a test taker. The prevailing rules are more closely related to definitions 1 and 2 above, requiring either the capacity to reason rationally or to arrive at a reasonable result. Throughout the Supreme Court's recent decisions we have seen a heavy emphasis on the presumption that children lack the capacity for informed judgment or to arrive at critical decisions in a mature manner. Justice Stevens, in his concurring opinion in *Matheson*, would have applied the Utah statute to all minor children, mature, emancipated, or otherwise, because he felt the notice requirement would tend to insure that the abortion decision was made as "wisely" as possible. Justice Marshall in dissent recognized Justice Stevens' argument for what it essentially is—a personal preference or value judgment for a particular outcome. Even the notice requirement, Justice Marshall asserted, was a state-imposed obstacle to the exercise of an adolescent's free choice to abort, a right which "by definition secures latitude of choice for the pregnant minor, without State approval of one decision over another" or the personal views of the Supreme Court (*H.L. v. Matheson*, 1981, p. 1188 n. 29).

Of course, the question arises, do children have sufficient maturity and stability to make life-important decisions? Or, are the courts correct in concluding that they do not? Justice Douglas, to support his claim in *Yoder* that students not only had the right but the competency to be heard, cited the work of such major developmental psychologists and sociologists as Piaget, Kohlberg, Gesell, Kay, and Ilg to the effect that cognitive capacity and moral judgment of young adolescents approximated that of adults. It must be said in the interest of intellectual honesty that while works cited by Justice Douglas lend substantial support to his assertion, many other scholars who have reviewed the research of those cited are not in total agreement with their colleagues. But the failure to corroborate centers mainly around adolescents' failure to evidence the judgment and reasoning associated with the most mature states of intellectual and moral development theoretically possible in adults. There is little evidence that those stages are reached by adults themselves.

The legal system, however, continues to uniformly assume that children are developmentally unable to render decisions equivalent to those of adults. But the increasing number of well-regarded, situation-specific, legally relevant studies indicates that the law's assumption of a generally uncrossable line of 18 years of age between dependence and autonomy is simply not empirically supportable. (Besides those studies reported in this text, see, *e.g.*, Cohen & Harnick, 1980; Lewis, 1980; Saks, 1981.)

One of the few literature reviews to investigate systematically the issue of consent with regard to treatment decisions (Grisso & Vierling, 1978) concluded that minors below the age of 11 generally did not have the intellectual ability or sense of independence to give competent consent but that those over 15 were not any less competent than their adult counterparts. But this and other more recent studies (*e.g.*, Grisso, 1980), even though challenging the validity of arbitrary age-graded distinctions, assume that increased ability to make decisions is predominantly the product of development. An alternative hypothesis is that society in general and the law, in particular, through its reinforcement of parental authority, even as against the mature minor, have retarded children's ability to make appropriate choices. What seems to be a developmental incapacity may be more the result of a failure to purposefully teach children to be capable.

> When John Stuart Mill eloquently argued against the subjection of women, he accepted, *arguendo*, that the women of his period were not effectively autonomous. He reasoned, however, that women ... possessed the capacity for autonomy even though such a capacity might be constricted by traditional prejudices and conventions. (Richards, 1980, p. 10)

Courts, legislatures, parents, and other promulgators of standards and values who view their function primarily as child protectors may, in actuality, perpetuate and promote incompetency. While the child, properly, may be protected, from taking actions that would preclude the development of independence, *i.e.*, lead to death or irremediable damage, it is antagonistic to the expansion of autonomy to prevent children from engaging in conduct in which they "take risks and make mistakes—even clearly irrational ones—because responsibility for the sting of one's own mistakes is a crucial part of the kind of independence we associate with autonomy" (Richards, 1980, p. 19). The Supreme Court's heavy reliance on the privacy of the family is, from one perspective, a salutary one, when balanced against the alternative of intrusion by the state. But, when the Court talks of the primacy of "family" prerogatives, it is speaking only of mothers and fathers. In the final analysis, the child is given no say in this family decision. Family, in reality, means only parents.

In light of the above, I would like to conclude with recommendations for two future courses of conduct. The first is a more precise formulation of an earlier comment. Researchers seeking to assess children's competence to consent must move out of the laboratory and into more realistic settings. "The point has frequently been made that developmental psychologists assume that in their laboratory experiments they investigate processes which operate in the real world, while in fact they investigate processes which occur for the first time *during* their experiments" (Houssiadas & Brown, 1980, p. 202). Recent etholog-ical and observational studies of parent-child interactions (*e.g.*, Baruch & Bar-nett, 1981; Gordon, Nowicki, & Wichern, 1981; Ishida, 1980) have revealed interesting data concerning the transactions that lead to the fostering of autono-my, independence, and increasing opportunities for children's decision making. These studies suggest that children can be taught to make decisions considered appropriate by adults at a much younger age than had heretofore been as-sumed and, as a result, cast doubt on the notion that reasoning and judgment are relatively fixed by development. Critiques of Piaget's classic experiments (*e.g.*, Garner & Plant, 1972) indicate that situational, rather than developmen-tal, factors, are responsible for his results and that it was the particular method-ology that Piaget used that produced the responses he described. Thus, what were once considered fundamental characteristics of young children's thinking may be, in reality, simply the products of a particular and inapproriate experi-mental situation. "Piaget's experiments have been found to have 'poor ecologi-cal validity,' since his results do not generalize to ordinary social contexts" (Houssiadas & Brown, 1980, p. 209). Thus, Piagetian stages (or those con-ceived by others relying on similar methodologies) may be more context- than age-dependent.

The problems with the traditional course of developmental research lead to my second recommendation. We need to study, in real-life settings and over the long term, what I would call "liberating parents and liberated children." Behavioral scientists must first discover parents who foster autonomy, inde-pendence, self-determination, and self-reliance and who view those as predomi-nant values to be transmitted to their children. Then we must study the effects of those overtly expressed values in a sample of children along the entire age span from infancy to later adolescence. The establishment of self-determination and emancipation is fostered not only through parental guidance and restraint, as the Supreme Court believes, but also through the creation by parents of the appropriate context for decision making and by offering choices to children, demanding maturity, and encouraging autonomy (Baruch & Barnett, 1981; Gordon *et al.*, 1981; Ishida, 1980). While some child developmental researchers are increasingly questioning the primacy of parental child-rearing attitudes and practices on children's ultimate behavior, until we engage in the kind of longitudinal, naturalistic study I have suggested we will have a difficult, if not impossible, time discerning whether children are genuinely developmentally incompetent for much of their childhood, or whether we have, indeed, subject-ed them to unnecessary dependency and learned helplessness.

Whatever the outcome, we need data, even at the risk of discovering that the Supreme Court's presumptions are correct. I think current legal formula-tions fall far short of recognizing the autonomy of children in those instances where, as in psychoeducational assessment, their significant interests are at stake. I believe that we need developmental, social, and educational psychologists to produce situation-specific research to help the legal system make more reality-oriented decisions. The present status of children's rights will not advance significantly unless there is strong, valid evidence that the "pages of human evidence" are wrong.

Note Added in Proof

As this chapter was going to press, the Department of Education issued proposed regulations modifying current rules in several significant respects. One of those modifications deletes the requirement for parental consent prior to an initial psychoeducational assessment. The proposals are presently mired in political and professional controversy.

References

Baruch, G., & Barnett, R. Competence-related behavior of preschool girls. *Genetic Psychology Monographs*, 1981, *103*, 79–103.

Bersoff, D. Silk purses into sow's ears: The decline of psychological testing and a suggestion for its redemption. *American Psychologist*, 1973a, *28*, 892–899.

Bersoff, D. The ethical practice of school psychology: Rebuttal and suggested model. *Professional Psychology*, 1973b, *4*, 305–312

Bersoff, D. Representation for children in custody proceedings: All that glitters is not *Gault. Journal of Family Law*, 1976–1977, *15*, 27–49.

Bersoff, D. Regarding psychologists testily: Legal regulation of psychological assessment in the public schools. *Maryland Law Review*, 1979, *39*, 27–120.

Bersoff, D. Children as research subjects: Problems of competency and consent. In J. Henning (Ed.), *Rights of children: Legal and psychological perspectives*, Springfield, Ill.: Charles C Thomas, 1981.

Bersoff, D. Larry P. and PASE: Judicial reports cards on the validity of individual intelligence tests. In T. Kratochwill (Ed.), *Advances in school psychology*, (Vol. 2). Hillsdale, N.J.: Lawrence Erlbaum, 1982.

Bricker, S. Children's rights: A movement in search of meaning. *University of Richmond Law Review*, 1979, *13*, 661–693.

Brim, O., Glass, D., Neulinger, J., Firestone, I., & Lerner, S. *American beliefs and attitudes about intelligence*. New York: Russell Sage, 1969.

Cohen, R., & Harnick, M. The susceptibility of child witnesses to suggestion. *Law and Human Behavior*, 1980, *4*, 201–210.

Department of Education. Individualized Education Programs. *Federal Register*, 1981, *46*, 5460–5474.

Department of Health, Education, and Welfare. Implementation of Part B of the Education of the Handicapped Act. *Federal Register*, 1977, *42*, 424474–42517.

Developments in the Law. The Constitution and the family. *Harvard Law Review*, 1980, *93*, 1156–1383.

Ellis, J. Volunteering children: Parental commitment of minors to mental institutions. *California Law Review*, 1974, *62*, 840–916.

Fischer, C. Collaborative psychological assessment. In C. Fischer & S. Brodsky (Eds.), *The Prometheus principle: Informed participation by clients in human services*. New Brunswick, N.J. Transaction, 1978.

Foster, H., & Freed, D. A bill of rights for children. *Family Law Quarterly*, 1972, *6*, 343–375.

Friedman, P. Legal regulation of applied behavior analysis in mental institutions and prisons. *Arizona Law Review*, 1975, *17*, 39–104.

Garner, J., & Plant, E. On the measurement of egocentrism: A replication and extension of Aebli's findings. *British Journal of Educational Psychology*, 1972, *42*,79–83.

Goldstein, J. On the right of the "institutionalized mentally infirm" to consent or refuse to participate as subjects in biomedical and behavioral research. In National Commission for the Protection of Human Subjects (Ed.), *Research involving those institutionalized as mentally infirm*, Appendix 2-1. Bethesda, Md.: National Commission, 1978. (DHEW Pub. No. (OS) 78–0006).

Gordon, D., Nowicki, S., & Wichern, F. Observed maternal and child behaviors in a dependency producing task as a function of children's locus of control orientation. *Merrill-Palmer Quarterly*, 1981. *27*, 43–51.

Grisso, T. Juveniles' capacities to waive *Miranda* rights: An empirical analysis. *California Law Review*, 1980, *68*, 1134–1166.

Grisso, T., & Vierling, L. Minors' consent to treatment: A developmental perspective. *Professional Psychology*, 1978, *9*, 412–427.

Hirshberg, B. Who speaks for the child and what are his rights. *Law and Human Behavior*, 1980, *4*, 217–236.

Houssiadas, L., & Brown, L. Egocentricism in language and space perception. An examination of the concept. *Genetic Psychology Monographs*, 1980, *101*, 183–214.

Holman, M., & Docter, R. *Educational and psychological testing*. New York: Russel Sage, 1972.

Holt, J. *Escape from childhood*. New York: Dutton, 1974.

Institute of Judicial Administration & American Bar Association, *Juvenile justice standards project: Standards relating to rights of minors*. Cambridge, Mass.: Ballinger, 1977.

Ishida, M. Mother–child management of interactions at choice points. *Psychiatry*, 1980, *43*, 71–77.

Katz, S., Howe, R., McGrath, M. Child neglect laws in America. *Family Law Quarterly*, 1975, *9*, 1–372.

Keasey, D., & Sales, B. An empirical investigation of young children's awareness and usage of intentionality in criminal situations. *Law and Human Behavior*, 1977, *1*, 45–62.

Kleinfeld, A. Balance of power among infants, their parents, and the state (I, II, III). *Family Law Quarterly*, 1970, 1971, *4*, *5*, 320–349, 410–443, 64–107.

Lewis, C. A comparison of minors' and adults' pregnancy decisions. *American Journal of Orthopsychiatry*, 1980, *50*, 446–453.

Macklin, R., & Sherwin, S. Experimenting on human subjects: Philosophical perspectives. *Case Western Reserve Law Review*, 1975, *25*, 434–471.

Mnookin, R. *Child, family, and state*. Boston: Little, Brown, 1978.

Moskowitz, J. Parental rights and state education. *Washington Law Review*, 1975, *50*, 623–651.

Note. Counseling the counselors: Legal implications of counseling minors without parental consent. *Maryland Law Review*, 1971, *31*, 332–354.

Note. Constitutional law–right of privacy–school program designed to identify and provide corrective therapy for potential drug abusers held unconstitutional. *Fordham Urban Law Journal*, 1974, *2*, 599–610.

Note. Parental consent requirements and privacy rights of minors: The contraceptive controversy. *Harvard Law Review*, 1975, *88*, 1001–1020.

Note. The psychologist as expert witnesses: Science in the courtroom? *Maryland Law Review*, 1979, *38*, 539–621.

Pitkin, H. *The concept of representation.* Berkeley: University of California Press, 1967.

Recent Cases. Constitutional Law—right of privacy—personality test used by school to identify potential drug abusers without informed consent of parents violates students' and parents' right of privacy. *Vanderbilt Law Review,* 1974, *27,* 372–384.

Recent Developments. Education—school-instituted program to identify potential drug abusers—right to privacy. *Journal of Family Law,* 1973–74, *13,* 636–638.

Richards, D. The individual, the family, and the Constitution: A jurisprudential perspective. *New York University Law Review,* 1980, *55,* 1–66.

Saks, M. (Chair). *Recent research on children's competence to consent.* Symposium presented at the Annual Meeting of the American Psychological Association, Los Angeles, August 1981.

Skolnick, A. The limits of childhood: Conceptions of child development and social context. *Law and Contemporary Problems,* 1975, *39,* 38–77.

Tapp, J. Psychology and the law: An overture. In M. Rozenzweig & L. Porter (Ed.), *Annual Review of Psychology* (Vol. 27.) Palo Alto, Calif.: Annual Reviews, 1976.

Wald, M. Children's rights: A framework for analysis. *University of California-Davis Law Review,* 1979, *12,* 255–282.

Wald, P. Making sense out of the rights of youth. *Human Rights,* 1974, *4,* 13–29.

Chapter 10

Children and Consent to Participate in Research

PATRICIA KEITH-SPIEGEL

The contemporary concept of consent for participation in scientific investigation utilizing minors provides an array of perplexing issues set against an unsettled backdrop. However, this situation compares favorably to but a few years ago when research consent issues were not actively examined. The recent and drastic increase in the literature on research consent issues generally, and consent issues when the participants are minors specifically, attests to the rising concern within the scientific community and regulatory agencies for those upon whom experimentation is conducted. But at this point one could hardly characterize the movement as a uniform set of marchers headed toward a well-defined horizon. Indeed, for every eloquent and well-reasoned view there exists an equally articulate and plausible counter-argument. And although it is not usually explicitly stated, diverse assumptions about the competency of minors appear to be at the base of most of these arguments. Whereas there may be an overall agreement that research participants, and especially those from vulnerable populations such as children, require respect and protection from harm and undue invasion, views about how to achieve these aims vary greatly.

A major reason for the complexity of the issues involves ambiguities and opinion differences over the distribution of authority among the child, the child's family, and the state and how proper it is to use a child for the good of society. Some of these issues, plus others, are evident in the literature and account for disparate conclusions. What is an appropriate or acceptable way of viewing

PATRICIA KEITH-SPIEGEL ● Department of Psychology, California State University, Northridge, California 91330.

consent and the procedures for obtaining it also vary markedly depending on whether researcher self-protection, lawfulness, efficiency, ethical ideals, developmental guideposts, society's right to know, parental rights, or minors' rights are the foundation upon which the arguments are based. Further, operational definitions of commonly used ethical and procedural terms (such as *reasonable* or *minimum risk*) are still unclear. Yet major implications for allowing minors some decision-making rights are often largely based on how such terms are interpreted.

Most writers and groups delving into the matter tend to make sweeping general recommendations while sticking to their own disciplines and, curiously, apparently fail to recognize that other research-oriented disciplines exist for which their specific set of recommendations are neither relevant nor applicable. For example, generally speaking consent is designed to protect the individual participating in biomedical research from bodily invasion, whereas it seeks to protect the social or behavioral research participant's privacy of thought and action and unexpected mental stress. Here the elements of the research procedures themselves are dissimilar enough to require distinct applications of consent acquisition even though the underlying ethical considerations are essentially the same. As Ramsey (1970) has pointed out, a difference exists between the *ethics of consent* and the *consent situation*. This critical difference often becomes obscured, and the result is either an absolutist position or a rag-tag bag of exceptions that become confusing or unusable to investigators seeking counsel as to how to implement their projects.

Other sets of tangling factors relate to the assessment of research as to its therapeutic or beneficial outcome potential for the minor participant and to risk factors and the propriety of "proxy consent" (or the rights of others to conscript a minor to participate in experimentation in this case). As we shall see, both minor *and* parental capacity tend to be viewed quite differently depending on the nature and purpose of the experimental procedure.

Because of the lack of clarity and conflict of opinion about the concept of consent itself in research situations, guidelines that do emerge from law, ethical codes of professional organizations, and regulatory policies obfuscate more often than enlighten. Whereas *malpractice* is a household word, *malresearch* is not. This is curious when one considers that scores of documented cases of participant abuse in research have received fairly widespread national attention and that opinions have been put forth indicating that researchers involved with some projects could be held legally accountable for their questionable procedures (Silverman, 1975). The reactions of a substantial minority of Wilson and Donnerstein's (1976) survey sample suggest that many members of the public would contact a lawyer for the pupose of taking legal action if they learned that they had been subjected to the procedures used in a number of already-published studies. Yet, according to Chalkley (1977), no physician in the United States has yet been found guilty of malresearch. The sole legal decision in the behavioral sciences is *Merriken v. Cressman*[1] described in detail in Chapter 9. Only one malresearch decision has been reached under English common law (*Halushka v. University of Saskatchewan.*[2]). Thus, disgruntled or abused research participants are not resorting to the courts—at least as a first line of action. Instead, attempts are often made by legal scholars to base their arguments about research situations on cases involving minors' capacity to consent unrelated to research situations (*e. g., Bonner v. Moran.*[3]). That the conclusions reached by such applications are usually debated and debatable is not surprising.

The federal government has been promulgating general guidelines and policies governing research conduct by its agencies for almost two decades. These are periodically restructured as power bases and prevailing viewpoints alter within Congress, the presidency, and the federal agencies themselves (Curran, 1974). And, as Chalkley (1977) aptly put it, "Unfortunately old policies seldom die—they just become more complex" (p. 913). The impact of the current lurch from a liberal, Democratic government to a conservative, Republican, and more active deregulation philosophy is yet to be felt.

Ethics code promulgated by research oriented professional organizations sometimes predate the involvement of the government and are also periodically refined. But with few exceptions (*e.g.*, the Society for Research in Child Development, 1973), the organization codes mention minor participants almost in passing if at all. Surely much of the disorganization is due to the fact that experimental work in the biomedical and social/behavioral sciences on a programmatic scale is a post-World War II phenomenon. The ethical dust is still settling.

Historical Background

References to experimentation are found in accounts of ancient scholarly and medical activivities, but voiced concern about procedure used to procure participants is recent. Similarly, ethics codes for medical practice have ancient

---

[1] Merriken v. Cressman, 364 F. Supp 913 (1973).

[2] Halushka v. University of Saskatchewan, 53 DLR2d 436 (1965).

[3] Bonner v. Moran, 126 F.2d 121, D.C. Cir. (1941). After being persuaded by a relative, a 15-year-old boy ageed to a skin graft after a donor could not be located for his cousin, who had been severely burned. The boy's ill mother knew nothing of the initial procedure. Additional operations were performed on the boy, presumably with the implied consent of the mother since she did not intervene. The boy spent a total of two months in the hospital. The physician was later sued for assault and battery, but the trial and appeals courts did agree that the boy did consent to the procedure. The complexity of the chronology of events and court opinions has led to varying interpretations of the meaning of the case. *See* Annas *et al.* (1976) for a more thorough analysis of the legal issues.

origins (*e.g.*, the Code of Hammurabi and the Oath of Hippocrates), but specific references to experimental investigation are not to be found until after World War II (Romano, 1974). Even children themselves were not of particular scientific curiosity until relatively recently. The ancient doctrine of preformationism, later echoed in the Judeo-Christian version of the Creation, held that a human being's characteristics were created instantaneously and determined prior to birth. The *developing* person was irrelevant. Lack of legal status and the high mortality rate of minors also contributed to their lower perceived value and interest. Ironically, however, the capacity of minors to perform and reason similarly to adults may have been viewed as greater than in more modern times as evidenced by the work they were expected to accomplish and the often harsh consequences condoned for lazy, irresponsible, or unlawful behavior.

By the mid-eighteenth century, recorded examples of experimentation emerged. Children from orphanages and "foundlings" were commonly conscripted for experimental purposes. Yet even when parents were available, references to asking permission to use their children for experimental purposes were rare (Mitchell, 1964).

Although the ethicality of research, including sophistication of designs and procedures, generally increased during the early twentieth century, it took the horrors of the experimentation conducted by the Nazis on political and war prisoners in Europe to bring the matter of participant consent to the fore. The first provision of the "Nuremberg Code," adopted as a judicial summary at the war trials where 23 Nazi physicians were indicted for crimes against humanity, deals specifically with consent, including competence to give it:

> The voluntary consent of the human subject is absolutely essential. This means that the person involved should have legal capacity to give consent; should be so situated as to be able to exercise free power of choice, without the intervention of any element of force, fraud, deceit, duress, over-reaching, or other ulterior form of constraint or coercion; and should have sufficient knowledge and comprehension of the elements of the subject matter involved as to enable him to make an understanding and enlightened decision. The latter element requires that before the acceptance of an affirmative decision by the experimental subject there should be made known to him the nature, duration, and purpose of the experiment; the method and means by which it is to be conducted; all inconveniences and hazards reasonably to be expected; and the effects upon his health or person which may possibly come from his participation in the experiment. The duty and responsibility for ascertaining the quality of the consent rests upon each individual who initiates, directs, or engages in the experiment. It is a personal duty and responsibility which may not be delegated to another with impunity[4]

Although the Nuremberg Code has never been used as legal precedent, nearly every writing about consent considers this document as the kick-off

[4] *Journal of the American Medical Association*, 1946, *132*, 1090.

point which subsequent codes and policies were developed. The Code is absolute on the question of consent, leaving virtually no room for exceptions, even if based on the highest standards of professional judgment and surveillance. Most commentators agree that a strict application of the Code would have resulted in a complete moratorium on research utilizing minor participants since they fail to meet the various tests and no provision for proxy consent is provided.

According to Alexander (1970), an author of the first draft of The Code, provisions were made for consent by the next of kin on behalf of incompetents. He reasons that the judges omitted this provision in the final version because it did not apply in the specific cases being tried.

Funding for scientific research increased steadily after World War II as a result of the establishment of the National Institutes of Health. Huge amounts of funding became available to thousands of investigators. NIH and its parent agency, the Public Health Service, began to develop formal standards for intramural clinical research. The ingrained concept of "academic freedom" mandated that principal investigators and their institutions be trusted to behave ethically and professionally. However, the results of the Law-Medicine Research Institute survey sponsored by the NIH during the early 1960s indicated that interest in and support for ethical and other guidelines in the medical research community was low, causing concern about leaving standards to the discretion of the individual researchers (Curran, 1969).

In 1965, the United States Public Health Service mandated that any PHS funded project must be reviewed at the institutional level to assure that participant rights were protected, including the use of appropriate consent procedures. By 1971, all Department of Health, Education and Welfare research was included. In 1973, DHEW began drafting separate guidelines for a number of "special category" research participants including children. The first draft version emerged promptly and contained concerns about properly obtained and monitored proxy consent and the minors' well-being, and according the minors themselves some rights to assent or withdraw, thus indicating some recognition of status if not competence. The general regulation has just been finalized by the Department of Health and Human Services (1981). The additional safeguard document for children was revised in 1978, but final regulations are still being considered as of this writing.

In the mid-1970s, the National Research Act (PL 93–348) established the National Commission for the Protection of Human Subjects of Biomedical and Behavioral Science Research (here-after referred to as "The Commission"). This group was mandated, among other things, to develop guidelines that would facilitate the application of ethical principles to actual research. In 1977, the Commission issued a report entitled "Research Involving Children." A number of recommendations emerged, including not only the requirements of consent for research with minors but also for the types of research (based primarily on risk levels) for which it can ethically be sought. This report and its appendices of commissioned background papers comprise the most thorough and definitive consideration of the issues to date. A concern with the minor participants' wishes is a theme throughout the document, but it is silent on *procedures* for assessing competence.

Professional organizations also began issuing ethical codes relative to research consent (including proxy consent) shortly after World War II. A major document, the Declaration of Helsinki, was adopted by the World Medical Association in 1964 and deserves a brief description because it does not differ markedly from basic practices used today. This code affirms the right to use experimental procedures when the "hope of saving life, reestablishing health, or alleviating suffering" pertains, but hedges on the issue of consent: "If at all possible, consistent with patient psychology, the doctor should obtain the patient's, freely given consent after the patient has been given a full explanation." The code also notes that, in cases of legal incapacity, consent should also be obtained from the legal guardian. Regarding nontherapeutic research, the document is more straightforward in that it mandates that the nature, purpose, and risk must be explained to the participants or their legal guardians. There was, however, no mention of the capacity of minors to participate in decision-making. In 1966, the American Medical Association endorsed the Declaration of Helsinki adding, for our interest here, that "consent, in writing, is given by a legally authorized representative of the subject under circumstances in which an informed and prudent adult would reasonably be expected to volunteer himself or his child as a subject." In the mid-1950s an interesting approach to consent and other research and general ethical issues was taken by the American Psychological Association. This society developed its code of ethics using empirical and participatory procedures based on member imput of critical case incidents. An extensive document entitled "Ethical Principles in the Conduct of Research with Human Participants" (1973) details and elaborates a host of issues, including all of the general consent-related ones to be discussed in this chapter. Unfortunately, however, the APA has not considered consent capacity issues related to minors themselves.

Today, controls over research, including consent procedures, are probably vested in neither common law nor statury law, but in regulation (Swazey, 1978). Voluntary codes and government regulations have slowly replaced the "intrinsic professional ethic" which presumed that right-minded professionals would act only in responsible ways (Ladimer, 1970). Yet the focus of these sources of controls have generally been on adult participants and "proxy consent" procedures which relegates the competence of minors themselves to secondary or non-status.[5]

---

[5] Space limitations preclude a thorough presentation of the history and development of the various

Functions and Requirements of
Consent to Participate in Research

The obligation to obtain informed consent from research participants is the keystone of the protective safeguard of ethical research although this obligation, and the term *informed consent* itself, came from medical malpractice cases rather than from experimentation or research ethics codes (Curran, 1974). Yet, as Katz (1972) has noted, "law has neither defined sufficiently well the substance and ambit of informed consent in therapeutic settings nor determined clearly its functional relevance for human experimentation" (p. 523).

Veatch (1976) details three alternative theories of the nature and purpose of informed consent in research. The first is the protection of participants from harm which holds, as an underlying assumption, that the individual is worthy of protection and possesses some rights. The second is the provision of the greatest good for the greatest number that subordinates individual rights but purports to uphold the highest regard for people collectively. The third, Veach's own favorite, is the individual's right to self-determination which implies that invasion into a person's body or privacy requires informed consent. The Commission (1977) also upholds this third concept by recommending that the primary requirement of consent be derived from the principle of respect for individual autonomy.

The concepts of *self-determination* and *autonomy* would seem to imply that the individual has some competence to make decisions for himself. Yet current thinking on the participation of minors in research shifts the exercise of these rights primarily onto others leaving us, logically-speaking, with somewhat of a contradiction. This same incongruity appears again when applying the legal requirement for consent. These are that an individual gives his permission *knowingly*, *intelligently*, and *voluntarily*. All three criteria will be discussed in the context of minor participation in research later. But because children, in most instances, have not been accorded the *legal* capacity to enter into such contracts with investigators, it means that others must be called in to consent for them.

That the quandary has at least been recognized is evidenced by the increasing use of the term *assent* as applicable when minors are willing to participate in a research procedure even through they may not fully understand the nature and purpose of the experiment. Similarly, the terms *parental* or *guardian permission* are used as a way of distinguishing what one is able to do for oneself—consent—and what may be done on behalf of another person—grant permission

---

government regulations and voluntary organization codes. For a more compete historical review, *see* Bower and de Gasparis (1978). Similarly, an account of post-War abuses of consent that have raised the consciousness of investigators and have influenced policy and law are not presented here. The interested reader is referred to Beecher (1966), Pappworth (1967), Ley (1970), Barber (1976), Bidlen (1978) and Swazey (1978) for examples.

(National Commission for the Protection of Human Subjects of Biomedical and Behavioral Research, 1977).

The most oft cited requirements for obtaining informed consent from human research participants are derived from the 1971 guidelines issued by the Department of Health, Education and Welfare. The six primary elements of consent are:

1. A fair and understandable explanation of the nature of the activity, its purpose, and the procedures to be followed, including an identificaion of those that are experimental
2. An understandable description of the attendant discomforts and risks that may reasonably be expected to occur
3. An understandable description of any benefits that may reasonably be expected to ensue
4. An understandable disclosure of any appropriate alternative procedures that may be advantageous for the participant
5. An offer to answer any inquiries concerning the procedures to be used
6. An understanding that the person is free to withdraw his or her consent and discontinue participation in the project or activity at any time without prejudice

Levine (1975) added four additional elements of information that should be communicated in order to fully meet *informed* consent criteria: (1) an invitation (as opposed to a request or demand) to become a participant along with a clear definition of the role the person is being asked to play as a participant; (2) informing the prospective participant as to why he or she has been selected, including any consequences of being found eligible; (3) an offer to the potential participant of consultation with a third party during the decision-making process; and (4) obtaining consent to any incomplete disclosure (as alternatives to complete deception or concealment). In addition, Levine elaborated on the first DHEW requirement by suggesting that prospective participants should also be told, when applicable, with whom they will be interacting, when and where the research activity takes place, how often the procedures will be administered, and how much time will be involved.

Reiss (1976) also expanded the list of DHEW consent acquisition requirements by specifically addressing features commonly at issue in behavioral and social research. Examples include the right of participants to know to whom information is given, sources of financial support, any possible limits of data confidentiality, and the conditions for disclosure of deception when practiced. He also stresses a sensitivity to "social harm" potential—that is, when social consequences to the participants or organizations involved may ensue as a result of conducting and/or publishing the research.

The newest policy issued by the Department of Health and Human Services (1981) reflects the elments presented above in a more concise format but adds that exculpatory language must be excluded, information about availability of compensattion and treatment if injury occurs must be conveyed, instructions as to who may be contacted for answers to pertinent questions must be provided, and a statment of the conditions of participation must be given. In addition, when appropriate, the participants should be told about the conditons of termination by the investigator, possible additional costs to the participants, consequences of participant withdrawal, the approximate number of participants in the study, and that significant new findings will be provided to the participant.

These various elements of proper consent are presumed applicable to adults (including parents or other approved proxy consent agents). But the question remains as to whether or to what extent minors are sufficiently competent to allow for the requirements to be fully understood and evaluated. So far, they are presumed not to be capable enough as the gatekeepers of consent. Without parental consent, conscripting even a bright, willing, and older minor to participate in a research project may well be considered unethical, professionally risky, and possibly unlawful.

Proxy Consent and Parental Competence

O'Donnell (1974) speaks of "vicarious consent" as occurring when someone consents, "as-if," for another. Proxy consent, as when a parent consents for a minor to participate in a research investigation, is an example of vicarious consent.

The concept of "proxy consent" is perhaps the most controversial issue relative to the participation of minors in research. All current guidelines and policies mandate that parental or guardian permission be obtained leaving the secondary procedure of child capacity to assent more flexible depending on the child's age and considerations of potential for needed benefit that might accrue to the minor.

Society has generally accorded parents considerable latitude within certain limits to determine what their minor children may or may not do during the course of their daily lives. The presumption is that parents are the primary source of advocacy or and well-being of their minor offspring despite the fact that the statistics on child abuse, neglect, and other negative influences perpetrated by parents are appalingly impressive. Even "good" parents, however, may be faced with circumstances that limit their ability to give responsible, fully informed and voluntary consent for children to participate in experimentation. These include lack of a research background, insufficient knowledge about alternatives to experimental procedure, fears that withholding permis-

sion will result in denying the best possible care for their child, lack of awareness of the potential stress of the experimental procedures on their child, or even
unconscious hostility toward their child (Lewis, McCollum, Schwartz, &
Grunt, 1969).

The State retains to itself the duty to assure that parents exercise their
authority in the child's best interest (*parens patriae*). But the issues with regards
to experimentation have no clear legal precedent. Although the courts have not
yet developed special rules for determining the legal rights of research participants, the general rule of law that would pertain if litigation arises relates to
compensation for malpractice and personal injury. Thus, the critical general
rule of law is that related to assault. Assault pertains when the legally valid
consent of a person has not been obtained prior to affecting the body or mind of
another (Hirsch, 1970). This means that the widely practiced use of "proxy
consent" for minors who participate in research may be tenuous if ever fully
tested in the courts.

Unfortunately, contemporary professional ethics codes are not too helpful
in resolving the proxy consent issues either. Frankel (1978) notes that it is not
surprising that codes of ethics for research professions almost unquestionably
support the notion of proxy consent since to do otherwise would severely limit
many areas of investigation. But most of them simply admonish investigators to
obtain permission from the proper parties and let it go at that.

The controversy that does exist over the propriety of proxy consent has
been focused on the use of minors in so-called nontherapeutic research (Cominskey, 1978; Lloyd, 1980). A resolution of the legal problems related to nontherapeutic experimentation on children is also difficult because of the lack of
statutory law and largely irrelevant case law (Annas, Glantz, & Katz, 1976).
And even if legal authority were clear, the ethical question as to whether
parents should approve their childrens' use for such experimentation remains
debatable (Lowe, Alexander, & Mishkin, 1974).[6]

The ethical argument that research that could not possibly benefit the
minor should not be permitted has been most vigorously pressed by Ramsey
(1970). Since children cannot meet the full requirements for informed consent,
he reasons that they cannot be used in research from which they will gain
nothing. Proxy approval for such research is not permissible because it constitutes a branch of fiduciary duty. This extreme view does not allow for consider-

---

[6] Neilsen v. the Regents of the University of California *et al.* (Civil Action No. 665–049, Superior
Court of California, County of San Francisco, 1973) was the first case based solely on the issue of
the legality of parental consent for participation of minors in nontherapeutic research and, as
such, attracted considerable interest within the scientific community. In 1975, Neilsen asked for a
partial summary judgment that the action of conscripting minor participants for a particular
study constituted child abuse under California criminal statutes. The motion was denied, and
Neilsen apparently did not pursue the case further.

ations of the child's willingness (which, it must be noted, is often enthusiastic) or competence, or for "non-beneficial" research that presents minimal risk. The Commission (1977) levels numerous criticisms of Ramsey's position. The members point out that his reasoning is based on a false dichotomy between research intended to benefit the participant and research intended to develop more knowledge since a considerable proportion of research does not easily fall into either category. The Commission further notes that the term *therapy* is, by definition, intended to benefit the individual whereas research, by definition, is for the purpose of developing general knowledge. *Therapeutic research*, then, mixes together two very different concepts and the meaning of this term is therefore rendered unclear and, as such, is of doubtful use as a pivotal concept.

Bartholome (1976) and Ramsey agree that interventions into the lives of children cannot be justified unless some benefit accrues to the child. However, improved moral character constitutes a benefit in Bartholeme's view and assenting to participate in nontherapeutic research may assist in teaching the importance of helping others. This view does reflect some competence on the part of the child if only a capacity to learn from the experience.

McCormick (1974) argues differently by assuming that children *ought* to engage in activity that would benefit others or society when there is little cost to themselves and that others (*e.g.*, parents) may morally and validly consent for the child because the act is right. Thus, proxy consent is legitimized for low-risk therapeutic research because all human beings should do for others as members of the human community. The Commission (1977) notes objections to McCormick's view as well. Basing arguments on a "natural law" assumption is tenuous since the presumed values may differ among cultures. Further, since obtaining consent is for the purpose of protecting an individual's autonomy, then invoking "oughts" becomes a conflicting prescription whenever a person may choose not to engage in an activity even if others justifiably believe that the person should do it. Finally, the Commission notes that if childrens' consent can be presumed because the child ought to be willing, then active consent by third parties on behalf of children undermines the proxy consent model by rendering it gratuitous.

Worsfold (1974) holds that others may justifiably decide for children who have not reached the age of reason when it can be reasonably assumed that, with additional development, the minor would likely have agreed that the decision made on his or her behalf was appropriate. He also notes that the preferences of even younger children should be taken into consideration by those who are making the decision on their behalf. This view approaches an inkling of according minors some competence to decide for themselves, but still gives considerable "as-if" power to others.

Another model of proxy consent holds that the minor's family should know what is best for the child and, therefore, the family *unit* is the appropriate consent agent for research participation by its minor members (Cooke, 1980). Hauerwas (1976) also holds to this view by asserting that a focus on "children's rights" is not entirely appropriate in the ethical analysis of research consent issues. He prefers an ethical model that holds parental duties and responsibilities as a central concept. Because the child is a family member, the guidance and consent of parents is a critical aspect of children's participation in many activities, including research. This sort of "group consent" model includes minors but does not accord them primary competence.

The issue in terms of ethical and philosophical considerations remains unresolved. But clearly the concern over involving minors in research not holding out the possibility of direct benefit has revealed itself in more stringent and protective federal policy.

Information Offered Participants

The consent criteria of *capacity* and *understanding* are not mutually exclusive since the quality of the information presented to prospective participants bears directly upon that individual's capacity to process and comprehend it.

Current guidelines require that a person or that person's legally authorized representative must be in position to exercise choice based on sufficient information about the research activity. But some, such as Barber (1980), have expressed concern that researchers may not be aware of the interests, motivations, and information needs of prospective participants.

The literature on the quality of the information given *to* adult participants as well as the impact of that information *on* participants is disconcerting. Epstein and Lasagna (1969) demonstrated that comprehension of medical information is *inversly* correlated with the elaborateness of information offered to the untutored participant. "Confused consent" may unwittingly occur when some participants are overwhelmed with factual but uncomprehensible information. It has also been shown, however, that giving more complete information may reduce the willingness to participate (Berscheid, Dermer, & Libman, 1973). Investigators have also been concerned about the possible "chilling effect" of requests for a signature on consent forms. Participants may assume that they are signing away some rights and/or solely providing legal protection for the investigator (Singer, 1977).

In their report prepared for the Commission, Tannenbaum and Cooke (1977) performed extensive analyses of consent forms used for research involving children. Using an "index of completeness"—inclusion of research purpose, procedures used, risks, benefits, statement of the right to withdraw, and an invitation to ask questions—they found the vast majority of forms lacking in one or more criteria. Further, most consent forms provided little understandable explanation of medical and technical terms. Even forms providing "lay explanations" were often very difficult to read due to such factors as excessive sentence length and complicated grammatical structure. Perhaps it is not surprising, then, that studies have indicated that many *adult* participants sign consent forms with a minimal understanding of what they have agreed to do (Cassileth, 1980, Gray, 1975; Martin, Arnold, Zimmerman, & Richard, 1968.) Although no systematic parallel work has been reported using children and their understanding of the bases of assent, it is assumed that the picture is at least as problematical.

Some remedies to the demonstrated problems surrounding the giving and impact of information have been proposed and deserve careful consideration. Improving the readability of consent forms can be assured (see Grunder, 1978, for ideas). A "counseling approach" to consent, wherein the investigator and participant discuss the study and its purpose and ramifications in a personal way as one would in partnership or alliance, has been proposed as one way of ameliorating the information gap (Denney, 1976; Jonas, 1969). It has even been suggested that the participants should routinely submit to a quiz as a means of assuring that the information has been correctly processed (Levine, 1975).

The Consent Survey (see Acknowledgment section, p. 207) responses gave an inkling that the practice of "counseling" during consent may be more prevalent than we realize. The vast majority of the respondents described how they took considerable time to discuss the project with, and encourage questions from, the parents *and* the minor participants. Although this procedure was often described in the context of techniques used to gain trust, build rapport, and allay any anxieties, it appears that considerable information was passed and clarified by most researches in this sample.

Capacity

The intent behind incapability law is to protect minors from harm resulting from ignorance or impulsivity and from situations involving persuasion that they may not be able to resist (Curran and Beecher, 1969). An arbitrary age (now under 18) is the general rule upon which to presume incapability. The *Restatement of Torts* (1939)[7] holds consent of a minor intelligent enough to understand the nature and consequences of the act as valid even in the absence of parental consent although this has been rejected, such as in *Bonner v. Moran*, in some cases (Curran, 1959).

In the context of professional practice, the legal system has been moving

---

[7] *Restatement of Torts*, § 59, comment a (1939).

towards the concept that professionals are responsible for informing clients not only about what will be done but also for assuring that this information is understood (Levine, 1975). In their extensive legal analysis, Annas *et al.* (1976) point out that the assumption of risk (*volenti non fit injuria*) is a defense in a negligence action. That is, if a person gives consent to accept the chance of injury from a *known* risk, then the defendant may be successful *if* it can be demonstrated that the plaintiff knew and understood the risk incurred. If one cannot comprehend the risk because of age, then the consent will not be held valid. However, the assumption of risk has been held up with minors a number of times (e.g., *Pouliot v. Black*,[8] *Porter v. Toledo Terminal Railway Co.*,[9] and *Centrello v. Basky*.[10] Annas *et al.* conclude that

> whether or not a child is capable of understanding the risks inherent in a dangerous endeavor, and whether or not those risks were voluntarily incurred are questions of fact, and the courts do not find that children are never incapable of assuming such risks. (p. 18)

However, it must be noted that in the examples offered there was substantial reason to believe that children had prior knowledge of risks involved based directly on their own experience. To presume that a child (or even his or her parents or guardians) would have sufficient knowledge of the kinds of risks that might be associated with scientific experimentation is far more problematical since the mechanics of scientific endeavor do not touch on most people's daily lives. Yet Annas et al. go on to point out many examples from law where minors have been given rights for decision making with consequences well beyond those incurred in most research projects (*e.g.*, the rights of females to consent to marriage at age 12).

Looking at the matter of capicity from a developmental perspective rather than a legal one and assuming that a given minor has been given sound and age-appropriate information about an experimental procedure, how can the minor's capability to decide to participate or not for him or herself be assessed? The "subjective rule," applying when a minor is judged to be of sufficient intelligence and maturity to comprehend and weigh the benefits and risks of the proposed experimental procedures, has been adopted by the National Commission (1977) as the primary criterion with respect to informed consent. However, this criterion is difficult to apply with ease since such capacities could vary markedly depending on the nature of the experimental procedure (Keith-Spiegel, 1976; Ferguson, 1978). Haber and Stephens-Bren (1981) found that some minors as young as 6 years of age could correctly recall the nature of a simple memory study design as well as the description of the experimental procedure they would experience even better than could some adults! By age 10, their entire minor sample was very similar to the capabilities of adults.

Tests of competence could also be devised for use with minor pariticipants, but one concern is that experimenters may be held liable if they were judged to have appraised the minor incorrectly. Committee screening is also a mechanism that could be called upon to evaluate the capabilities of individual minor participants to decide for themselves, but already considerable doubt has been expressed about the capabilities of review committees to do their already prescribed duties effectively, leaving one to wonder how competently this even more complicated task would be executed. The "easy out" is to specify an age limit below which minors are assumed incapable of self-determination and decision making. Various ages for various rights to control one's own destinies in varied situations dot recorded history. Unfortunately, the critera are often either seemingly capricious or they are obsolete as when, in Europe, males were given many rights at age 15 when they were physically capable of bearing arms, later to be increased to age 21 when the weight of military equipment substantially increased. It becomes easier to see why our system has relied so heavily on adult permission (proxy consent) in the context of the equivocal alternatives. Yet, for those who believe that minors should have considerable say in what happens to them if they are capable of doing so, seeking to refine or develop those alternatives remains an inperative activity.

But, meanwhile, various ages have been assigned by policies as to when consent/assent should be obtained from minor participants in research, especially nontherapeutic research. For example, drafts, including the most recent one, of the DHEW research guidelines (1973, 1978) provide that assent be obtained from children 7 years of age or older. The Consent Survey sample was asked to specify an age, generally speaking, that minors are *as capable* as adults to meaningfully consent to participate in a study that was relatively easy to fully describe to potential participants. Keeping in mind that all respondents are among the leading American authorities in the field of child development, the results well illustrate the problems with age-based criteria. The answers ranged from 2 to 17, with a mean age of 11. However, the spread was wide with no truly "modal age agreement" emerging.

The Consent Survey respondents were also asked to share their ideas as to how a child's capacity to decide could be evaluated. Many suggested that the minor might be gently quizzed after receiving information about the study purpose and techniques to assure that the information was processed correctly (although one suggested that a rigid "grilling" might well be more noxious than any experimental trial itself). Some suggested the utilization of standard mental abilities test, but others warned that a too-intense focus on cognitive capacity misses the emotional aspects of the process of asserting self-determination. Several noted that obtaining assent based on utilizing any assessment of capacity was not sufficient to assure that the minor really wants to participate. This answer, regardless of capacity, may not become clear until the experimental trials are actually in process. These respondents noted that responsible investigators have an obligation to remain sensitive to the minor throughout the course of data collection and to be vigilant to any indication that the child may wish to cancel out of his or her role.

Voluntariness

The requirement of voluntariness bears on consent capacity of minors since the tactics used by investigators to conscript children (and their proxy consent agents) require evaluation prior to reaching a decision. Here we are dealing less with cognitive competence and more with the type of competence that emerges from emotional and social maturity and self-confidence.

Whereas it seems simple enough to mandate that consent to participate in research must be done without exercising coercion, duress, pressure, or undue enticement or influence, it does not follow that the absence of these not-easily-defined conditions means that the decision was freely made. Few investigators would report that people have shown up at their laboratory doors requesting to be subjected to experimental procedures for no particular reason. The remarkably high level of compliance exhibited by adult research participants, even under adverse conditions or for prolonged periods of time, led Orne (1964) to assert that one of the basic characteristics of human beings is that they will ascribe purpose and meaning to the experimental task even when there is none.

Grisso and Vierling (1978) make the important point that registering consent or dissent in treatment is a *social* act. That is, one is asked to respond to a request made by a person of some prestige and authority. Researchers (who also often have the title of "doctor" before their name) may well share the powerful mystique accorded physicians in the eyes of parents. To children, of course, any large persons who seem to know what they want and what they are doing may elicit conformity responses. Noncompliant behavior has often led to penalties that, in the research situation, may also reduce their ability to exercise the right of withdraw even after assent has been obtained. Thus, most minors probably have not had sufficient experience with free choice and decision making to perceive the research situation as apart from the demands imposed upon them in their daily lives.

Children come into the research situation with varying degrees of a socialized self. With perhaps the exception of tiny infants, all have idiosyncratic needs for attention, novelty, dependency, and so on. These needs will affect "voluntariness" aspects of research participation and, although these cannot be controlled, the investigator should be sensitive to them. Thus, it becomes important, as Grisso and Vierling (1978) also note, to seek consent that is not merely an acquiescent or deferent response to authority.

Attracting Consent

It has been argued that there is *some* element of coercion involved in any investigator-participant transaction (Ingelfinger, 1972). Whereas Chan's (1961) position that the "engineering of consent" constitutes a major malpractice of our era is probably excessive, the potential for undue inducements to consent to experimentaion are everpresent and children are among the categories of participants who may be especially vulnerable to them. What is the difference between "acceptable persuasion" and "undue influence"? Hirsch (1970) notes that what may pass as acceptable persuasion on the part of a physician to partake of a medical treatment judged as advisable and in the best interests of the patient may be judged as undue influence when applied to clinical investigation.

Parents, especially those concerned about their child's physical or emotional condition, may be persuaded by very subtle, even unconscious inducements by an investigator. The researcher's authority, enthusiasm, and involvement may be sufficient to alter the decision-making process of a guilty, desperate, or insecure parent. In his frank account, Shaw (1973) illustrated how his personal opinions may have influenced medical life-or-death decisions about the fate of parents' severely impaired newborns.

One subtle form of coercion consists simply of not offering potential participants any alternatives. Rosen (1977) demonstrated how easily people will sign away their rights, privacy in this case, if they are not given other options. The percentage of compliant responses dropped considerably when alternatives were given.

The majority of respondents in the Consent Survey sample indicated that they refrained from using any form of coercion with a reluctant child (or parent) and many added they would not engage in the kind of research that required undue influence to gain cooperation. Most respondents reported that the child participants were usually quite eager to cooperate regardless of any altruistic appeals or little prizes that might be offered. Children often enjoy individual attention and new experiences which serve both as an incentive and a reward. The majority of the respondents agreed that age was a primary determinant of what would constitute an inducement. The "beads and trinkets" approach is persuasive to young children whereas an adult would find such offers trifling or insufficient. These views correspond to findings that children would be somewhat more persuaded by rewards in the lower monetary value ranges than would adults (Keith-Spiegel & Maas, 1981). For parents not under stress, satisfaction from "contributing to knowledge" or to the hope of learning how to raise their children more successfully are more likely to serve as reinforcers to agree to involve their children in research.

However, age *per se* may not always be a major determinant of what kinds of approaches are persuasive. One respondent in the Consent Survey Sample noted that economic need is the greatest determinant of the differential effects of enticement regardless of age. Another respondent offered this thoughtful comment:

> Any organism's consent response can be modified: The question is how difficult it will be. A small part of the answer is knowing what their reinforcers are and they are likely to change with age. A large part of the answer is knowing what their skills, alternatives, and resources are and these are likely to change with age. Skilled, resourceful people with many alternatives are difficult to control; their opposites are quite easy to control. Age is a marker for this fact but not its essence.

Altruistic appeals are often used with research participants of all ages and range from personal statements of a need for help by the investigator to declarations that cooperation will benefit society or advance science. A number of Consent Survey respondents indicated that personal appeals for assistance are extremely persuasive to children. Children may, as one respondent put it, be more open to adult definitions of what is "good," "valuable," and "healthy," although Keith-Spiegel and Maas (1981) did not find great differences between adults and minors when a strong altruistic appeal was used to attempt to induce participation in painful or upsetting procedures. Ferguson (1978) does not view appeals to altruism as inappropriate just so long as "undue social pressure" is not involved. She asserts that altruistic appeals may be not only legitimate but may even contribute in constructive ways to the child's social development.

Right to Withdraw

Directly related to the issue of voluntariness is the right to withdraw from an experimental procedure after the initial consents or assents have been negotiated. This right also bears directly on capacity issues since even if minors are not viewed as capable of consenting, according them the opportunity to leave suggests some consideration of their capacity for self-determination. Although the exercise of this right creates headaches for investigators if an elaborate or lengthy procedure was well underway (such as in longitudinal studies of child development), most contemporary ethical and policy guidelines mandate that this right must be not only honored but made explicit during the initial consent phase. However, with regards to children, the Commission's (1977) recommendations allow for exceptions. Whereas an objection by a child of any age should normally be respected, intervention from which the child might derive significant benefit to her health or welfare and when that intervention is available only in a research context, the objections of the child may be overridden. The Commission report adds, however, that the child's wishes carry more weight with maturity and as the ability to perceive and act in his or her own best interest increases.

The Consent Survey respondents were asked how they handled a child's explicit request to withdraw from research after initial assent was given. The vast majority reported no instance of this situation as ever occurring. Those few who did experience such requests noted that they were rarely made by either the parents or the children.

When asked about instances when the investigators decided to terminate a child participant because of indicators other than explicit requests, most of the respondents to the Consent Survey had more experiences to share. Signs interpreted to mean that a minor participant did not want to fulfill the obligations of participation once assent was given fell into two categories. Among the behavioral indicators commonly mentioned were passivity, distractiveness, off-task behavior, lack of cooperation, random responses, shyness, fussiness, silence, crying or puckering, going to sleep, hand or foot dancing, constant looks towards the door, excessive nervousness, lack of eye-contact with the experimenter, and signs of boredom such as multiple yawns. Among the verbal expressions on the part of children that indicated a desire to disengage from the research trials were, "I want to go to the bathroom," "I'm tired," "When will I be done?," responding repeatedly to direct and age-appropriate questions with "I don't know," and any expression of a desire to be doing something else. Several of the respondents noted that they did not necessarily interpret these reactions as indicating a blanket unwillingness to participate in the project. Rather, such behavior or verbal expressions may indicate a temporary lack of cooperation and an attempt could be made to schedule the session at another time.

Anticipated Benefit

An intriguing observation arises relative to presumed competence of minors to consent in discussions of potential benefit versus no benefit to the participants. For beneficial or therapeutic research, minor participants are viewed as uncomprehanding and vulnerable people who require help and protection by adults who are then accorded the authority to do just that. However, for nonbeneficial/nontherapeutic research, minors are suddenly transposed into persons with the same rights as adults to privacy, self-respect, and self-determination rendering the right of anyone to decide on their behalf as morally questionable. Although Ramsey (1976) may not agree with this author's application of his term *accordian morality*, it appears that the very essence of minors is viewed as markedly different depending on the needs of ethicists and other authorities to defend their positions. Thus, a discussion of the "benefit test" is relevant here primarily because the competencies of minors are viewed so differently depending on whether or not a project has been judged to have met it and because, after the surface is scratched, such tests are of doubtful validity.

The first obvious problem is that experimentation, by definition, cannot assure a beneficial result. A related question is how much possible benefit is enough to conscript a minor to participate, especially if there are risks of harm?

Aside from life-or-death situations, the definition of benefit may exist largely in the eye of the beholder. This is especially true for social and behavioral research where the concept of benefit is particularly difficult to define or assess. Much social and behavioral research deals with normal, healthy children with the goal of further improving their capabilities (such as teaching them how to read better or to engage in more prosocial behavior or to adjust to the traditional school system) or simply to learn more about them. Here "benefit" becomes defined by the value systems of the society and is justified on these grounds. The concept of benefit has not been construed as applicable only to the research findings either. The actual experience of participating has been interpreted as potentially profitable. Bower and de Gasparis (1978) note that benefits can accrue to participants in social and behavioral research on the bases of "feeling good" about contributing to science, enjoying the experimental procedure, and learning something new and interesting (especially if experimenters are sensitive to their ethical obligation to explain their procedures and purposes and provide feedback if requested). Baumrind (1976) and Ferguson (1978) both speak of benefits to child research participants as consisting of a positive learning experience that somehow contributed to the child's growth.

Another obstacle provided by the application of the "benefit test" is that it assumes that a definitive answer or result will be forthcoming from a single study. The process of scientific problem solving is typically, in fact, an evolving and continuous process. If benefit does not accrue to a participant as a direct result of one study, the results may be part of a pathway that will lead to direct benefit later on. Others have rejected the "benefit test" outright on the grounds that it negates the value of accumulating knowledge for its own sake.

Formal guidelines remain unclear as to the definition of benefit. Yet such distinctions remain important relative to current consent practices. The child's wishes can be overridden *and* additional risks can be "ethically" introjected into the design if the research project meets the "benefit test" applied, somewhat unevenly we can presume, by review bodies. Baumrind (1977a) argues that the meaningful relevant distinction bearing on the right of consent by proxy is "harmful" and "not harmful" research. Whereas assessment of harm (to be discussed in more detail next) is not devoid of entanglements either, it seems to cut somewhat more smoothly across the obfuscation inherent in determining consent procedures by assigning value to yet unknown outcomes, or to goals upon which agreement as to worthiness does not exist.

Potential Risk

In biomedical research, the concept of risk applies largely to physical or bodily harm. It can be transitory (*e.g.*, a painful experimental procedure) or long-lasting. Or, risk could be said to have been incurred by withholding standard treatment for the purposes of an experiment that caused a prolongation or aggravation of symptoms (Mitchell, 1964). It has been asserted that the risks involved in social science research are usually trivial as compared to those in biomedical research (Reynolds, 1972). However, it should be candidly admitted that "harm" is usually easier to detect and link to a biomedical research procedure than to a social or behavioral research procedure. Among the risks that may be present in social or behaviorl research are invasion of privacy, breach of confidentiality, stress or other negative emotional reactions such as loss of self-esteem, and "collective risks" wherein harm to others may result from study results (see Bower & de Gasparis, 1978; Reiss, 1976).[11]

Conducting research with minor participants that carries potential risk of harm poses a number of dilemmas related to consent. The primary one with regard to competence is the general presumption that minors are incapable of fully evaluating risk factors. Of course, the question can be asked regarding *any* person's capabilities of assessing possible risk of harm prior to experiencing it regardless of how heroic the attempt to describe it. Actually defining risk, or agreeing that a possible aspect of participation may constitute a risky procedure, is also often very difficult to do with any precision before the fact. The impact of the potentially risky procedure may also vary tremendously depending on the personal characteristics, not necessarily determined by age, of the participants themselves. For example, what one child might find frightening, another child might find pleasantly exciting.

The Commission (1977) considered risk levels in some detail and recommends that any research involving "more than minimal risk" (defined as presenting experiences to participants that are reasonably commensurate with

---

[11] Curran (1974) notes that a certain amount of discretion about risk information is allowable, depending on the emotional state of the participant, in the case of therapeutic research. But, he stresses, this discretion does not pertain to nontherapeutic research where *any* risk must be discussed.

those inherent in their actual or expected medical, psychological, or social situations) and is likely to yield generalizable knowledge about the participants' disorder or condition. Although one gets the gist of the Commission's concern about minor protection, the vague definitions of significant terms pose obvious problems for application.

Another complicating factor relative to risk is that solutions to many significant problems of interest to contemporary investigators require the use of completely new approaches and techniques. Many kinds of problems are unique to immature humans rendering pretesting or use of alternative samples inappropriate. The degree of risk in these instances may simply be unknown. A useful example is the current drug situation. Many chemical agents have not been approved for use with children because the definitive research has not been executed. But using child participants to test drugs, including the use of healthy children to gather normative data for dosage regulation, may do harm. Reichler (1976) concludes that without further research on the effects of drugs on children. we are caught between the extremes of withholding treatment that may be significantly effective for some children or subjecting others to unnecessary risk.

Certainly all investigators must remain sensitive to posssible risks of all sorts and take precautions to reduce the potential of harm despite the difficulties that often arise in defining and communicating what they might be. (See Zeisel, 1970, for ideas as to how risk factors can be reduced or eliminated.)

Deception

The deliberate distortion of the consent acquisition stage by misinforming the participant (deception) or omitting information that might have otherwise altered the consent decision (concealment) constitute the most profound ethical issues relative to consent. The reason is obvious. At best consent is uneducated and at worst it is an outright sham. Questions of *competence* to consent are rendered meaningless.

Clearly, deception is not a simple all-or-nothing thing and can range from outright lies and concealment of risks to mild and ambiguous forms of dissembling (Bower & de Gasparis, 1978). Deception and concealment can be *nonintentional*, occurring whenever a full disclosure of the research design and/or objectives are not offered to or understood by the participants. Nonintentional deception probably cannot be entirely avoided, especially when the participants are young children (Baumrind, 1977a). *Intentional* deception is the more perilous issue. Baumrind argues that intentionally decptive research practices always constitute a violation of the fiduciary relationship between investigators and their research participants. Such acts are a violation of the investigators' duty as a fiduciary and, in her view, are both morally reprehensible and possibly unlawful. Whereas the ethics codes of professional associations implicitly or explicitly recognize the profound moral dilemmas surrounding the use of deceptive practices, their use is not entirely forbidden and they are actually relatively commonly practiced in the social and behavioral sciences. The deliberate witholding of information from participants and/or their legitimate proxies in biomedical research, particularly if the research is not intended to benefit the participant directly and risks are involved, is increasingly and vigorously disallowed. However, just as the biomedical researchers require that the physical body be in a certain condition, the behavioral/social scientists sometimes require that the "state of mind" be in a certain condition. That required state may be of a particular "set" or one of "ignorance" lest responses be distorted or biased by full knowledge of the study design or purpose (see Berscheid *et al.*, 1973; Corwin & Nage, 1972; Resnick & Schwarts, 1973; Ruebhausen & Brim, 1966).

When deception is utilized, contemporary ethical guidelines mandate that the participants must be "disabused" or "debriefed" in a timely fashion upon completion of the data gathering. Whereas this procedure is designed to erase the temporary "lapse in honesty," it too is fraught with difficulty (see Holmes, 1976; Mills, 1974; Ring, Wallston & Corey, 1970; Tesch, 1977). According to Baumrind (1976) the investigator is faced with two alternatives: "deceptive debriefing" (the deception may be perpetrated because, for example, the investigator believes that divulgence of the true nature of the study may disturb the blissful ignorance enjoyed in the absence of such disclosures) or "inflicted insight." Many suspect that the reestablishment of trust and respect for the investigator (and perhaps the entire scientific discipline represented) cannot be fully restored through any post-investigation clarification (Baumrind, 1977a; Fillenbaum, 1966)

The effects of deception and debriefing on minors may be even more insidious than for adults. Children, during the formative years when value systems are being constructed, may be left with the distinct impression that lying is an *appropriate* way for adults to achieve their goals. Debriefing may be especially perplexing to child participants who leave the study feeling disoriented and unsure of what they just did really meant. The American Psychological Association (1973) treats deception as a delicate technique to be avoided if at all possible. It is used only when the study is extremely significant and unamenable to alternative approaches and investigators are warned to take full responsibility to detect and remove any stressful aftereffects. However, the APA allows for some special considerations when the participants are children.

> With children, the primary objective of the postinvestigation clarification procedure
> is to assure that the child leaves the research situation with no undesirable afteref-
> fects of his participation. This may mean, for example, that certain misconceptions

should not be removed or even that some new misconceptions should be induced. If
a child erroneously believes that he has done well on a research task, there may be
more harm in trying to correct this misconception than in permitting it to remain.
Similarly, ameliorative efforts are needed when a child feels that he has done poorly.
(p. 81)

Although this guide can be justified on "kindness" grounds, it implicitly
singles out children as being incapable of handling the truth. The vast majority
of the Consent Survey respondents supported the reasoning behind the APA
guideline. But several were uncomfortable about lying to children even if instil-
ling such misconpcetions might make them feel better. These respondents suggested other ways of dealing with poor performances such as focusing on ex-
pressing appreciation to the child for his or her assistance.

The Consent Survey respondents were also asked about their attitudes
towards the use of deceptive techniques with minor participants. The respondents were split almost evenly into the three camps that one might expect to
find among social and behavioral scientists. About a third of the sample did
justify the use of deception when valuable data that could benefit many could
not be collected otherwise. The second group believed that deception was justified *sometimes* but focused on the features of the procedures used rather than on
the merit of the project. Common limitations criteria included no use of outright lies or tactics that would make the child feel foolish or a failure and no use
of any technique that would betray a trust or encourage the child to act in a
way that might create guilt or anxiety or the expression of feelings or attitudes
that the child might not ordinarily express. False negative feedback was also
discouraged. This group generally found deception or concealment as also
acceptable if such techniques assisted the child or the parents in feeling better
about their participation than they might have otherwise. Respondents in both
of these groups upholding the use of deception often noted that its use still
requires justification and must meet certain standards. Debriefing was mentioned as a requirement by most respondents in both groups.

The final group consisted of respondents who found no justification for
deceptive techniques, usually on ehtical grounds. Reasons ranged from viewing the use of deception as a quick-and-dirty substitute for quality work to a
concern that professionals who presumably care about children should be the
last to deceive or mislead them. "Who is left *then* to trust?," one respondent
asked.

Deceptive procedures in research are deceptively complicated, and a full
discussion is beyond the scope of this chapter. (For further reading, see
Baumrind, 1972, 1976, 1977a; Bower & de Gasparis, 1978; Brandt, 1978;
Kelman, 1967; Menges, 1973; Oetting, 1975; Seeman, 1969; Shipley, 1977;
Striker, 1967; Striker, Messick, & Jackson, 1969; Warwick, 1975.)

Competence of Investigators

The public images of researchers are often somewhat negative and sometimes downright unsavory. In the popular fictional vein we find the deranged scientist, daring to defy the "natural order," carting off his research participants despite their desperate and wriggling protests. He creates evil, misshapen monstrosities before he, himself, is eventually destroyed—often by one of his own participants-turned-creature. The coldly objective, insensitive research scientist whose essence is intellect is another unfortunate image. This sort of investigator is viewed as categorizing human participants as "guinea pigs" and according them little regard as thinking and feeling beings. Another image is the impassioned experiementer whose zest for knowledge far exceeds any other considerations including the rights of participants. Lack of regard for others is not so much an error of active commission as a casualty of obsession. A fourth image is the brilliant but arrogant and paternalistic investigator who does not consult with research participants because of a conviction that they could not possibly comprehend the intricacies of science or the reasons why they were selected to participate. In all four perceptions, the research participants are viewed literally as "subjects"[12] without recourse to self-determination. That the primary definition of "a person or thing under the control, influence, and authority of another person or power" should emerge as the primary term for human beings who are being scientifically studied is probably not a spurious observation.[13]

Interestingly, the image of the treatment or service provider is more often one of a warm and caring person whose primary concern is for his patient. As Reichler (1976) has noted, poor clinical treatment is often more readily tolerated than quality treatment research. Unproven, faddish, and even fraudulent treatments may be unregulated and clamored for by the public while attempts to evaluate or improve treatment in the context of experimentation are criticized and often impeded.

Obtaining study populations and proper consents prior to administering a research procedure is, objectively speaking, a tedious chore. Investigators require sufficient numbers of participants to execute their studies and do not wish to scare anyone off. Thus lurks the additional temptation to offer enticements, make the consent phase presentation attractive, downplay information that might be disturbing, and so on. When investigators are under pressure to produce and publish lest their own positions be jeopardized, a conflict of interest may emerge and influence the ethicality of the procedures used (see Barber,

---

[12] From the Latin, *subjectus*: "thrown under."

[13] A movement to switch from "subject" to the somewhat cumbersome but more egalitarian "research participant" is catching on in some circles.

1976). Exposing participants to excessive risks, or involving them in poorly designed experiments, or using them as samples of convenience in a trivial manner, or executing the procedures hurriedly or carelessly are all possible consequences when the motivations or values of the investigators are focused on their own needs (Lewis *et al.*, 1969). Clearly the entire scientific enterprise is jaded as well since no meaningful knowledge results from poorly designed, carelessly executed, or unethical research (Mitchell, 1964). Indeed, it is the documentation of such abuses that has contributed to the push for increased regulation of research including the necessity of obtaining proper consent.

Is it true that expecting research investigators to be in charge of protecting the welfare and rights of those upon whose cooperation they are dependent for their livelihoods and professional status constitutes yet another version of entrusting henhouses to the foxes? Most investigators would reject the proposition that the negative images and conduct of researchers actually prevail. Safeguarding the rights of participants do not need to clash with the investigators' legitimate interests. There are few "either-or" dilemmas for the compassionate, competent investigator. Nevertheless, the concern about the integrity or sensitivity of investigators has led to increasing external control mechanisms such as protection committees, institutional review boards, and other third-party consent arbitrators. (See Barber, 1976; Baumrind, 1976; Bower & de Gasparis, 1978; Chalkley, 1977; and Levine, 1975; for fuller discussions of the assets and limitations of external review systems.)

Researchable Questions

It is unfortunate that child development research has provided little information about children's capacity to consent in the variety of situations presented in this volume. Perhaps in a frenzy to outgrow its "soft-science" image of the 1930s through the early 1950s, developmental psychology has overemphasized the importance of laboratory settings, design sophistication, and controls. The result may be that we know a great deal about how children will behave in highly atypical and abnormal environments while performing tasks that have little relevance to their daily lives. Smith and Stone (1961) issued an early warning:

> To require a human being to spin a web or peck at corn would be hardly less appropriate than some of the tasks carried over directly, say, from rats or pigeons, which have been set for children. Some of these seem more like studies of how to limit conditions so children cannot learn than attempts to determine true dimensions of capability. (pp. 1–2)

Although more recent research has reflected the daily behavior of children in more natural settings, including the experiential conditions that affect the development of general cognitive competence, the dependent variable more often than not is a child's performance on measures of intellectual ability, rather than his or her ability to make decisions in real-world situations.

Research assessing the impact of information offered during the consent phase of research participation has been conducted on adult populations. These studies should be replicated with children. As was discussed earlier, the adult data illustrate profound dilemmas and it is important to learn the degree to which (if at all) children are confused and/or hesitant to participate, depending on the level, complexity, and completeness of the information. A corollary area of inquiry would involve exploring formats that investigators might use to assure the maximum level of understanding in minors at various ages. Empirical tests of the "counseling approach" to research consent or "consent quizzes," as examples, would at least tell us if such notions have merit.

Since incapability laws assume the need to protect minors from their own impulsivity and the ease with which they can be dominated or persuaded, it is important to put these presumptions to some empirical test. Are children far more easily persuaded by authority figures than are adults in research-consent situations? Can they say "no" despite the assumption that their restricted opportunities to decide may lower their capabilities of noncompliance to requests? Are altruistic appeals for assistance by the researcher more effective with children than with adults? Are promises of rewards more effective and, if so, in what magnitude ranges and under what conditions are they effective? Will children be able to withdraw during the experimental trial any less often that will adults? If there are personality differences or other circumstances such as socioeconomic status that account for any differences, do these override considerations of age?

The concept of *risk* and the presumed incapacity of minors to understand it are consistently discussed as primary reasons for heavy reliance on proxy consent. Thus, a further exploration of children's understanding of the concept of risk would be another important area of inquiry. Are there developmental trends in ability to balance potential risks and benefits? Are there particular kinds of risks that are especially salient at various ages? What situational factors impinge up on a child's ability to balance risks and benefits? Are these factors substantially different from those affecting adults?

Assessing children's understanding of research and experimentation generally would be of interest, since it is assumed that adults are more knowledgeable about scientific endeavor. But with the development of educational media for children, in addition to their daily involvement with school learning, the "competence gap" may not be nearly as wide as has been imagined.

Finally, researching into the specific questions raised by various extant or proposed standards for assent or consent to participate in research would be helpful in formulating appropriate procedures that involve children as substantially as possible in the consent decision.

Concluding Remarks

At this time it is abundantly clear that the profound dilemmas posed by competency and other consent issues when research participants are minors are far from resolved. At best we can say that they are out of the closet and are being more actively examined from ethical, legal, and theoretical perspectives.[14] Yet to suggest that research utilizing minor participants should be foreclosed until such time as the dilemmas are fully resolved would neither be in the best interests of science nor of minors themselves.

The benefits to children that have been derived directy from research conducted with them are already impressive. Examples from biomedical research include vaccines for poliomyelitis, rubella, rubeola, diptheria, and tetanus as well as antimicrobial agents that have drastically reduced the mortality rate for acute suppurtive diseases in early childhood (Lowe, 1970). The Commission (1977) report offers numerous examples of misadventures in the treatment of children due to untested therapies and iatrogenic diseases that were eliminated as a result of research findings.

A trial-and-error approach to socializing children in concert with unfounded tradition as to their essence and nature have perpetuated practices that have caused developmental distortion, stunting, or considerable harm. Social and behavioral science research findings have formed the basis of discoveries of unique attributes and response capabilities of immature human beings that are essential to the welfare of minors as developing psychosocial entities.

It will not be possible to learn all we need yet to know from subhuman and adult human populations. One of the insights research has provided is that children are neither complicated animals nor simple adults. Whereas most would agree that alternative populations should be studied if at all possible, the fact that infants and young children are among the least able to consent, assent, or object should not preclude altogether conducting high quality, ethical experimentation that is important to their well-being as a class, (Cooke, 1980; Lloyd, 1980; Lowe *et al.*, 1974; Shirkey, 1968).

It is unlikely that even the most responsible and meticulous investigators

---

[14] There are a number of specialized study approaches often utilizing minor participants that pose additional problems relative to consent competency beyond those discussed in this chapter. For further information, *consult* Gray (1971) and Curran (1974) for intervention/longitudianl research and Baumrind (1988b), Silverman (1975), Deiner and Grandhall (1978), Bower and de Gasparis (1978), Denzin (1968), and Erikson (1967) for disguised and unobtrusive research practices.

can design consent procedures that guarantee that the participants emerge with a consummate understanding of the project purpose, design and experience of participating prior to the actual experimental session. However, *caveat emptor* has no place in research either. The competent investigator who is sensitive to and well-informed about the ethical issues and who remains vigilant to the needs and competencies of children and their families is a large part of the resolution. These attributes cannot be dictated by any law or administrative fiat.

ACKNOWLEDGMENTS

The author wishes to express gratitude to Diana Baumrind and Lisa Soule for their invaluable assistance in providing materials critical to the preparation of this chapter. Appreciation is also given to the 45 social science researchers specializing in child development for responding to a lengthy, open-ended survey on consent issues. This population is referred to as the "Consent Survey sample" throughout the chapter.

References

Alexander, L. Psychiatry: Methods and processes for investigation of drugs. *Annals of the New York Academy of Sciences*, 1970, *169*, 347–351.

American Medical Association. *Declaration of Helsinki and AMA Ethical Guidelines for Clinical Investigation*, 1966.

American Psycholigical Association. *Ethical principles in the conduct of research with human participants.* Washington, D.C.: American Psychological Association, 1973.

Annas, G. J., Glantz, L. H., & Katz, B. F. *Law of informed consent in human experimentation: Children.* Paper prepared for the National Commission for the Protection of Human Subjects of Biomedical and Behavioral Research. Washington, D.C.: U.S. Department of Health, Education, and Welfare, 1976.

Barber, B. The ethics of experimentation with human subjects. *Scientific American*, 1976, *234*, 25–31.

Barber B. *Informed consent in medical therapy and research.* New Brunswick, N. J.: Rutgers University Press, 1980.

Bartholome, W. G. *The ethics of non-therapeutic clinical research on children.* Paper prepared for the National Commission for the Protection of Human Subjects of Biomedical and Behavioral Research. Washington, D.C.: U.S. Department of Health, Education, and Welfare, 1976.

Baumrind, D. Reactions to the May 1972 draft report of the Ad Hoc Committee on Ethical Standards in Psychological Research. *American Psychologist*, 1972, *27*, 1083–1086.

Baumrind, D. *Nature and definition of informed consent in research involing deception.* Paper prepared for the National Commission for the Protection of Human Subjects of Biomedical and Behavioral Research. Washington, D.C.: U.S. Department of Health, Education and Welfare, 1976.

Baumrind, D. *Informed consent and decit in research with children and their parents.* Paper presented at the Biennial Meeting of the Society for Research in Child Development. New Orleans, March 17–20, 1977. (a)

Baumrind, D. *Snooping and duping: The application of the principle of informed consent to field research.* Paper presented at the Society for Applied Anthropology meetings, 1977. (b)

Beecher, H. K. Ethics and clinical research. *New England Journal of Medicine*, 1966, *274*, 1354–1360.

Berscheid, E. R. S., Dermer, M., & Libman, M. Anticipating informed consent—An empirical approach. *American Psychologist*, 1973, *28*, 913–925.

Biklen, D. Consent as a cornerstone concept. In J. Mearig (Ed.), *Working for children: Ethical issues beyond professional guidelines.* San Francisco: Jossey-Bass, 1978.

Bower, R. T., & de Gasparis, P. *Ethics in social research.* New York: Praeger, 1978.

Brandt, L. W. Don't sweep the ethical problems under the rug: Totalitarian versus equalitarian ethics. *Canadian Psychological Review*, 1978, *19*, 64–66.

Cahn, E. The lawyer as scientist and scoundrel. *New York University Law Review*, 1961, *36*, 1–2.

Cassileth, B. R. Informed consent—Why are its goals imperfectly realized? *New England Journal of Medicine*, 1980, *302*, 896–900.

Chalkley, D. T. Federal constraints: Earned or unearned? *American Journal of Psychiatry*, 1977, *134*, 911–913.

Comiskey, R. J. The use of children for medical research: Opposite views examined. *Child Welfare*, 1978, *57*, 321–324.

Cooke, R. W. Clinical research on children. In *Issues in Research with Human Subjects* (NIH Publication No. 80–1858). Washington, D.C.: Department of Health, Education, and Welfare, 1980.

Corwin, R. G., & Nagi, S. Z. The case of educational research. In S. Z. Nagi & R.G. Corwin (Eds.), *The social contexts of research.* New York: Wiley, 1972.

Curran, W. J. A problem of consent: Kidney transplantation in minors. *New York University Law Review*, 1959, *34*, 891–898.

Curran, W. J. Government regulations of the use of human subjects in medical research: The approach of two federal agencies. *Daedalus*, 1969, *98*, 542–594.

Curran, W. J. Ethical and legal considerations in high risk studies of schizophrenia. *Schizophrenia Bulletin*, 1974, *10*, 74–92.

Curran W. J., & Beecher, H. K. Experimentation in children. *Journal of the American Medical Association*, 1969, *10*, 77–83.

Declaration of Helsinki. Code of ethics of the World Medical Association with regard to human experimentation. *British Medical Journal*, July 18, 1964, *2*, 177.

Denny, M. K. Informed consent—Doctor's friend or foe? *Modern Medicine*, 1976, August, 74–76.

Denzin, N. On the ethics of disguised observation. *Social Problems*, 1968, *15*, 502–504.

Department of Health, Education, and Welfare. *Institutional guide to DHEW policy on the protection of human subjects* (NIH Publication No. 72–101). Washington, D.C.: U.S. Government Printing Office, 1971.

Department of Health, Education, and Welfare. Protection of human subjects: Policies and procedure. *Federal Register*, November 16, 1973.

Department of Health, Education, and Welfare. Protection of human subjects: Research involving children. *Federal Register*, July 21, 1978.

Department of Health and Human Services. Final regulations amending basic HHS policy for the protection of human research subjects. *Federal Register*, January 26, 1981.

Diener, E. and Crandall, R. *Ethics in social and behavioral research.* Chicago: University of Chicago Press, 1978.

Epstein, L. C. and Lasagna, L. Obtaining informed consent: Form or sustance. *Archives of Internal Medicine*, 1969, *123* 682–688.

Erickson, K. A comment on disguised observation in sociology. *Social Problems*, 14 366–373.

Ferguson, L. R. The competence and freedom of children to make choices regarding participation in research: A statement. *Journal of Social Issues*, 1978, *34*(2), 114–121.

Fillenbaum, R. S. Prior deception and subsequent experimental performance: The faithful subject. *Journal of Personality and Social Psychology*, 1966, *4*, 532–537.

Frankel, M. S. Social, legal, and political responses to ethical issues in the use of children as experimental subjects. *Journal of Social Issues*, 1978, *34*, 101–113.

Gray, B, H. *Human subjects in medical experimentation*. New York: Wiley, 1975.

Gray S. W. Ethical issues in research in early childhood intervention. *Children*, 1971, *18*, 83–89.

Grisso, T., & Vierling, L. Minors' consent to treatment: A developmental perspective. *Professional Psychology*, 1978, *9*, 412–427.

Grunder, T. M. Two formulas for determining the readability of subject consent forms. *American Psychologist*, 1978, *33*, 773–774.

Haber, S. & Stephens-Bren, S. *Do children understand enough to consent to participate in research?* Paper presented at the meetings of the Western Psychological Association, Los Angeles, April 1981.

Hauerwas, S. *Rights, duties, and experimentation on children: A Critical response to Worsfold and Bartholome.* Paper prepared for the National Commission for the Protection of Human Subjects of Biomedical and Behavioral Research. Washington, D.C.: U.S. Department of Health, Education, and Welfare, 1976.

Hirsch, B. D. The medicolegal framework for clinical research in medicine. *Annals of the New York Academy of Sciences*, 1970, *169*, 308–315.

Holmes, D. S. Debriefing after psychological experiments. *American Psychologist*, 1976, *31*, 858–875.

Ingelfinger, F. J. Informed (but uneducated) consent. *New England Journal of Medicine*, 1972, *287*, 465–466.

Jonas, H. Philosophical reflections on experimenting with human subjects. *Daedalus*, 1969, *98*, 219–247.

Katz, J. *Experimentation with human beings*. New York: Russell Sage, 1972.

Keith-Spiegel, P. Children's rights as participants in research. In G. P. Koocher (Ed.), *Children's rights and the mental health professions*. New York: Wiley, 1976.

Keith-Spiegel, P., & Maas T. *Consent to research: Are there developmental differences?* Paper presented at the Annual Meeting of the American Psychological Association, Los Angeles, August 1981.

Kelman, H.C. The rights of the subject in social research: An analysis in terms of relative power and legitimacy. *American Psychologist*, 1972, *27*, 989–1015.

Ladimer, I. Protecting participants in human studies. *Annals of the New York Academy of Sciences*, 1970, *169*, 546–572.

Levine, R, J. *The nature and definition of informed consent in various researech settings.* Preliminary paper prepared for the National Commission for the Protection of Human Subjects of Biomedical and Behavioral Research. Washington, D.C.: U.S. Department of Health, Education, and Welfare, 1975.

Lewis, M., McCollum, A. T., Schwartz, A. H., & Grunt, J. A. Informed consent in pediatric research. *Children*, 1969, *16*, 143–148.

Ley, H. L. Federal law and patient consent. *Annals of the New York Academy of Sciences*, 1970, *169*, 523–527.

Lloyd, J. K. Clinical research with children. In *Issues in research with human subjects* (NIH Publication No. 80–1858). Washington, D.C.: Department of Health, Education, and Welfare, 1980.

Lowe, C. U. Pediatrics: Proper utilization of children as research subjects. *Annals of the New York Academy of Sciences*, 1970, *169*, 337–343.

Lowe, C. U., Alexander, D, & Mishkin, B. Nonttherapeutic research on chidren: An ethical dilemma. *Pediatrics*, 1974, *84*, 468–472.

Martin, D. C., Arnold, J. D., Zimmerman, T. F., & Richard, R. H. Human subjects in clinical research—A report on three studies. *New England Journal of Medicine*, 1968, *279*, 1426–1431.

McCormick, R. A. Proxy consent in the experimentation situation. *Perspectives in Biology and Medicine*, 1974, *18*, 2–20.

Menges, R. J. Openness and honesty vs. coercion and deception in psychological research. *American psychologist*, 1973, *28*, 1030–1034.

Mills, D. H. Whither informed consent: *Journal of the American Medical Association*, 1974, 229, 305–310.

Mitchell, R. G. The child and experimental medicine. *British Medical Journal*, 1964, *1*, 721–727.

National Commission for the Protection of Human Subjects of Biomedical and Behavioral Research. *Research involving children.* (Publication No. OS 77–004). Washington, D.C: Department of Health, Education, and Welfare, 1977.

O'Donnell, T. J. Informed consent. *Journal of the American Medical Association*, 1974, *227*, 73.

Oetting, E. R. A response to "Science, psychology and deception." *Bulletin of British Psychology and Sociology*, 1975, *28*, 268–269.

Orne, M. T. On the social psychology of the psychological experiment: With particular reference to demand characteristics and their implications. *American Psychologist*, 1964, *17*, 776–783.

Pappworth, M. H. *Human guinea pigs.* Boston: Beacon Press Press, 1967.

Ramsey, P. *The patient as person.* New Haven: Yale University Press, 1970.

Ramsey, P. The enforcement of morals: Nontherapeutic research on children. *Hastings Center Report*, August 1976, *21.*

Reichler, R. J. Testimony to the National Commission for the Protection of Human Subjects of Biomedical and Behavioral Research on behalf of the American Academy of Child Psychiatry. April 1976.

Reiss, A. J. *Selected issues in informed consent and confidentiality with special reference to behavioral/social science research/inquiry.* Paper prepared for the National Comission for the Protection of Human Subjects of Biomedical and Behavioral Research. Washington, D.C.: U.S. Department of Health, Education, and Welfare, 1976.

Resnick, J. H., & Schwartz, T. Ethical standards as an independent variable in psychological research. *American Psychologist*, 1973, *28*, 134–139.

Reynolds, P. D. On the protection of human subjects and social science. *International Social Science Journal*, 1972, *24*, 693–719.

Ring, K., Wallston, K., & Corey, M. Mode of debriefing as a factor affecting subjective reaction to a Milgrim-type obedience experiment: An ethical inquiry. *Representative Research in Social Psychology*, 1970, *1*, 67–88.

Robbins, L. N. Problems in follow-up studies. *American Journal of Psychiatry*, 1977, *134*, 904–907.

Romano, J. Reflections on informed consent. *Archives of General Psychiatry*, 1974, *30*, 129–135.

Rosen, C. E. Why clients relinquish their rights to privacy under sign-away pressures. *Professional Psychology*, 1977, February, 17–24.

Ruebhausen, O. M., & Brim, O. G. Privacy and behavioral research. *American Psychologist*, 1966, *21*, 423–444.

Seeman, J. Deception in psychological research. *American Psychologist*, 1969, *24*, 1025–1028.

Shaw, A. Dilemmas of "informed consent" in children. *New England Journal of Medicine*, 1973, *289*, 885–890.

Shipley, T. Misinformed consent: An enigma in modern social science reearch. *Ethics in Science and Medicine*, 1977, *4,* 93–106.

Shirkey, H. C. Therapeutic orphans. *Journal of Pediatrics*, 1968, *72*, 119–120.

Silverman, I. Nonreactive methods and the law. *American Psychologist*, 1975, *30*, 764–769.

Singer, E. *Informed consent: Consequences for response rate and response quality in social surveys.* Paper presented at the meeting of the American Sociological Association, Chicago, 1977.

Smith, H. T. and Stone, L. J. Developmental psychology. *Annual Review of Psychology*, 1961, *12*, 1–26.

Society for Research on Child Development. *Ethical standards for research with children.* Chicago: Society for Research in Child Development, 1973.

Striker, L. J. The true deceiver. *Psychological Bulletin*, 1967, *68*, 13–20.

Striker, L. J., Messick, S., & Jackson, D. N. Evaluating deception in psychological research. *Psychological Bulletin*, 1969, *71*, 343–351.

Swazey, J. Protecting the "animal of necessity": Limits to inquiry in clinical investigation. *Daedalus*, 1978, *107*, 129–145.

Tannenbaum., A. S., & Cooke, R. A. *Research involving children*. Paper prepared for the Natioal Commission for the Protection of Human Subjects of Biomedical and Behavioral Research. Washington, D.C.: U.S. Department of Health, Education, and Welfare, 1976.

Tesch, F. E. Debriefing research participants: Though this be method there is madness to it. *Journal of Personality and Social Psychology*, 1977, *4*, 217–224.

Veatch, R. *Three theories of informed consent: Philosophical foundations and policy considerations*. Paper prepared for the National Commission for the Protection of Human Subjects of Biomedical and Behavioral Research. Washington, D.C.: U.S. Department of Health, Education, and Welfare, 1976.

Warwick, D. P. Deceptive research: Social scientists ought to stop lying. *Psychology Today*, 1975, *10*, 38–40.

Wilson, D. W., & Donnerstein, E. Legal and ethical aspects of nonreactive social psychological research. *American Psychologist*, 1976, *31*, 765–773.

Worsfold, V. L. A philosophical justification of children's rights. *Harvard Educational Review*, 1974, *44*, 142–157.

Zeisel, H. Reducing the hazards of human experiments through modifications in research desigh. *Annals of the New York Academy of Sciences*, 1970, *169*, 475–486.

Part IV

Implementing Consent Standards

CHAPTER 11

Preparing Children for Decision Making

Implications of Legal Socialization Research

JUNE LOUIN TAPP
and
GARY B. MELTON

Over the past 20 years, psychologists and legal scholars alike increasingly have recognized the expanding activity of the law (Bermant, Nemeth, & Vidmar, 1976; Konecni & Ebbesen, 1980; Monahan & Loftus, 1982; Sales, 1977; Sarat, 1977; Tapp, 1969, 1976, 1977, 1980). Its role as a primary socializing agent parallel to church, home, and school has been recognized in both the East and the West. With increased recognition of the importance of law and normative ordering, there has been increased study of the acquisition of legal values within and between rule/justice systems (*e.g.*, home, school, union, community) as well as the characteristics of particular legal cultures (*e.g.*, Adelson, 1970, 1971; Friedman, 1971/1977, 1975; Hess & Tapp, 1969; Minturn & Tapp, 1970; Sarat, 1977; Tapp, 1971, 1976). This search has included investigations dealing with the development of legal reasoning patterns and the configuration of legal beliefs (Levine, 1979; Levine & Tapp, 1977; Tapp, 1970, 1974; Tapp &

JUNE LOUIN TAPP ● Institute of Child Development, University of Minnesota, Minneapolis, Minnesota 55455. **GARY B. MELTON** ● Department of Psychology, University of Nebraska, Lincoln, Nebraska 68588. Portions of this chapter were presented in an invited address by the first author at the 18th Inter-American Society of Psychology Congress, Santo Domingo, June 1981. The ideas presented in some other sections of the chapter were published by the second author in a chapter in J. S. Henning's volume on *The Rights of Children: Legal and Psychological Perspectives* (Melton, 1982).

Keniston, 1976; Tapp & Kohlberg, 1971; Tapp & Levine, 1970, 1974, 1977). The reported trends, based on developmental, cross-cultural, and occupational group data, "provide an important key to the structure of legal culture" (Sarat, 1977, p. 453).

Legal socialization has been a distinct area of inquiry since the late 1960s (Tapp, 1969, 1970, 1971, 1974; Tapp & Levine, 1970, 1974). After a cross-national, six-country, seven-culture study of some 5,000 urban preadolescents' socialization into compliance systems (*e.g.*, family, school, religion, local or national government, friendship) discussed in Hess and Tapp (1969) and Minturn and Tapp (1970), Tapp separated legal development from political and moral to underscore the importance of understanding reasoning about "legal" norms such as a rule-guided *or* law-consciousness sense and a fair-play *or* justice sense. Legal socialization delineates that aspect of the socialization process dealing with legal beliefs and behaviors, the internationalization of "rule" norms, the conditions of obtaining legal compliance, and competence. It focuses on development of individual standards for making sociolegal judgments *and* for using the legal network—the law—to press claims or obtain rights as well as resolve conflicts and settle disputes.

The Relevance of Legal Socialization Research

The legal socialization literature is of particular import in consideration of children's competence to consent. First, much of the research on legal socialization has focused on development of concepts (*e.g.*, law, rights) basic to a competent understanding of the power to give or refuse consent (see Chapter 12, for a discussion of competence as *understanding*). This research is useful in identifying the level of competence of children at various ages, or at least in clarifying expectable developmental sequences in understanding of these key concepts. However, it should be noted that the relevance of such conceptualizations is dependent upon the elements of understanding legally required for competence to consent in a particular situation. Thus, the standard for competence to consent to treatment might be limited to an understanding of what a particular treatment entails and of its probable consequences. Nonetheless, it is arguable that such understanding is moot without an appreciation that the patient is *entitled* to make a choice in the matter, that it is his or her *right* to decide. Otherwise, the "voluntariness" of the decision may be suspect, regardless of the child's sophistication about the medical procedures themselves.

Second, research on factors enhancing legal socialization may provide indications of methods of preparing children for exercising legal rights and of the degree to which such preparation is likely to be helpful. Such information may be useful in setting age-based thresholds for competence to consent. Even if the *average* age of attainment of understanding of key concepts underlying legal reasoning were attained at age 12 (hypothetically), there still might be reason to permit children to consent at younger ages if there were evidence that younger children (at age 9, for example) could be *taught* to exercise competent decision making. The issue here is the need to attend to developmental indicators as much as chronometric ones (*i.e.*, stage-based criteria as well as age-based ones for competence to consent. Additionally, knowledge of the process by which such "early" competence is attainable might also be helpful in teaching children to exercise power of consent meaningfully, regardless of the age at which *per se* competence to consent (or a rebuttable presumption of competence) is set. Essentially, then, it is important (a) to consider the age and stage relation in developing criteria for an individual's ability to consent, and (b) to identify the processes and educative (socializing) strategies that could move persons to more complex, competent levels of legal reasoning (understanding). Legal socialization research identifies some characteristics and conditions necessary to the preparation of materials or experiences that enhance legal understanding and exercise legal rights (Tapp, 1974; Tapp, Gunnar, & Keating, 1982).

Third, the legal socialization literature may indicate possible socializing effects of the consent process itself. As Melton suggests in Chapter 2, if the exercise of power of consent increases a child's appreciation of the application of law to himself or herself, there may be reason to support increased self-determination for minors, independent of their level of competence. The experience of giving or refusing consent may enhance a child's sense of himself or herself as a full participant in the legal process, broadly defined, and consequently may help to prepare the child for exercise of the rights and responsibilities of citizenship in a democracy. Of particular import is the possibility that such empowerment may increase a child's conceptualization of the law as a "mobility belt" (Tapp & Levine, 1974), a means of achieving change of social status and redress of grievances. Tapp and Levine (1974) have succinctly indicated the social significance of legal socialization in this respect:

> In broader terms, the socialization of conceptions of rights, justice, and claims-consciousness is essential if individuals are to develop their capacities as creators as well as consumers of law. As persons develop greater experience in mobilizing the law, other legal behaviors beyond simple legal compliance are stressed. In providing a legitimate mechanism for participation and conflict, the law demonstrates a potential for stimulating just, humane, and autonomous modes of legal reasoning. Furthermore, to the extent that the law functions as a mobility belt, it can have a crucial impact on socializing a more pervasive sense of competence in individuals—especially among the variously "poor." (p. 8)

In short, legal socialization research is relevant to the question of the ages and social conditions under which children can be expected to be competent to give or refuse consent (at least insofar as a standard of *understanding* is used). Moreover, this literature may inform decisions as to whether the threshold for competence should be low or high. That is, the legal socialization literature may provide important information as to whether there are particular benefits from encouraging children to exercise consent; such research may also provide clues as to means of educating children to exercise consent more competently. Therefore, the legal socialization literature is likely to have import for both "kiddie libbers" and "child savers" in making policy decisions about children's attainment of power of consent (see, for discussion of this distinction among child advocates, Mnookin, 1978; Rogers & Wrightsman, 1978). For those who seek to increase self-determination by minors, the legal socialization literature will provide clues as to points in development at which privacy of decision making can be respected without undue concern that the child's decision will be "unknowing." Legal socialization research may also inform the child liberator as to means of preparing the child to be a decisionmaker. On the other hand, for those interested in "saving" children, particularly children from disadvantaged backgrounds, the legal socialization literature may provide information concerning the kinds of opportunities required for children to begin to exercise a sense of empowerment (cf. Rappaport, 1977) and eventually to work for improvement of the status of themselves and their community.

Cognitive Theory of Legality

For this chapter, we briefly describe the Tapp-Levine cognitive model of legal reasoning plus some developmental and cross-cultural as well as occupational and situational findings, with primary emphasis on the implications of this work for consent by children. More detailed presentations of the Tapp-Levine theory are available elsewhere (Levine & Tapp, 1977; Tapp, 1969, 1970, 1974, 1976; Tapp & Kohlberg, 1971/1977; Tapp & Levine, 1971, 1974, 1977). The utility of the model is its identification of underlying reasoning structures with definable characteristics, basic to sociolegal judgments. This model of legal reasoning applies Piaget's (1932, 1947) and Kohlberg's (1963, 1969) moral stage typology to the realm of law. While the Tapp-Levine model adapts Kohlberg's descriptive labels to characterize levels of legal reasoning, and so describes "ideal" types, the theoretical (epistemological) and empirical roots reside more with Piaget who attends to the impact of cultural/social determinates on cognitive capacities (Piaget, 1969; Piaget & Inhelder, 1969; see also Berg & Mussen, 1975).

Drawing from cognitive developmental stage theory (Kolberg, 1963, 1969; Piaget, 1932, 1947) and social learning/psychological theory (Aronfreed, 1968; Bandura & McDonald, 1963; Berkowitz, 1964; Hoffman, 1970; Kelman, 1958), Tapp and Levine formulated a model of legal reasoning that adapted Kohlberg's terminology for three legal levels—I: Preconventional; II: Conventional; III: Postconventional. I is a law-deferring, sanction-oriented stance; II is a law-maintaining, conformity posture; III is a law-creating, principled perspective. Each level represents a qualitatively distinctive way of characterizing one's rights, roles, and responsibilities in relation to the legal system. Together, the three comprise a developmental (but not always invariant) sequence wherein higher levels (III > II > I) reflect more accommodative, integrative, and complex structures of reasoning.

A brief description of the three legal levels follows (see Tapp & Levine, 1974, for more detailed discussion). A Level I (preconventional) view of law and of legal obligation focuses on external consequences and authority; an instrumental hedonism tempers these legal valuations. At Level II, the conventional law-maintenance level, people worry about fulfilling role expectations; they obey or disobey for personal and social conformity reasons. The postconventional Level III is the law-creating, principled thinking perspective. Here developmentally advanced (cognitively complex) persons see the need for social systems, but differentiate between the values of a given social order and universal principles. In the United States, Martin Luther King may have been a twentieth-century example with such a postconventional reasoning capacity; Thomas Jefferson, an eighteenth-century one.

The implications of this broad theory of legal socialization may be illustrated in terms of the development of a specific legal concept, that of rights, particularly as applied to children themselves (Melton, 1980, in press). Briefly, Level I reasoning involves a confusion of rights with what one can in fact do or have. By such a conceptualization, children have rights only if adults allow them. Level II involves a confusion of rights with privileges associated with being "nice" or accorded by one's role, physical competence, or social status. Finally, Level III concepts of rights are based on abstract ethical principles, such as freedom of the press and right to privacy. In such a framework, rights may exist "naturally" without respect to their legal recognition because of their logical necessity for maintenance of human dignity. Perhaps the best-known example of such thinking was Jefferson's declaration of the "unalienable rights" of "life, liberty, and the pursuit of happiness."

Each characterization in the Tapp-Levine theory is based on empirically derived categories from open-ended classic jurisprudential-type questions in the Tapp-Levine Rule-Law Interview (TLRLI). Examples include: "What is a right? What is a rule? A law? A fair law?" The TLRLI focuses on five substantive areas: the value and function of rules and law; the conditions of legal compliance; the changeability and breakablility of rules; the dynamics of justice/fairness; and the nature of rights consciousness. It measures legal reasoning about such basic jurisprudential concepts as rules, laws, rights, fairness, and compliance and permits classification of legal reasoning according to three cognitive developmental levels. The basic 15-item version of the TLRLI is appended to this chapter.

The TLRLI has been standardized cross-culturally and developmentally over age and occupational groups in classroom, courtroom, and cellroom contexts on samples totaling nearly 6,000 (Hess & Tapp, 1969; Levine, 1979; Levine & Tapp, 1977; Minturn & Tapp, 1970; Tapp, 1974, 1978; Tapp & Kohlberg, 1971/1977; Tapp & Keniston, 1976; Tapp & Levine, 1974, 1977). The initial cross-national scoring reliability was 77%; earlier U.S. developmental studies averaged 83%; recent U.S. reliabilities ranged between 86.2 and 98% (Levine, 1979; Tapp, 1978).

Results: Cross-Cultural, Developmental, Occupational, and Situational

Basic research using this framework yielded aggregate data from four types of populations: (a) primary age school children from kindergarten to grade 3 (5 to 8 years); (b) middle school preadolescents from grades 4, 6, and 8 (10 to 14 years); (c) college men and women in diverse university settings (17 to 21 years); (d) adult groups of graduating law students, parents, elementary/ high school teachers, federal penitentiary inmates, and jurors (20 to 60 years). Results from these studies confirmed (a) that responses to the TLRLI questions are classifiable into the three legal levels; (b) that there were age differences in response to classic jurisprudential questions; (c) that these differences paralleled a developmental progression from preconventional (I) to conventional (II) to postconventional (III) levels found in moral and political socialization studies; (d) that across cultures, status (age), or occupational groups similar patterns were observed; (e) that the conventional level of legal reasoning (II) was modal for adolescent and for most adult groups; and (f) that socializing strategies (such as legal information, conflict, participation, and legal continuity) affected jurisprudential norms.

Studies of the U.S. youth from kindergarten to college, middle school preadolescents from six nations, and three adult groups (*i.e.,* law students, teachers, prisoners) vividly showed these patterns (Levine & Tapp, 1977; Tapp & Kohlberg, 1971/1977; Tapp & Levine, 1971, 1974). Moreover, recent research has moved beyond consideration of *aggregate* responses on a series of questions to a focus on *individual* legal reasoning. Levine's study (1979) of fifth-, tenth-, and eleventh-graders demonstrated that there was sufficient consistency across an individual's responses to permit their meaningful classification into preconventional, conventional, and postconventional modes of thought. Furthermore, her data analyses clearly indicated that the differences that emerged in reasoning modes were true differences that could not be attributed to measurement error (Levine, 1979, pp. 69–71). Other data from samples of jurors (Tapp & Keniston, 1976), upper and lower division college students (Tapp, 1978), incarcerated mothers (Stanton, 1978), and, in a recent investigation, day care parents further confirmed such patterns (Tapp, Vopava, Kolmar, & Richardson, 1982).

Related investigations similarly confirm the viability and utility of a cognitive model and measure of legality (e.g., Morash, 1979; Melton, 1980; Stanton, 1978). For example, in a study of children's concepts of rights, Melton (1980) found a developmental progression and conceptual characterization that paralleled earlier work (Aliotta & Tapp, 1979; Levine, 1979; Tapp, 1978). Ample research in political and legal psychology and in moral development likewise supports the hypothesis of an age-related sequence in the growth of ideas concerning law, justice, and morality (e.g., Adelson, 1971; Berg & Mussen, 1975; Damon, 1975, 1977, 1979; DePalma & Foley, 1975; Gallatin, 1972, 1976; Gallatin & Adelson, 1971/1977; Torney, 1971/1977; Torney & Brice, 1979).

In addition to identifying a developmental progression in legal reasoning, work has also focused on the relationship between legal and moral judgment. As early as 1971, Tapp and Kohlberg conceived of a congruence between legal and moral development, but Levine's study (1979) was the first to examine empirically this relationship as well as the utility and validity of the legal levels theory for characterizing individuals' perspectives toward law and justice. Administering the TLRLI, Kohlberg's moral judgment scale, and other instruments to approximately 100 children, Levine corroborated that legal reasoning was significantly related to age and to moral judgment controlling for age. In addition, she found that legal reasoning and moral judgment continued to be positively and significantly related to age independent of the other, confirming that these are distinct, albeit related, cognitive developmental processes. Finally, her work pointed to particularly attitudinal but also behavioral linkages with both these constructs. Thus, Levine's work underscores the construct validity of a cognitive model of legal reasoning, its potential for explaining beliefs and behaviors, and the reliability of the TLRLI at both aggregate and individual levels.

Apart from coming to better understand the components and correlates of legal reasoning, research in legal socialization over the past decade has also been directed to studying the impact of socializing strategies such as legal information, continuity, participation, and conflict on development of an ethical legality (Tapp, 1978, Tapp & Keniston, 1976; Tapp & Levine, 1971, 1974; see also Tapp, Gunnar, & Keating, 1982). Analyses of courtroom data confirmed that rights-consciousness can be "leveled" I, II, or III paralleling the reasoning progression of attitudes toward law and justice (Aliotta & Tapp,

1979). They also suggested that decision making in small groups such as juries—involving acquistion of legal information, participation (roleplaying), conflict, and connection of legal concepts across social systems—can affect legal level positively (Smolka & Tapp, 1979; Tapp & Keniston, 1976).

Basically, then, findings from varying age cohorts and other groups support several recurrent and pertinent themes on the origins of jurisprudence and the psychological limits of legality. First, there are distinct and classifiable patterns of legal reasoning that progress from a preconventional law-obeying to a conventional law-maintaining to a postconventional law-creating orientation (I to II to III). Second, this progression is marked by more developmental (age) than situational or cultural effects, but the variation among occupational groups reveals the interactive nature of legal development. Third, over all groups, the conventional perspective is modal. Nevertheless, by late adolescence, and particularly by college age, sizable minorities exhibit postconventional principles. Fourth, while no person's answers are 100% at any one level, primary school children show more preconventional reasoning, adolescents typically give conventional responses, and college and adult groups are more postconventional than preconventional. This was the case in classroom, courtroom, and cellroom contexts. Fifth, although postconventional legal reasoning did not dominate in any age group, there is evidence that certain intense ecologically valid socializing settings (like a jury) may move persons to higher levels. The same effect may occur when children participate in settings in which their legal reasoning is challenged.

An Empirical Example

To illustrate more graphically the configuration of legal reasoning—and thus the bases of legal competence—we describe the patterns of response to the question, "Are there times when it might be right to break a rule (law)?" The five general findings delineated in the preceding section, and the three reasons stated earlier about the relevance of legal socialization research, are further demonstrated by data drawn across age groups and different settings (*e.g.*, classroom, courtroom, home, prison).

United States Youth

With regard to the legitimacy of rule violation, a developmental progression emerged among youth: 80% of the primary schoolers revealed a preconventional legality, with 55% adopting an absolutist stance against rule breaking. The youngest children equated rule breaking *per se* with badness; by preadolescence, youth accepted that certain conditions preclude compliance:

73% of the middle schoolers focused on the morality of the circumstance. An eighth-grade boy reasoned, "Well, it depends on what's going on. If it's a matter of life and death or you know something pretty important, then it's all right. But is should be followed as much as possible." Underscoring a sequential progression in legal development, by college a postconventional legality emerged as the dominant mode for the majority. College students argued that compliance must be assessed against the inherent rightness or morality of the rule, independent of the circumstance. A college woman's response typified the position: "[I would break a rule] when the rule is immoral or unjust because I believe that people are morally accountable for their actions and, thus, above the law or rules." To these youth, an act following from a valid application of "universal" moral principles is the essence of legality even if it necessitates violating a particular rule or law.

Cross-Cultural Youth

Congruent cross-cultural results further supported the hypothesis of universality in legal development. In five of the seven cultures, children accepted the possibility of rule departure; only in two cultures was the preconventional, "no rule is breakable" orientation the modal response. Although reasons varied, in five out of seven cultures more eight-graders maintained that rules or laws are breakable than did their fourth-grade counterparts. Adopting a strongly conventional posture, they demonstrated increased acceptance of the morality of circumstances legitimizing rule breaking. Postconventional reasoning that emerged in the United States study was not a dominant justification for rule violation cross-culturally among preadolescents. Yet this child's answer captured the transition:

> When you're hungry you go in the store and steal something. When you need the money, like for someone kidnapped in your family, then you steal money from the bank, pay the ransom, and try to pay the money back to the bank. Money and food could be replaced, but the person's life couldn't.

Adult

Overall, the majority response for adult figures fell short of a principled legality. For example, of the fledgling law professional, 67% reflected a conventional orientation as did 54% of the teachers and 36% of the prisoners. Twenty percent of the inmates also manifested preconventional modes of thought. While the adult groups generally gave conventional responses to this question, sizable minorities among them *did* attain a postconventional legality, ranging from teachers at 34% to lawyers at 46% to prisoners at 40%.

These patterns in the adult data attest to the progression and continuity in legal reasoning between childhood and adulthood. Like the youth, most adults had not fully developed their capacities to shape their systems of law. For example, in Levine's (1979) study of elementary and high school youth, both groups gave conventional (Level II) answers—83% and 73%, respectively.

In the Tapp Wounded Knee jury study, however (where jurors experienced "socialization"), the impanelled jurors stressed fairness and universal morality to a greater extent than the other juror groups that had not been exposed to the clash of ideas in the trial itself: 67% gave Level III answers in comparison to 43% for prospective jurors who had been removed by challenge by one of the parties and 26% for persons randomly selected from the jury pool. Basically the impanelled jurors gave significantly more *morality of the rule* answers than *morality of the circumstances* ones. A Level I answer was "no," while a juror at Level II observed, "Yes, I would. Well, I think a rule is just a guideline that is not hard and fast; you just . . . try to stay within 'em and if you can't, well you do it the way you see it best," and one at Level III said, "Yes. When you feel yourself that it's really wrong, that it'll do a lot of harm, and it does no good discussing it with people. Also, if there's a general consensus that it's wrong, but you can't get it changed. Because I think some of them aren't good. I think if they aren't good and you care enough about the fact that they're not good, then you have to break them" (see Tapp, Gunnar, & Keating, 1982).

In addition to the illustrative patterns of response, other indicators showed the positive socializing effects of involvement as a juror in a controversial trial. For example, while no juror groups were at a preconventional level (I) of legal reasoning before the trial, nine months later at the conclusion of the Wounded Knee trial, all (100%) of the impanelled jurors scored at the postconventional level (III).

As we know, home and school are important "legal" institutions for teaching and learning rules and norms for children and youth. One place where adult figures can experience the socializing role of the law is through jury service. A parallel participating experience in making and maintaining laws (*i.e.*, legal rules) is available to children in other legal decision-making contexts, such as the experience of giving or refusing consent. While age is a crucial variable in the socialization process, situational variables and socialization experiences also vitally affect the rate of development. Since socialization and resocialization continue through the life cycle, one basic question is the extent to which legal experiences use—or can use—socialization strategies to stimulate competence for both child and adult.

Implications of the Developmental Findings

The general finding from legal socialization studies conducted thus far suggest that "liberal" acceptance of children's decision-making ability is well-founded. The research results strengthen the case insofar as competence to consent is predicated on a basic understanding of concepts inherent in legal decision making (*i.e.*, definitions of law/rule, fairness/justice, rights/right). Comprehension of the situations in which such dilemmas arise also further enhance children's capacity to make specific decision based on basic principles. Tapp's report of the striking similarity of children in six countries on the meanings of law, rule breakability, and compliance adds more fuel (1970; Tapp & Kohlberg, 1971/1977). Aliotta and Tapp's later report on the parallel developmental progression on adult jurors and their kin's concepts of rule and right (1979) provided another case in point. Melton's (1980) finding that the average third-grader has some understanding of the concept of a right is illustrative. Moreover, while Level III reasoning based on abstract and ethical legal principles is generally not observed before a person reaches adolescence, it is important to note, for both legal and social purposes, that the majority of adults also do not use such principled reasoning. Indeed, as noted earlier with respect to rule-making, early adolescents generally achieve conventional legal reasoning, the modal level of reasoning among adults. This finding is supportive of the conclusion of others (*e.g.*, Grisso & Vierling, 1978) that there is no empirical basis for depriving adolescents of power of consent, insofar as the rationale is incompetence. Holding children to a standard of competence not attained by most adults may violate fundamental fairness, given the nature of the privacy and liberty interests involved.

Moreover, while developmental sequences in acquision of legal concepts are well established, it is also true that the rate of these progressions may be highly affected by the nature of socialization experiences. Indeed, Tapp's Wounded Knee jury study suggest that *adults'* legal reasoning may be enhanced by experience with conflict of ideas and participation in decision making. Melton's finding of marked social class differences in the age at which children achieve Level II reasoning in concepts of their rights may be interpreted similarly. Presumably lower-class children are less likely than more privileged peers to experience both entitlement itself (cf. Coles, 1977) and modeling of diverse social roles and decision making. Thus, while maturation may account for much of the variance in level of legal socialization, social factors clearly affect the rate and endpoint of such development.

Several policy inferences may be drawn from this general finding. First, children's level of competence to consent at various ages may vary systematically across situations and social-class groups and may make purely age-based thresholds for competence difficult to draw, if such thresholds are to be based on the functioning of the average child at a given age—rather than concomitantly with stage also. In other words, use of a chronometric measure or age standard only rather than a developmental one too (*i.e.*, age and stage) may be "unfair" to the child and the legal system. On the other hand, to the extent that distinctions in personal liberty of minors based on class distinctions are politically and ethically undesirable (or even legally proscribed), purely individual tests of competence to consent may also present difficult dilemmas. This possibility is greater with children from disadvantaged groups who are less likely to have incurred the kinds of socializing experiences that enhance sense of entitlement and general legal development.

However, these dilemmas may be less troublesome than they appear at first glance. Given requisite cognitive development, children's legal, political, and moral development may be enhanced by appropriate educational experiences. It is probable that social-class differences in legal socialization could be substantially reduced by systematic efforts to increase a sense of entitlement among disadvantaged children. Indeed, to the extent that *participation* in legal decision making is itself a conflict-inducing experience, exercise of power of consent itself may actually be socializing. Practitioners and researchers alike need to know the educative and experiential conditions that move children, regardless of social heritage, to make autonomous, informed decisions (*i.e.*, consent choices) in legal settings. The means by which socialization might occur will be explored in the remainder of this chapter.

Principles of Legal Education

To date, the conventional or system maintenance level (II) has been modal among adults in most societies. The presence of conventional and postconventional (I and III) legality in children, youth, and adults suggests that social experiences in particular environments can limit or extend an individual's natural capacity (Rest, 1973, 1979; Tapp & Keniston, 1976). As psychologists, we want to know the socializing conditions that move persons to make autonomous choices and to use law in a just manner.

In efforts toward such socialization, it is important to stimulate both vertical and horizontal development of moral and legal reasoning. That is, one hopes to induce successively higher level *structures* of moral and legal judgment. At the same time, as transitions occur to higher levels, it is desirable to extend the new level of reasoning to continually broader ranges of concerns. Thus, legal education may be conceptualized both as a means of exposing children to higher levels of reasoning and as providing an opportunity to extend existing reasoning to specific concepts (*e.g.*, rights) that have important implications for full participation in a democratic society.

As developed by Tapp and Levine (1974, 1977; see also Melton, 1982), four socializing strategies, derived from experimental settings, seem basic to stimulating movement to a higher level of legal reasoning and thus socializing for an ethical legality. The four are listed below.

1. *Legal knowledge.* This strategy involves transmitting information. Effective socialization includes "schooling" about rights, rules, and remedies. Such education allows individuals to become creators as well as consumers of law. Without substantive knowledge of law and the legal process, individuals cannot as effectively use a service, invoke a right, redress a grievance, question a police officer, or hire a lawyer. However, knowledge alone is not a sufficient condition to stimulate integrative, independent, and critical thought.

From a cognitive-developmental or interactionist perspective, development of new cognitive structures or schemata is more significant than mere acquisition of information or memorization of facts. While rights are theoretically absolute, in practice the application even of legal rights requires much more complex cognitive processes than simply "knowing" the law. While natural rights obviously involve complex abstractions, legal rights also require high-level judgments. As Freund (1977) has noted, there is a danger that an emphasis on learning the rules of law will result in a neglect of the dialectical process by which such rules are developed, tested, and revised.

Furthermore, exposure to legal dicta will not in and or itself create a higher-level legal reasoning. For example, most law students do not exhibit postconventional legal reasoning (Levine & Tapp, 1977; Tapp & Levine, 1974).

Nonetheless, without a basic knowledge of what rights are and of procedures for their assertion, even a principled thinker may not be able to apply (or create) the law. If children, and perhaps parents, do not know their rights, then children's rights may in fact be moot. (Melton discusses this point in more detail in Chapter 2 of this volume.)

2. *Mismatch and conflict.* Mismatch in value orientations or value conflicts stimulates the construction of more complex forms of thought. Some argue that increases in disequilibrium afford excellent conditions for development. In both cognitive-developmental and social learning theories, conflict has been identified as a strategy in value education. As Haan, Smith, and Block (1968) said: "Conflictless experiences are probably incompatible with both moral and cognitive growth" (p. 200).

While the literature concerning factors affecting attitudes toward children's rights is still sparse, the available literature on attitudes toward civil rights generally confirms the importance of exposure to conflicting points of view. There is broad consensus among adults in favor of such democratic principles as freedom of speech (Erskine & Siegel, 1975; Prothro & Grigg, 1960; Wilson, 1975; Zellman, 1975). However, that consensus breaks down when opinion is gathered concerning concrete applications of the principles (*i.e.*, whether a Communist should be allowed to give a public speech). The best demographic predictor of whether an individual will espouse civil liberties in specific situations is educational level (Montero, 1975; Prothro & Grigg, 1960;

Wilson, 1975; Zellman, 1975). Prothro and Grigg found, for example, that regional and income differences in attitudes toward civil liberties disappeared when education was held constant.

The most common explanation of such findings is that higher education results in exposure to diverse points of view and increases tolerance for them. Education is thought to reduce tendencies to see issues in black and white. As students explore issues in depth, they come to appreciate their complexity and to understand how people can reach different conclusions. Furthermore, as people become more sophisticated in their thinking, illogical reasoning may arouse more dissonance for them. Educated people may be less likely to tolerate the inconsistency in advocating free speech for all and then denying it to an unpopular group. (See Melton, 1982, for more extensive discussion of the relationship between education and libertarianism.)

3. *Participation.* Through participation, an individual can gain an appreciation of someone else's framework. The centrality of such perspective taking to mature moral thought and action is emphasized by cognitive-developmental psychologists (Damon, 1977; Flavell, Botkin, & Fry, 1968; Selman & Damon, 1975). In addition to role-taking opportunities, participation emphasizes reciprocity and cooperation. To the extent that participatory experiences stimulate empathy, enhance tolerance for dissent, and foster critical abilities and internal controls, they embody a postconventional legality. In short, while advanced levels of legal and moral reasoning require increasingly abstract cognitive operations, such cognitive skills are not sufficient. Such reasoning is also dependent upon an awareness of the circumstances and needs of others and the interdependence of people. One implication of such a view is that psycholegal development is facilitated by the child's actually *experiencing* rights and participating in roles that allow for some degree of self-determination.

4. *Legal continuity.* Rule-creating and fair-play opportunities (and thus experience of justice and injustice, obedience and disobedience, and so on) occur in many daily contexts: home, school, church. All these rule-guided systems are experientially "legal." This broader view of the law emphasizes the rule-making power and connection of various legal systems from family to school to government. Recognition of the continuity among various compliance, rule, or justice systems should help persons define the interdependent nature of legal activity.

To the extent that these principles are valid, the implications for preparation of children for decision making are clear. First, at a minimum, children need to be informed of their rights. However, teaching rights in list fashion is not sufficient. Second, in order to enhance children's legal reasoning when they are in fact able to exercise or refuse consent, children need to have been exposed to divergent and higher level points of view. Third and perhaps most importantly, they should have an opportunity to experience rights in everyday situations. Legal education is likely to be most effective when children are in fact shown respect and given some responsibility for governance. Fourth, the law is taught in terms of common, real-life situations. Children's sense of the law is likely to be different in a school where "due process" is taught in terms of school disciplinary proceedings from one where it is defined solely in terms of distant abstractions. Similarly, knowledge of the legal system generalizable across diverse settings is more likely to occur when discussion centers on specific issues of consumer protection than when instruction focuses on abstractions about the function of the courts. In other words, children's sense of right in the legal realm needs to be continuous with home and school contexts and experiences if they are to be experienced as more than a list of claims yet to be achieved.

While the general principles of effective preparation for legal decision making may be clear, three important qualifiers should be noted. First, even informing children of their rights in list fashion may require substantial changes in schools as social institutions. Inclusion of material about children's rights and social justice within social studies curricula, even in a purely didactic nonparticipatory format, is likely to require substantial changes in the curricula and probably in many educators' attitudes toward their students. As one of us (Melton, 1982) has noted previously:

> [E]ven this basic spoon-feeding approach to rights education may be threatening to many adults. It is hard to imagine many principals telling students that they are free to express political opinions by wearing armbands or writing controversial articles in the school newspaper. Similarly, many may find it objectionable to tell students that they have the right to access to school records or, as some courts have ruled, that their lockers are private and subject to search only if the authorities have a warrant. Doubtlessly many would view telling minor women about their rights to contraception and abortion as unconscionable. The point is that, although they do not mesh with other principles ... discussed here, purely didactic approaches to teaching rights may themselves represent major steps for many school systems and individual educators.

Second, research on typical legal reasoning of teachers suggests that their reasoning is often not sufficiently different from their students, at least in high school, to provide much conflict (Tapp & Levine, 1974). In view both of this fact and of the attitudinal and organizational changes required, significant school-based legal socialization interventions will probably have to begin with efforts to change the legal development of the *adults* in schools. The lack of postconventional reasoning among many teachers may be mitigated, however, if they can learn to present arguments at a level in fact higher than their own modal level of legal reasoning (*cf.* Kohlberg, 1966).

Third, there has been little research on the *specific* approaches to legal education that are most likely to enhance children's competence in decision making. In part as a result of the efforts of the American Bar Association's

Special Committee on Youth Education for Citizenship, literally scores of law-related education projects have developed (ABA, 1978). However, many of these projects have emphasized *responsibilities* rather than *rights*. Moreover, while there have been some evaluations of the impact of such programs on juveniles' compliance with the law,[1] there are no studies specifically evaluating legal education programs in terms of the effects of such programs on children's sense of entitlement and their competence to consent.[2] Given the impressive body of data on legal socialization in terms of developmental sequences and of socializing experiences in adulthood, such studies of the effects of efforts to enhance legal socialization in childhood would be likely to have considerable theoretical significance as well as to contribute to the applied concerns discussed in this volume.

Keeping in mind these three qualifiers, however, it is important not to lose sight of the state of the literature with respect to the three children's-competency issues we noted early in this chapter. First, the legal socialization literature suggests that basic legal concepts are typically acquired in elementary school, and that early adolescents are typically capable of conventional legal reasoning, the modal level of reasoning among adults. Consequently, insofar as a standard of understanding is used, there is likely to be no reason in most situations to deprive adolescents of power of consent on the basis of competence. Second, there is reason to believe that legal development may be facilitated by provision of legal information, presentation of mismatch and conflict in legal reasoning, opportunities for participation in legal decision making, and instruction in the continuity of the legal system across diverse settings. Thus, children *can* be taught to be more sophisticated legal thinkers. Third, it may be reasonably hypothesized that exercise of the power of consent will itself be socializing, particularly in enhancing an appreciation of the protections of the law as applicable to oneself. Evaluation research on programs designed to increase children's participation in decision making would be useful in testing this hypothesis.

References

Adelson, J. What generation gap? *New York Times Magazine*, January 18, 1970, pp. 1–11.

Adelson, J. The political imagination of the young adolescent. *Daedalus*, 1971, *100*, 1013–1050.

Aliotta, J., & Tapp, J. L. *Developmental, legal, and social aspects of rights—Consciousness*. Unpublished manuscript, University of Minnesota, 1979.

---

[1] Some work in this area is currently underway under the direction of Robert Hunter at the Center for Action Research in Boulder, Colorado.

[2] Melton is currently developing such a research program in collaboration with colleagues in the Department of Psychology and the College of Law at the University of Nebraska-Lincoln and with staff of the Nebraska State Bar Association.

American Bar Association, Special Committee on Youth Education for Citizenship. *Directory of law-related education projects* (3rd ed.). Chicago: ABA, 1978.

Aronfreed, J. *Conduct and conscience: The socialization of internalized control over behavior.* New York: Academic Press, 1968.

Bandura, A., & McDonald, F. J. Influence of social reinforcement and the behavior models in shaping children's moral judgments. *Journal of Abnormal Social Psychology*, 1963, *67*, 274–281.

Berg, N., & Mussen, P. The origins and development of concepts of justice. *Journal of Social Issues*, 1975, *31*(2), 183–201

Berkowitz, L. *The development of motives and values in the child.* New York: Basic Books, 1964.

Bermant, G., Nemeth, C., & Vidmar, N. (Eds.). *Psychology and the law.* Lexington, Mass.: D. C. Heath, 1976.

Coles, R. *Privileged ones.* Vol. 5 of *Children in crisis.* Boston: Little, Brown, 1977.

Damon, W. Early conceptions of positive justice as related to the development of logical operations. *Child Development*, 1975, *46*, 301–312.

Damon, W. *The social world of the child.* San Francisco: Jossey-Bass, 1977.

Damon, W. The genesis of social responsibility in the child. In J. L. Tapp (Chair), *Children's rights and the development of social responsibility.* Symposium presented at the meeting of the American Psychological Association, New York, September 1979.

DePalma, D. J., & Foley, J. M. (Eds.). *Moral development: Current theory and research.* Hillsdale, N.J.: Lawrence Erlbaum, 1975.

Erskine, H., & Siegel, R. L. Civil liberties and the American public. *Journal of Social Issues*, 1975, *31*(2), 13–30.

Flavell, J. H., Botkin, P., Fry, C., Wright, J., & Jarvis, P. *The development of role-taking skills in children.* New York: Wiley, 1968.

Freund, P. A. Law in the schools. In J. L. Tapp & F. J. Levine (Eds.), *Law, justice, and the individual in society.* New York: Holt, Rinehart & Winston, 1977.

Friedman, L. M. *The legal system.* New York: Russell Sage, 1975.

Friedman, L. M. The idea of right as a social and legal cocept. In J. L. Tapp & F. J. Levine (Eds.), *Law, justice, and the individual in society.* New York: Holt, Rinehart & Winston, 1977. (Reprinted from *Journal of Social Issues*, 1971, *27*(2), 189–198.)

Gallatin, J. *The development of political thinking in urban adolescents.* Washington, D.C.: U.S. Department of Health, Education, and Welfare, 1972.

Gallatin, J. The conceptualization of rights: Psychological development and cross-national perspectives. In R. Claude (Ed.), *Comparative human rights.* Baltimore: Johns Hopkins University Press, 1976, 302–325.

Gallatin, J., & Adelson, J. Legal guarantees of individual freedom: A cross-national study of the development of political thought. In J. L. Tapp & F. J. Levine (Eds.), *Law, justice, and the individual in society.* New York: Holt, Rinehart & Winston, 1977. (Reprinted from *Journal of Social Issues*, 1977 *27*(2), 93–108.)

Grisso, T., & Vierling, L. Minors' consent to treatment: A developmental perspective. *Professional Psychology*, 1978, *9*, 412–427.

Haan, N., Smith, B., & Block, J. Moral reasoning of young adults. *Journal of Personality and Social Psychology*, 1968, *10*, 183–201.

Hess, R. D., & Tapp, J. L. *Authority, rules, and aggression: A cross-national study of the socialization of children into compliance system: Part I.* Washington, D.C.: United States Department of Health, Education, and Welfare, 1969.

Kohlberg, L. The development of children's orientations toward a moral order: I. Sequence in the development of moral thought. *Vita Humana*, 1963, *6*, 11–33.

Kohlberg, L. Moral education in the schools: A developmental view. *School Review*, 1966, *74*, 1–30.

Kohlberg, L. Stage and sequence: The cognitive developmental approach to socialization. In D. A. Goslin (Ed.), *Handbook of socialization theory and research.* Chicago: Rand McNally, 1969.

Konecni, V. J., & Ebbesen, E. B. (Eds.). *Social-psychological analysis of legal processes*. San Francisco: Freeman, 1980.

Levine, F. J. *The legal reasoning of youth: Dimensions and correlates*. Unpublished doctoral dissertation, University of Chicago, 1979.

Levine, F. J., & Tapp, J. L. The dialectic of legal socialization in community and school. In J. L. Tapp and F. J. Levine (Eds.), *Law, justice, and the individual in society*. New York: Holt, Rinehart & Winston, 1977.

Melton, G. B. Children's concepts of their rights. *Journal of Clinical Child Psychology*, 1980, *9*, 186–190.

Melton, G. B. Teaching children about their rights. In J. S. Henning (Ed.), *The rights of children: Legal and psychological perspectives*. Springfield, Ill: Charles C Thomas, 1982

Melton, G. B. *Child advocacy: Psychological issues and interventions*. New York: Plenum Press, in press.

Minturn, L., & Tapp, J. L. *Authority, rules, and aggression: A cross-national study of children's judgments of the justice of aggressive confrontations: Part II*. Washington, D.C.: United States Department of Health, Education and Welfare, 1970.

Mnookin, R. H. Children's rights: Beyond kiddie libbers and child savers. *Journal of Clinical Child Psychology*, 1978, *7*, 163–167.

Monahan, J., & Loftus, E. F. The psychology of law. *Annual Review of Psychology*, 1982, *33*, 441–475.

Montero, D. Support for civil liberties among a cohort of high school graduates and college students. *Journal of Social Issues*, 1975, *31*(2), 123–236.

Morash, M. A. *Implications of the theory of legal socialization for understanding the effect of juvenile justice procedures on youths*. Unpublished doctoral dissertation, University of Maryland, 1978.

Piaget, J. *The moral judgment of the child*. New York: Kegan, Paul, Trench, Trubner, 1932.

Piaget, J. *The moral development of the adolescent in two types of society: Primitive and modern*. UNESCO Seminar on Education for International Understanding, July 1947.

Piaget, J. *Science of education and the psychology of the child*. New York: Basic Books, 1969.

Piaget, J., & Inhelder, B. *The psychology of the child*. New York: Basic Books, 1969.

Prothro, J. W., & Grigg, C. W. Fundamental principles of democracy: Bases of agreement and disagreement. *Journal of Politics*, 1960, *22*, 276–294.

Rappaport, J. *Community psychology: Values, research, and action*. New York: Holt, Rinehart & Winston, 1977.

Rest, J. Patterns of preference and comprehension in moral judgment. *Journal of Personality*, 1973, *41*, 86–109.

Rest, J. *The D. I. T.* Minneapolis: University of Minnesota Press, 1979.

Rogers, C. M., & Wrightsman, L. S. Attitudes toward children's rights: Nurturance of self-determination. *Journal of Social Issues*, 1978, *32*(2), 59–68.

Sales, B. D. (Ed.), *Psychology in the legal process*. New York: Spectrum, 1977.

Sarat, A. Studying American legal culture: An assessment of survey evidence. *Law and Society Review*, 1977, *11*, 427–488.

Selman, R., & Damon, W. The necessity (but insufficiency) of social perspective taking for conceptions of justice at three early levels. In D. DePalma & J. Foley (Eds.), *Contemporary issues in moral development*. Hillsdale, N.J.: Lawrence Erlbaum, 1975.

Smolka, P., & Tapp. J. L. *The jury as a socialization experience*. Unpublished manuscript, University of Minnesota, 1979.

Stanton, A. M. *Female offenders and their children: The effects of maternal incarceration on children*. Unpublished doctoral dissertation, Stanford University, 1978.

Tapp, J. L. Psychology and the law: The dilemma. *Psychology Today*, 1969, *2*, 16–22.

Tapp, J. L. A child's garden of law and order. *Psychology Today*, 1970, *4*, 29–31; 62–64.

Tapp, J. L. Reflections. *Journal of Social Issues*, 1971, *27*(2), 1–16. In J. L. Tapp (Ed.), Socialization, the law, and society. *Journal of Social Issues*, 1971, *21*(2) (whole issue).

Tapp, J. L. The psychological limits of legality. In J. R. Pennock & J. W. Chapman (Eds.), *The limits of law: Nomos XV*. New York: Lieber–Atherton, 1974.

Tapp, J. L. Psychology and the law: An overture. In M. R. Rosenzweig & L. W. Porter (Eds.), *Annual review of psychology* (Vol. 27). Palo Alto, Calif.: Annual Reviews, 1976.

Tapp, J. L. Psychology and the law: A look at the interface. In B. D. Sales (Ed.), *Psychology in the legal process*. New York: Spectrum, 1977.

Tapp. J. L. *The classroom as a socializing experience in legality: Working paper*. Unpublished manuscript, University of California at San Diego, 1978.

Tapp, J. L. Psychological and policy perspectives on the law: Reflections on a decade. *Journal of Social Issues*, 1980, *36*(2), 165–192.

Tapp, J. L., & Keniston, A. Wounded Knee—Advocate or expert: Recipe for a fair juror? In J. L. Tapp (Chair), *"What is a Fair Jury?" Psychological and Legal Issues*. Symposium presented at the meeting of American Psychological Association, Washington, D.C., September 1976.

Tapp. J. L., & Kohlberg, L. Developing senses of law and legal justice. In J. L. Tapp & F. J. Levine (Eds.), *Law, justice, and the individual in society*. New York: Holt, Rinehart & Winston, 1977. (Reprinted from *Journal of Social Issues*, 1971, *27*(2), 65–91.)

Tapp, J. L., & Levine, F. J. Persuasion to virtue: A preliminary statement. *Law and Society Review*, 1970, *4*, 565–582.

Tapp, J. L., & Levine, F. J. *The jurisprudence of youth*. Unpublished manuscript, American Bar Foundation, 1971.

Tapp, J. L., & Levine, F. J. Legal socialization: Strategies for an ethical legality. *Standford Law Review*, 1974, *27*, 1–72.

Tapp, J. L., & Levine, F. J. (Eds.). *Law, justice, and the individual in society: Psychological and legal issues*. New York: Holt, Rinehart & Winston, 1977.

Tapp, J. L., & Gunnar, M., & Keating D. Socialization: Three ages, three rule systems. In D. Perlman & C. Cozby (Eds.), *Social psychology and social issues*. New York: Holt, Rinehart & Winston, 1982.

Tapp, J. L., Vopava, J. R., Kolman, A. S., & Richardson, R. M. *Rights consciousness and child care: A report on the right-to-care project*. Unpublished manuscript, University of Minnesota, 1982.

Torney, J. V. Socialization of attitudes toward the legal system. In J. L. Tapp & F. J. Levine (Eds.), *Law, justice, and the individual in society*. New York: Holt, Rinehart & Winston, 1977. (Reprinted from *Journal of Social Issues*, 1971, *27*(2), 137–154.)

Torney, J. V., & Brice, P. J. Children's concepts of human rights and social cognition. In J. L. Tapp (Chair), *Children's rights and the development of social responsibility*. Symposium at the American Psychological Association meeting, New York, September 1979.

Wilson, W. C. Belief in freedom of speech and press. *Journal of Social Issues*, 1975, *31*(2), 69–76.

Zellman, G. L. Antidemocratic beliefs: A survey and some explanations. *Journal of Social Issues*, 1975, *31*(2), 31–54.

APPENDIX

Tapp-Lavine Rule Law Interview (TLRLI)

Open-ended Items[a]

1. What is a rule? Why is that a rule?
2. What is a law? Why is that a law?
3. Why do we have laws? Why should we have laws?
4. Can some things be fair and right to do even when there are no laws about them? How can this be?
5. What is a fair law? Why is it fair?
6. What is a right?
7. What kinds of rights should people have? Why?
8. What kinds of rights do people have? Why?
9. What would happen if there were no laws anywhere at all? Why?
10. Why should people follow laws?
11. Why do you follow laws?
12. How and why can laws be changed?
13. Are there times when it might be right to break a law? When, if ever?
14. What does it mean to be right?
15. Can a person be right and break a law? How can this be?

---

[a] Rank-order, forced-choice items are also available.

CHAPTER 12

Involving Children in Decisions Affecting Their Own Welfare

Guidelines for Professionals

LOIS A. WEITHORN

The foregoing chapters have provided analyses of legal, psychological, and social issues relevant to children's "competency" to make decisions affecting their own welfare. Scholars, scientists, and practitioners have focused attention on these issues in response to the courts' involvement in cases concerning the rights of legal minors to make autonomous decisions. Most publicized have been the United States Supreme Court's 1979 decisions in the cases of *Parham v. J. R.*[1] and *Bellotti v. Baird*[2]. The first case involved the rights of minors whose parents petition for their admission to psychiatric hospitals. In *Bellotti*, the Court considered the right of minor females to obtain abortions independent of their parents' consent.

Attention also has been focused upon the rights and capacities of children to self-determination in other situations, such as: provision of consent or refusal for other types of medical and psychological treatment (Brown & Truitt, 1979; C. C. Lewis, 1980; Holder, 1977; Schowalter, Ferholt, & Mann, 1973; Weit-

---

[1] Parham v. J.R., 442 U.S. 584 (1979).
[2] Bellotti v. Baird, 443 U.S. 622 (1979).

LOIS A. WEITHORN ● Institute of Law, Psychiatry, and Public Policy, University of Virginia, Charlottesville, Virginia 22901. This work was supported in part by research grant SOC 79-09760, Law and Social Sciences Program, National Science Foundation.

horn, 1979; Wilkins, 1975) including health care procedures of no direct benefit to themselves, such as organ and tissue donation (Fost, 1977; Herman,
1979); provision of consent or refusal for participation in research (Curran &
Beecher, 1969; Glantz, Annas, & Katz, 1977; Katz, 1975); provision of input
into the disposition of child custody cases of which they are the subject (Bersoff,
1976–77; Ellsworth & Levy, 1969); cooperation with attorneys in civil and
criminal cases (Leon, 1978); waiver of *Miranda* rights when taken into police
custody (Grisso, 1981); and decision making regarding educational assessment
and placements (Chapter 9) or leaving high school prior to completion of
degree requirements (C. C. Lewis, in press). The media reported the dilemma
faced by a juvenile court judge in Chicago required to decide the legal custody
of a 12-year-old immigrant boy who preferred not to accompany his parents
when they relocated in their country of origin: the Soviet Union (Castillo,
1980)

The competency or capacity of legal minors to make personal and autonomous decisions in such situations is but one of many complex considerations
relevant to empowering minors to self-determine. Most relevant to courts' decisions are interpretations of legal precedent and the constitutional issues related to
the balancing of the interests of the parents, the child, and the state. Historically,
the courts have respected the rights of parents to exercise discretion and control
relating to the activities, welfare, and destinies of their minor chidren.[3] However,
as Melton (1982) points out, there also has been a judicial recognition of the rights
of minors as "persons" under our Constitution, regarding such interests liberty,[4]
privacy,[5] and free speech.[6] The state's interests are well articulated in the Supreme
Court's majority opinion in *Prince v. Massachusetts:*

> The state's authority over children's activities is broader than over like actions
> of adults. . . . A democratic society rests, for its continuance, upon the healthy, well-
> rounded growth of its young people into full maturity as citizens, with all that
> implies.[7]

It appears that opinion as to the competency of minors probably is not a
key factor in judicial determinations of whether or not to expand minors' rights.
However, given that the law recognizes minors' interests as paramount in a
particular case, notions of minors' capacities may influence the mechanisms by
which expansions in rights are granted. That is, if certain minors are perceived

[3] Parham v. J.R., 442 U.S 584 (1979); Wisconsin v. Yoder, 406 U.S. 205 (1972); Pierce v. Society of
Sisters, 268 U.S. 571 (1924); Meyer v. Nebraska, 262 U.S. 390 (1923).

[4] *In re* Gault, 387 U.S. 1 (1967).

[5] Bellotti v. Baird, 443 U.S. 662 (1979); Planned Parenthood of Central Missouri v. Danforth, 438
U.S. 52 (1976).

[6] Tinker v. Des Moines Independent Community School District, 393 U.S. 503 (1969).

[7] Prince v. Commonweath of Massachusetts, 321 U.S. 158 (1944) at 168.

to be competent, they may be more likely to be empowered with some degree of decision-making authority. If certain minors are perceived as incapable of exercising a right of self-determination in a competent manner, they may be provided additional protections from the state, such as due process protections, but little voice in decision making.

Children's rights, specifically with respect to the right of self-determination, can no longer appropriately be referred to as a "legal vacuum" (Forer, 1969). Yet, few consistent standards have emerged to guide practitioners who work with children. Legal standards governing consent requirements vary considerably across jurisdictions and decision-making contexts. Health and mental health professionals, educators, researchers, attorneys, and others often must consider under what circumstances, to what degree, and in what ways to involve children and adolescents in decision making. In the following pages, an attempt will be made to identify certain key issues and concepts relevant to involving children in decisions affecting their own welfare.

Why Involve Children in Decisions Affecting Their Own Welfare?

Generally, a minor's parents retain the legal authority to make most important decisions affecting the welfare of that minor. it is probably true that in most instances this allocation of decision-making responsibility adequately serves the needs of the child. Yet, in certain predictable situations, the prevailing doctrine of parental discretion and control regarding minor children may not be in the child's best interests. Among these situations are instances where parental capacity to act in a child's best interests may be diminished or compromised due to a "conflict of interests" as well as instances in which a minor might not seek needed heath care or other services if parental consent or involvement were required. Before reviewing these specific situations, it is relevant to comment on certain more general points.

It is important to differentiate between the concept of *de jure* incompetence and actual or demonstrated incompetence to make personal decisions. *De jure* incompetence results from either a judicial determination of incompetence or from a legal standard that defines an entire class of persons as incompetent by virtue of their status as members of that class (Meisel, 1981). Minors generally are, by law, considered to be incompetent due to their minority status. By contrast, adults are considered *de jure*, to be competent, absent formal adjudication of incompetence. Although one would hope that *de jure* incompetence would correlate highly with actual capacities in the proscribed situations, this may not be the case. Thus, one's legal status as incompetent or competent, while determining the degree to which one may participate in personal decision making, may not accurately reflect one's actual or demonstrated capacities.

Some suggest that minors should be permitted legally to self-determine to the maximum extent that their capacities permit, in many or all of those situations reviewed at the beginning of this chapter (Bersoff, 1979; Ellis, 1974; Rodham, 1973; Weithorn, 1979; Wilkins, 1975). This perspetive is consistent with concepts that define our nation's legal tradition, such as the individual rights guaranteed by our Constitution. In general, the rights of individuals to exercise personal control over their lives is recognized and protected, as in the example of the law of informed consent, which forbids unauthorized intrusions upon an individual's bodily integrity by health care professionals. Ethical standards promulgated by various bodies and professions generally reflect this tradition. Yet, our current legal and ethical standards also require that we "protect" more vulnerable and less capable individuals from their own deficits and assure that their best interests are considered. The National Commission for the Protection of Human Subjects of Biomedical and Behavioral Research, in its *Belmont Report*, reviews "basic ethical principles" that are generally accepted in our cultural tradition:

> Respect for persons incorporates at least two basic ethical convictions: first, that individuals should be treated as autonomous agents, and second, that persons with diminished autonomy are entitled to protection. . . .
> An autonomous person is an individual capable of deliberation about personal goals and of acting under the direction of such deliberation. To respect autonomy is to give weight to autonomous persons' considered opinions and choices while refraining from obstructing their actions unless they are clearly detrimental to others. To show a lack of respect for an autonomous agent is to repudiate that person's considered judgments, to deny an individual the freedom to act on those considered judgments, or to withhold information necessary to make a considered judgment, when there are no compelling reasons to do so.
> However, not every human being is capable of self-determination. The capacity for self-determination matures during an individual's life. . . . Respect for the immature or incapacitated may require protecting them as they mature or while they are incapacitated.
> Some persons are in need of extensive protection, even to the point of excluding them from activities which may harm them; other persons require little protection beyond making sure they undertake activities freely and with awareness of possible adverse consequences. . . . The judgment that any person lacks autonomy should be periodicaly reevaluated and will vary in different situations. (1978, pp. 4–5)

Differences in philosophy exist regarding the degree to which the state should exercise its *parens patriae* power to allow or initiate benevolent limitations of individuals' right of self-determination. Several authors have noted that the "children's rights" movement may be characterized by two ostensibly opposing perspectives. Rogers and Wrightman (1978) contrast the orientations advocating "self-determination" and "nurturance." Mnookin (1978b) refers to the "kiddie libbers" and the "child savers." The former attitude encourages legal policies that extend adult rights to children (Rodham, 1973), allowing them to exert personal control in matters of their own welfare. The latter philosophy is more paternalistic, and emphasizes that children have special needs and vulnerabilities that render them deserving of additional protection by adults and by law.

These two perspectives need not be considered contradictory nor mutually exclusive. They may, at times, be conceptualized as complementary, as in the *Belmont Report*. However, in practice, these perspectives lead to dramatically different public policy recommendations. Such discrepancies may be due to two aspects of the arguments presented by those favoring the "protection" and "nurturance" model: a categorical presumption that minors are not as capable as adults of exercising decision-making autonomy; and a commitment to absolute control by adults over the activities, destinies, and welfare of minors. The latter argument is determined largely by values and is reinforced by certain interpretations of constitutional law. The former point, relating to the capacities of minors, however, can be subjected to empirical study.

The debate as to whether minors are entitled to the right of self-determination has led us to reexamine the traditional presumption that legal minors categorically are incompetent to make decisions as to what is in their own best interests. Such incapacity has been attributed to lack of intellectual and emotional maturity, lack of experience, and a diminished capacity to exercise free will. All of these deficits have been viewed as inherent in the minors' age and status of minority. The physiological and psychological immaturity of many minors is undeniable, as is the dependency upon adults intrinsic to this immaturity and our social structure. Yet, the ages of 18 and 21 delineating majority are arbitrary and stem from currently irrelevant historical concerns such as sufficient physical strength to bear heavy armor (Glantz *et al.*, 1977). Recently, the presumption that minors are incompetent to make decisions affecting their own welfare has partially given way to focused analyses of the existing cognitive-developmental literature (Grisso & Vierling, 1978; C. C. Lewis, in press; Weithorn, 1980) and requests for criterion-relevant research directed toward learning more about children's specific capacities in the specific decision making contexts (Grisso, 1979; Leon, 1978; Mnookin, 1978b; M. Wald, 1976). Some writers have pointed out that our assumptions regarding the capacities and decision-making modes employed by adults may not be accurate (Skolnick, 1975). That is, neither children nor adults may categorically and routinely make important life decisions in a manner commensurate with the legal standards applied when judging decision-making competency (Glantz *et al.*, 1977; Bersoff, 1979; Weithorn, 1980). Therefore, it is critical that in our evaluations of the capacities of minors, we compare them to adults in similar situations, rather than to the hypothetical standard of the "reasonable" adult.

Returning again to the question of why children should be involved in decisions affecting their own welfare, let us examine the notion that unilateral parental decision making is in the best interests of the child. The concept of children as the "property" of parents, and as having no personal rights regarding their well-being has been replaced by the notion that children's best interests should be considered paramount in specific situations affecting their welfare. Parental judgment regarding what are a child's best interests in such situations often is unchallenged by the court. In other situations, the state may impose its judgment of a child's best interests in place of the parents'. Yet, Mnookin (1978b) points out that what is "'best' for a particular child . . . is often indeterminate and speculative," and that such judgments are strongly influenced by subjective and personal values. Consider, for example, the case of a child with terminal cancer, for whom an amputation may briefly prolong life. One who values length of life most highly might favor the amputation, whereas one who values quality of life more highly might reject this procedure. Given the subjective nature of such decisions, it seems reasonable in a society concerned with protecting the best interests of the child that the child be provided with an opportunity to voice personal preferences and priorities. The degree to which the child's preferences would be controlling or given weight would be related, in part, to the child's capacity to make meaningful decisions about his or her own welfare.

Rodham (1973) points out that the law has presumed, traditionally, that a child's best interests are identical to those of the parents, or the state, when it substitutes its judgment for that of the parents. The law also presumes that parents have the capacity and motivation to determine and act in accordance with the child's best interests. Yet, certain situations present a "conflict of interests" for parents. The conflict may relate to the competing interests of two children, as when one child is a suitable organ donor for another child. The choice of whether to place the health of one child at risk in order to improve the health of another child unquestionably presents a conflict. The conflicts also might relate to a blurring of what is in the interests of the parent versus the child, as might occur when two divorcing parents each desire child custody. Weithorn (in press) comments that many parents also may experience such "conflicts of interest" when a child is manifesting psychological or behavioral problems. If the stress upon the family is sufficient, the parent might consent to psychiatric hospitalization, psychotropic medication, or aversive conditioning for the child when these alternatives are not in the child's best interests. In these situations, suggesting that treatment alternatives are in the child's best interests allows the adult decisionmaker to avoid confronting the possibility that the treatments may benefit the child's caretakers more than they do the child.

Parental judgment as to what is in the best interests of a child may blur in instances when a child wishes to obtain birth control devices or an abortion. Parent and child might have different attitudes about sexuality and pregnancy. Parental anxiety and concerns about the relationship between availability of contraception and teenage sexual activity may cause a parent to attempt to impose his or her morality upon the child. The parent's preferences may not adequately take into consideration the context of the child's social situation and may deny the realities of the child's sexual activity.

It also has been noted that in the case of these and other "sensitive" health care situations minors might not seek needed services if parental consent or involvement was required (Pilpel, 1972; M. Wald, 1979). In addition to situations relating to birth control and termination of pregnancy, older minors have been permitted by law to obtain treatment for such problems as drug or alcohol abuse and emotional disorders (Wilkins, 1975).

Finally, it can be argued that permitting minors' involvement in decisions affecting their own welfare, *as a process*, is in the child's best interests. The Subtask Panel on Infants, Children and Adolescents of the President's Commission on Mental Health (1978) recommended "youth participation as a sound strategy to enable young people to undertake responsible and rewarding involvement in the adult world" (p. 636). Involving children in decisions that affect their welfare affords them a learning opportunity that better prepares them for future joint or independent decision making. Involving children in such decisions respects the autonomy, individuality, and privacy of each child, and may increase the children's sense of themselves as active and responsible participants in their own care, rather than as powerless victims of the whims of adults (Weithorn, 1980). Lewis, Lewis, Lorimer, and Palmer (1977) found that children between the ages of 5 and 11 who utilized a health care system permitting them independent access to services provided by a school nurse practitioner placed a greater emphasis on personal responsibility for health care. Melton (Chapter 2) predicts that increased autonomy may heighten children's sense of "personal causation" (*i.e.*, their experience of being in control). The experience of being in control and having a sense of mastery over what happens to one has been suggested as directly related to a person's adaptive and healthy psychological functioning (Frank, 1976; Thoresen & Mahoney, 1974). Melton also suggests that "increased autonomy would increase children's performance in those spheres in which they had the opportunity to make choices." Thus, children who participate in decisions regarding their own care may be more likely to follow through with a particular treatment regimen. Some initial findings reported by C. E. Lewis (Chapter 5) suggest that increasing children's participation in decision making related to treatment of a chronic illness (*i.e.*, asthma) actually improves treatment compliance. Day and Reznikoff (1980) found that inappropriate expectations of children regarding psychotherapy were related to attrition. If we presume that participation in decision making regarding one's own treatment contributes to the appropriateness of one's expectations for treatment, we might speculate that such participation will reduce the likelihood of premature termination.

Melton cautions that increased autonomy for children might have certain negative effects, particularly in instances when the choice is complex or may have negative consequences, or where particular children may become anxious in response to autonomy. It is relevant to emphasize that implicit in the right of a child to choose for himself in a particular situation is the right of that child to defer to others whom he/she invests with decision-making responsibility, such as the parents. Full decision-making autonomy may be viewed as an option available to those minors who have both the capacity and the desire to exercise it.

Factors Related to Children's Involvement in Decisions Affecting Their Own Welfare

When considering under what circumstances and in what ways to involve children in decisions affecting their own welfare, professionals may wish to give thought to the following factors: existing legal standards governing allocation of decision-making power among child, parent, and state (Mnookin, 1978a) in the specific context; the minor's capacity to exercise "decisional autonomy" (Meisel, 1981); the "risk/benefit ratio" that may be thought to characterize the specific situation requiring a decision; and the degree and mode of the minor's desired involvement.

Allocations of Decision-Making Power

The law stipulates that in particular situations relating to the welfare of minors, decision-making authority rests either with the minor's parents, the minor, or the state. Such delineations are based upon the law's balancing of interests of these parties, as discussed earlier in this chapter. However, within these legally proscribed delineations, there is significant flexibility regarding each party's actual role in decision making. Parent, child, or state can, in the practical sense, permit the preferences of another to be influential or controlling in aspects of the decision making. For example, parents may invite children to share with them in decision making for which unilateral parental consent is legally binding. A minor legally empowered with the right to obtain an abortion independent of her parents' wishes, consent, and knowledge may choose to solicit her parents' opinions. A judge, wielding ultimate power in determining the outcome of a child custody case, may allow the child's preferences to guide the disposition of the case.

It is imperative that professionals who work with children in contexts where such decision making is regulated by law ascertain what are the relevant standards.[8] Once it is determined how decision-making authority is distributed by law, a professional can attempt to work within these standards to foster the degree and type of involvement by minors that appears to be consistent with the minor's needs, desires, and capacities. A professional such as a provider of health or mental health services, an educator, or an attorney can serve as an effective advocate for the child by representing the child's point of view to other adults, where appropriate, or by facilitating that minor's open expression of relevant preferences. Further, a professional who is cognizant of relevant legal standards can choose to observe certain more stringent ethical codes as well. Thus, a researcher, or a health care provider may opt not to include a child in a study or not to perform certain health care procedures unless the child has provided fully informed and voluntary consent, even if such consent is not required by law. Finally, within a given professional relationship, such as ongoing psychotherapy, there is significant opportunity to allow a child a meaningful role in determining the goals of the process and that relationship (Melton, 1981).

The Capacity of Minors to Exercise Decisional Autonomy

Capacity to exercise "decisional autonomy" is not an "all-or-none" capability: children and adults evidence varying degrees of competency to render informed decisions affecting their own welfare. "Competency" is but a construct, or set of constructs, with somewhat differing meaning in different situations. An individual may appear competent in one situation, but not another, and competency may vary over time. It is not clear that most adults do, in fact, make important life decisions in a manner that would be judged competent according to prevailing legal standards (Fellner & Marshall, 1970). Therefore, it is emphasized again that, when assessing the "competency" of minors, we compare them directly to adults, rather than to our theoretical notions of the "reasonable" person.

The Concept of "Competency"

In recent years, writers and investigators have evidenced increasing inter-

---

[8] Such information about statutory and case law and relevant considerations in one's jurisdiction can be obtained through consultation with legal experts.

est in varying legal definitions of "competency" and strategies for assessing the relevant skills and performance (Applebaum & Roth, 1981; Friedman, 1975; Gert & Culver, 1981; Grisso, 1981; McGarry, 1973; Meisel, 1979, 1981; Roth, 1980; Roth, Meisel, & Lidz, 1977; Stanley, 1981; Weithorn & Campbell, in press). *Competency, competence, capacity,* and, in the case of minors, *maturity,* are terms often used interchangeably to refer to one of the three conditions necessary for a treatment decision to be considered legally valid (Weithorn, in press). *Voluntariness and knowledge* are the other conditions. Used more generally, the term *competency* refers to having certain skills, abilities, or a capacity to perform in a certain manner. Among the many situations in which competency to make decisions may be relevant regarding children are medical and psychological treatment situations, research and educational contexts, exercise of rights upon entrance into the criminal justice system, and representation by an attorney. Various tests or standards of competency have been defined by law and professional practice, and these tests differ across situations, as might individual skills and performance. However, there also are varying standards applied to judge competency within the same or similar situations. A large proportion of the relevant empirical and theoretical work in this area has focused upon competency to make decisions regarding participation in treatment or research, and therefore, this analysis will focus upon these contexts.

Applebaum and Roth (1981) provide a useful framework with which to analyze the various tests of competency. They point out that the different standards of competency can be characterized as representing varying levels of "stringency" and as fostering different sets of public policy goals. For example, in a treatment situation, a more lenient test requiring minimal demonstration of skills promotes individual autonomy by maximizing the likelihood a person will be found competent and therefore allowed to self-determine. Meisel (1979) suggests that a standard that considers a decision to be competent if the outcome coincides with the choice the so-called hypothetical reasonable person might make "unduly honors the concerns of the medical profession at the expense of the patient's autonomy." This may be true because the choices attributed to the hypothetical "reasonable" person usually are the choices recommended by the attending professionals or by a consensus of prevailing medical opinion. Thus, preference for the "self-determination" versus "nurturance" models regarding children's rights may relate to the standards courts or professionals set for demonstrations of competency by children.

The *Restatement (Second) of Torts,* a summary and analysis of American standards of torts law, suggests the following test of competency:

> If a person consenting is a child or one of deficient mental capacity, the consent may still be effective if he is capable of appreciating the nature, extent and probable consequences of the conduct consented to.[9]

---

[9] *Restatement (Second) of Torts,* Ch. 45, Section 892A(2) (1979).

Meisel (1979) and Roth *et. al.* suggest that, in general, the following tests of competency in treatment situations are at times applied: evidence of choice (*i.e.*, simple expression of a preference relative to the treatment alternatives); reasonable outcome of choice (*i.e.*, that the option selected coincides with a choice the hypothetical "reasonable" person might make, often determined by prevailing medical opinion); reasonable decision-making process (*i.e.*, that the treatment preference was derived from "rational" or logical reasons) and understanding. Different applications of the latter standard might require either a demonstration of a more concrete "factual understanding" (Applebaum & Roth, 1981) or a more abstract "appreciation" of consequences as specified in the *Restatement (Second) of Torts*. Or, the concept of understanding may refer more to a hypothesized capacity or ability rather than a skill that is measured in the decision-making situation. Appreciation as a standard of competency may be the most stringent legal test; by contrast, evidence of choice may be the most lenient.

The Competency of Minors

Many authors have reexamined the presumption that minors are incompetent to make decisions regarding their own health care or research participation (Ferguson, 1978; Grisso & Vierling, 1978; Schowalter, 1978; M. Wald, 1979; P. Wald & P. Friedman, 1976; Weithorn, 1980, in press; Weithorn & Campbell, in press. The conclusions drawn by these writers are strikingly similar. On the basis of cognitive-developmental theory and research, all authors suggest that children age 14 and older possess the requisite cognitive and intellectual capacities to render them comparable to adults, as a group, relative to competency. And, most of these authors recognize that many children attain this highest level of cognitive functioning by age 12. Initial empirical findings support these conclusions. Weithorn and Campbell (in press) compared demonstrations of competency by minors age 9 and 14 to those of adults aged 18 and 21 relative to four hypothetical medical and psychological treatment "delimmas." Although there were certain differential patterns of developmental change related to the specific test of competency employed, the investigators conclude that the findings do *not* support the denial of the right of self-determination in treatment situations to adolescents age 14 and older on the basis of a presumption of incapacity. They conclude further that minors age 9 do not appear to be as competent as adults according to the standards concerned with demonstration of "reasonable" decision-making process and "understanding." Yet, these children did voice clear and sensible preferences that did not differ from those chosen by the adults for three of four hypothetical dilemmas.

In another study, Lewis, Lewis, and Ifekwunigue (1978) offered children between the ages of 6 and 9 the choice of participating in a swine flu vaccine research trial. After presenting information to them regarding the study, a group question-and-answer session was held to allow the children to clarify their understanding of the information. The investigators did not attempt to evaluate each child's individual competency. However, the authors suggested that their findings "indicate that children of this age can be involved meaningfully . . . in decisions related to informed consent." Korsch (1974) drew similar conclusions from group discussions with children age 9 to 11 who considered hypothetical dilemmas regarding participation in a research study.

In general, therefore, we might conclude that minors age 14 and older should be considered by professionals to be as competent as adults to make decisions affecting their own welfare. As in the case of adults, if an individual initially presumed to be competent demonstrates otherwise, options are available to insure that the individual's best interests are considered. Preadolescence (ages 10 to 13) is a period characterized by significant shifts in cognitive capacities. In relevant situations, certain minors in this age group may perform as competently as adults, whereas others may not. Case-by-case determinations of capacity may be relevant for this age group, as well as for younger children. It is possible that in some instances children between the ages of 7 and 9 will not appear competent according to the more stringent standards. Yet, research and experience suggests that children have "considerable capacity for self-determination" (Ferguson, 1978). Their understanding and decision-making skills may not be as sophisticated as an adults' yet, they appear to be able to arrive at meaningful and logically derived choices and are often eager to become active participants in the decision-making process (Weithorn & Campbell, in press). Regarding children below the age of 7 Ferguson suggests that preschool and primary-age children "have some capacity for understanding verbal explanations and some ability to communicate their own questions and concerns." Although it is unlikely that children younger than age 7 will be judged competent according to the more stringent standards, it is likely that many may have reasonable preferences and ideas about what happens to them.

It is important to comment here that competency or capacity is but one of three conditions required for the provision of informed consent. Although this text and much of the recent literature focus upon competency, consideration of "voluntariness," that is, freedom "from coercion and from unfair persuasions and inducements" (Meisel, Roth, & Lidz, 1977), are also relevant. Grisso and Vierling (1978) concluded that minors younger than age 15 might be more likely than older minors and adults to defer to authority. Grisso (1981), who studied juveniles' competence to waive *Miranda* rights, concludes that certain such factors inherent in the actual interrogation situation tend to inhibit juveniles from making decisions that they, themselves, would otherwise believe to be in their own best interests. Grisso questions the voluntariness of the rights waivers by many juveniles. Thus, when we examine the competency of minors to make decisions affecting their own welfare, we must recognize that such capacity is but one dimension (albeit, a critical dimension) relevant to that minor's performance in the specific decision-making situation. Additional relevant factors include decreased effectiveness or increased motivation due to the effects of physical illness or psychological disturbance and reactions to stress engendered by situations such as illness, child custody disputes, or involvement in the criminal justice system. Such factors may hamper or facilitate the use of one's decision-making capacities. Although the legal definitions of competency refer, primarily, to cognitive variables, emotional or situational variables may mitigate against or facilitate use of cognitive skills. It is suggested, however, that reactions to stress, illness and other such variables, and their subsequent effects upon functioning probably are determined must strongly by individual differences and specific situational factors than by cognitive development or chronological age (Weithorn, 1980).

Determinations of Competency

In the precious section, it was suggested that, for minors of specific age groups, case-by-case determinations of competency might be appropriate. The prevailing legal standards against which to judge the minors' competency is the "mature minor" rule, which is quite similar to the test reviewed in the *Restatement (Second) for Torts*. The "mature minor" exception in the statutes of some states, and in the case law of others, holds that a minor may consent to any surgical or medical treatment or procedures if that minor is "of sufficient intelligence to understand and appreciate the consequences of the proposed treatment or procedures for himself."[10] For these definitions, the emphasis is upon the minor's capacities rather than an actual demonstration of such ability in the specific decision-making context. It is not clear, in practice, how courts and professionals actually assess such capacity. However, this author concurs with Roth *et al.* (1977), who suggest that this test defines competency as a "construct or intervening variable in the decision-making process" and does not focus upon "concrete and observable elements of behavior." It is thus suggested that we employ the Roth *et al.* concept of "actual understanding" which must be demonstrated in the specific instance for which a consent or refusal is obtained. Judging competency, therefore, becomes one aspect of obtaining informed consent. As Meisel and co-workers (1977) suggest, fully informed consent can be obtained only after the following information has been provided to prospective patients: the nature of the problem for which treatments are recommended; a description of the alternative treatments; the anticipated benefits of such treat-

---

[10] Arkansas Statutes Annotated, Section 82–363 (1976); Mississippi Code, Section 41–41-3(h) (Supp. 1972).

ments; the risks, discomforts, and side effects of such treatments; and the consequences of failure to be treated at all. Also relevant is the likelihood of occur-
rence of any of the aforementioned possibilities, if known. Similar, although
expanded, procedures are suggested for obtaining informed consent for research (American Psychological Association, 1973; National Commission for
the Protection of Human Subjects of Biomedical and Behavioral Research,
1977). In other situations, such as decision-making regarding educational
placements or one's defense in a criminal case, the "elements of disclosure"
(Meisel, 1979) are similar. Professionals are required to inform the individual of
the nature of the situation: the alternative courses of action available to that
person; the potential benefits, risks, or discomforts attendant to each alternative
as well as the likelihood of each occurring.

Evaluation of "understanding" or "appreciation" may require two phases.
One should assess the individual's basic understanding of the facts and possibilities described. Second, one should determine the degree of the individual's
appreciation of the personal consequences of each alternative course of action.

The standard of understanding and appreciation is among the most stringent applicable. Although such a definition may require that minors demonstrate capacities that many adults could not demonstrate, it probably is the
only standard that would justify, *legally*, the self-determination of a minor
whose parents retain decision-making authority and have not concurred with
the minor's decision. However, one also can apply increasingly more lenient
standards when determining how much weight to give to a minor's stated
preferences in other instances. In the following section on " risk/benefit ratios,"
it is suggested that stringency of one's standards regarding competency may
vary with the specifics of the decision-making situation.

Risk/Benefit Ratios and Specific Decision-Making Contexts

The weighting of potential risks and benefits is necessarily a subjective
process. Yet, our laws and professional standards appear to lean in the direction
of certain predictable weightings of these factors in specific situations. When
considering the involvment of children in decisions affecting their own welfare,
our implicit or explicit weightings of perceived risks and benefits may determine the types of standards and proscriptions we set for such involvement. Let
us consider the following examples relating to how personal values and societal
mores may empower minors with or deprive them of decision-making autonomy.

Schowalter, Ferholt, and Mann (1973) cite the case of a 16-year-old girl
who chose to terminate hemodialysis when her severe renal disease became
intractable. Her parents supported her decision. The authors suggest that by

age 14 or 15, most adolescents can understand the "meaning of death." Schowalter *et al.* cite Piaget and suggest that "grasping of the possibilities and limitations of one's self in relation to a finite future develop within the stage of formal operations" (p. 99). Holder (1977) suggests a hypothetical case where a competent adolescent wishes to refuse life-saving treatment, and the parents do not concur with the decision. It is likely that the courts would support tthe parents' wish to prolong the child's life as long as possible. By contrast, if it is the parent who wishes such treatment be refused, and the minor prefers to undergo the proposed treatment, it is likely that the court would support the minor. Holder states "in most cases involving conflicts between parents and children, the legal system automatically assumes that the parent is correct." She continues by pointing out, however, that "it does seem that where the child's life is at stake, a conflict between the parents and the child should be resolved in favor of the preservation of the child's life" (p. 130). The foregoing analysis supports Applebaum and Roth's (1981) contention that we often apply different standards to consent situations depending upon particular policy goals. When the life of a minor is in jeopardy, our social values dictate that the potential loss of life outweighs other considerations. Unfortunately, if it is the minor who is stating a preference that is contrary to the socially acceptable norm, that minor probably will be labeled incompetent. By contrast, if the parents are choosing to refuse treatment, their competency probably will not be discussed. Rather, it will be determined that they are not acting in the child's best interests. A slightly different picture emerges when considering the situation of a child who is a potential participant in research.

In its report and recommendations relating to *Research Involving Children*, the National Commission for the Protection of Human Subjects of Biomedical and Behavioral Research (1977) stated that:

> The Commission believes that children who are seven years of age or older are generally capable of understanding the procedures and general purpose of research and of indicating their wishes regarding participation. Their assent should be required in addition to parental permission. . . . The objection of a child of any age to participation should be binding except as noted below. (p. 16)

The exceptions to this standards are of particular interest, given the preceding discussion:

> If the research protocol includes an intervention from which the subjects might derive significant benefit to their health or welfare, and that intervention is available only in a research context, the objection of a small child may be overridden. . . . As children mature their ability to perceive and act in their own best interests increases; thus, their wishes with respect to such research should carry increasingly more weight. When school-age children disagree with their parents regarding participa-

tion in such research, the IRB[11] may wish to have a third party discuss the matter with all concerned and be present during the consent process. Although parents may legally override the objections of school-age children in such cases, the burden of the decision becomes heavier in relation to the maturity of the particular child. (p. 16)

In the case of research not expected to be of direct benefit to the subject through the provision of needed services (*i.e.*, "nonbeneficial research"), the National Commission proposed that children as young as age 7 be given an absolute right of refusal.[12] Such minors do *not* also have an independent right to choose to participate in such research. Rather, their affirmative decision to participate is a necessary, although not sufficient condition for participation, and must be supplemented by parental permission. The terms assent and permission are used to highlight that neither, in isolation, is sufficient to include the child in the research study. However, all other elements of the obtaining of informed consent are identical to the more traditional consent requirements: subjects must be free from duress and must be provided the relevant information.

Regarding nonbeneficial research, the Commission's recommendations tip the balance in favor of nonparticipation. That is, since the proposed research is not expected to benefit the subject, the subject is afforded maximum protection regarding participation, including a right of absolute refusal by the young subject, and the need for supplemental parental approval for participation. No case-by-case evaluation of the minor's competence is required. However, as the possibility increases that the research might hold some therapeutic benefit for the subject, that subject's absolute veto power decreases. If children are, by virtue of attainment of a particular age, considered to be competent to make a particular decision, why should their decision be rendered invalid if the research holds some therapeutic value? Obviously, this discrepancy follows from the social value placed upon therapeutic procedure and the potential benefit such procedures might hold for the minor.

It appears that, in general, the United States Supreme Court has been more responsive to minors' requests for autonomy when those requests involve *access to* rather than *refusal of* particular treatments.[13] This pattern is consistent with the social value placed upon "therapeutic interventions."

---

[11] Institutional Review Board.

[12] The recommendations of the National Commission were amended and published as proposed rules at 43 Federal Regeister 31786 (July 28, 1978). The amendments included three alternative proposals regarding the age at which a child's assent should be required (*i.e.*, age 7, age 12, and allowing each IRB discretion in this matter). At the time of this writing, the final regulations have not yet been signed or published.

[13] *Compare* Bellotti v. Baird, 443 U.S. 584 (1979); Planned Parenthood v. Danforth 438 U.S 52 (1976); Carey v. Population Services International, 431 U.S 678 (1977) with Parham v. J.R., 442 U.S 584 (1979).

Consider a somewhat different perspective on a risk/benefit formula. If a parent-child conflict exists and the decision involves the child's liberty (such as in the case of involuntary admission to psychiatric hospitals, or possible incarceration in a juvenile detention facility after some type of judicial hearing) or privacy of body or mind (such as in the case of reproductive rights, or rights to be free of psychotropic medication), "competent" minors should be allowed an absolute right of self-determination. Further, minors of questionable competence should be provided input into these decisions to the maximum extent their capacities permit, and a third party should be involved to represent the child's interests. Implicit in such a position is a belief that threats to constitutional rights, such as liberty and privacy, are so significant as to outweigh the loss of potential therapeutic gains in those instances where such gains are relevant.

It is crucial that professionals who work with children be alert to the ways in which societal and personal values affect their evaluations of the risk/benefit ratios in situations involving the welfare of children. When considering the welfare and interests of a minor, no aspect of one's perspectives and judgments can be completely free of such values. If the professional is aware of personal biases, that professional is better able to determine whether his or her actions are consistent with the formal and personal ethical standards relevant to work with that minor.

The Minor's Desired Involvement

An important aspect of the right of self-determination is the right to decide what role one wishes to play in decision-making regarding one's own welfare. It is possible that if all age barriers constraining the decision making of minors regarding their own interests were removed, most minors would continue to defer to their parents or to rely upon their parents' judgment when making most important life decisions. This may be due, in part, to Melton's (Chapter 2) point that the concept of civil liberties may not be immediately relevant for most children and that they may not be likely to experience themselves as "owning" such rights. Obviously, in order for children to learn to exercise the right of self-determination, their socialization must include relevant experiences. Children's hypothesized reluctance to make fully autonomous decisions also may relate to the likelihood that, in most families, children and parents are relatively content with their intrafamilial and idiosyncratic patterns of decision making regarding the welfare of a minor. Parental experience, judgment, and protection can be quite beneficial to children facing important life decisions.

In some situations, however, such as those where the decision is sensitive in nature, where parent and child disagree regarding the child's interests, or where the parents may be faced with a conflict of interests, a minor may desire to make a particular decision relatively independently. Such independent decision making may be particularly important to the personal growth and privacy of an adolescent.

Apart from those situations in which minors initiate an effort to participate in decision making, they may display more subtle indications of interest in participating. These indications may range from simple expressions of curiousity or preference to clear and meaningful ideas about what they believe should happen to them. However, it is likely that, in most cases, unless their involvement is solicited, minors may not attempt to play a role in relevant decisions. Thus, it is imperative that all professionals who work with children make an active attempt to encourage the minor's participation. Many may not realize they have the right or opportunity for such participation unless it is made explicit. Some minors may demonstrate a clear preference *not* to be placed in a decision-making role. They may be uncomfortable with such responsibility and may prefer noninvolvement. Such a preference should be respected, as would an affirmative preference regarding a specific decision.

Models for Involving Children in Decisions Affecting Their Own Welfare

There are various ways in which children and adolescents can be involved in decisions that affect their own welfare. One way of conceptualizing such involvement is on a continuum that relates to the degree of involvement: full decisional autonomy; some type of shared decision making with a parent or other adult; or noninvolvement in decision making. Another dimension to a child's involvement in decision making relates to his or her role in charting the course of the relationship with the professional. Thus, once a decision has been made for a child to enter ongoing treatment (*e.g.* psychotherapy) or to take part in a particular educational program, a child can collaborate with the professional regarding continually revised goals and strategies. Finally, children can be involved in decisions through the provision of information to them about their situation. Regardless of the degree of decision-making autonomy minors may be granted by law, or in practice, they can remain participants in the process if they are educated and encouraged to ask questions throughout.

Self-Determination

Minors may be granted full decisional autonomy in a particular situation involving their own welfare either by law or by the individuals who have legal authority to delegate such decision-making responsibility. If a professional wishes to abide by a particular child's decision, regardless of the distribution of decision-making authority, he or she may attempt to intervene in such a way as to secure decisional autonomy for the minor. Such intervention might involve serving as an intermediary with parents, articulating the child's point of view, and encouraging that the parents consider it. Or it may involve seeking legal remedies, such as a court-mandated judgment.

When securing the judgment of a minor who has been given authority to self-determine, the professional must abide by the legal and ethical standards for informed consent. This minor must be situated so as to choose free from coercion or persuasion; all relevant information about the minor's particular treatment (or other) situation and options must be clearly provided; and one must ascertain that this information has been comprehended.

Respecting an individual's right to self-determine does not mean that a professional must refrain from offering recommendations. In fact, having access to the practitioner's considered opinions is a valuable aspect of the relationship between client and professional. Optimally, a professional can express such recommendations without limiting the client's freedom to act autonomously. Particularly with children, the perceived and actual authority of professionals can be a formidable impediment to a truly free choice. Practitioners must avoid giving the impression that there is only one "right' decision. They must recognize their natural feelings of "paternalism" or protectiveness toward their clients and consciously work to keep in check the desire to have the client concur with their recommendation. This is most difficult when a caring practitioner believes that a client's choice may have deleterious results. However, if one is committed to the ethic of permitting those who are capable to self-determine, one must abide by this standard, even if one believes the client is making a poor or destructive choice.

Joint Decison Making

The models for joint or shared decision-making between a minor and parents, or other adults, are many. Two will be discussed here. Wherever possible and whenever not invasive of a minor's privacy, it is suggested that joint decision-making between parent and child is a preferred alternative. Exceptions to this model are those situations in which it is determined that full decisional autonomy is in the child's best interests, with no input from parents. This may be the case when mature adolescents prefer full personal responsibility for their choice or when it appears that joint decision making may be nonproductive or destructive.

One model for joint decision making requires the active participation of

parent and child as a decision-making *team*. The parent and child could prob-
lem-solve together, involved in an ongoing give-and-take and sharing of perspectives. An important and additional benefit of such efforts is the simultane-
ous training of parent and child regarding the potential for processing and
respecting the viewpoints of the other. It may be a positive learning experience
for all family members, and may increase parental respect for and attention to
the personal preferences of children in important decision-making contexts.
The professional may serve as a facilitator if necessary. Another advantage of
this model is that it decreases the likelihood that breaches in family relationships will result from parent-child conflict regarding decision outcome. Practically, such shared decision making may be the only way in which many minors
may be able to exercise greater autonomy, since legal authority regarding their
welfare rests with the parents. Even young children who may not be competent
according to most legal standards can have some input together with the protection of the parent's experience and judgment. The professional may need to
coach both parent and child in this process, since it may be new to both. And, if
the parent appears unwilling and unable to discuss such issues with the child,
the professional can solicit the preference and concerns of the minor, and can
serve as an intermediary, representing the child's perspectives where necessary.

A second model of joint decision making does not stipulate the *process* by
which the decision should be reached, as does the above mode. Rather, it
stipulates a distribution of decison-making power. As reviewed below, regarding informed consent for research, it is possible to structure a decision-making
situation so that both child and parents have an absolute right of refusal. That
is, both the child's assent and the parent's permission are necessary conditions
for that child's participation in research. Neither individual's decision is sufficient, however, to volunteer the child for the study. Some consider that the
prospective donation of a kidney by a minor is quite similar to participation in
research regarding the risk/benefit ratio. The donor is subjected to some risk,
and moderate discomfort, with no direct or apparent personal benefit. However, in some instances, the courts have found that a psychological benefit
would accrue to a minor whose donated kidney saves the life of a loved sibling
(Glantz *et al.*, 1977). Yet, such benefit varies with each individual situation, and
some may wish to permit both parent and child absolute right of refusal in this
or related situations. Obviously, this model can be extended to various other
contexts.

Proxy Consent

In some instances, it is impractical to consider involving a minor in personal decision making. Infants and children who are unconscious or severly
disabled so as to be unable to register a preference cannot participate in the

process. Other minors may *prefer* not to become involved in the decision-making process. In these instances, parental judgment will provide an absolute determinant regarding the welfare of the minor, unless the state intervenes.

Proxy consent refers to the provision of consent (or refusal), particularly regarding research or treatment participation, by one person on behalf of another. Glantz *et al.* review certain types of proxy consent: decisions made through an attempt to "substitute judgment" for another person; determinations of what is in the patient's or subject's "best interests"; or decisions based upon the standard of what a "reasonable" person might decide in a similar situation. Substitute judgment requires that the patient's or subject's representative actually try to determine how the incompetent individual would act in the particular situation. This test is next to impossible to apply when the individual in question is an infant or young child with no history of decision making in similar contexts. However, in the case of older minors who may be temporarily or permanently incapacitated, it may be possible to draw some conclusions based upon past behavior.

The best interests standard requires that the chosen procedure or course of action will benefit the individual. This test protects the individual from being inappropriately volunteered by another for nonbeneficial or risky procedures. However, it allows decisionmakers considerable leeway in determining what is in the individual's best interests. Sterilization of a mentally retarded teenaged girl may be judged by some to be in her best interests, since it may be feared that she might be psychologically harmed by pregnancy. However, such determinations are speculative and value-laden. As noted earlier, the phrase *in the child's best interests* may be inappropriately applied when the decision is actually more in the caretaker's best interests.

Finally, the "fair and reasonable" test applies to the standard of whether the proposed action meets the subjective criterion of matching what a hypothetical reasonable person might do in a similar situation. Thus, it seems quite appropriate for parents to decide that an infant should have benefit of all of those health care procedures that are reasonable and necessary for that child's well-being. What is reasonable and necessary is less clear in the hypothetical case of a parent who volunteers a child with no serious physical defect for plastic surgery to improve appearance. Since there is substantial variability in what reasonable persons decide regarding such surgery, it would be difficult to draw a generalization supporting the parent's wishes.

Collaboration by Child and Practitioner within the Professional Relationship

Certain types of professional relationships, such as those between a psychotherapist and client, educator and student, attorney and client, and, in some

cases, physician and patient, lend themselves to an ongoing collaboration between the practitioner and child. Once a decision is made to establish a particular professional relationship, that relationship can be conceptualized as a working partnership. Koocher (Chapter 7) and Melton (1981) suggest that
children's input into goal setting and therapeutic strategies should be incorporated into treatment planning whenever possible. The rationales for such involvment have been discussed earlier in this chapter: respect for the individual's right of self-determination, it may be a positive psychological experience,
and it may facilitate treatment success. Further, professionals should never
underestimate the degree to which children's ideas relative to their own needs
and goals will provide essential and valuable information.

Access to Information

Apart from children's actual input into decision making, they can remain
active participants in the professional relationship through access to information about their situations and options. Children's capacities to understand,
process and utilize information about their own situation and alternatives will
vary and professionals often wonder how much and what types of information
are helpful to the client. Some express concern that too much information may
overload the client or cause undue anxiety. There are, of course, no answers.
Professional experience and careful observation of the ongoing reactions of the
client may be one's best guide. Adult clients and patients vary dramatically in
their desire and need for information, and there is no reason to believe that
children are any less heterogeneous.

Although some clients and patients are less able to hear disturbing facts,
professionals also may tend to underestimate their capacity to deal with reality.
Early recognition of disturbing information may be difficult and even traumatic. But, most individuals, with the appropriate support, have a surprising capacity to adapt themselves to unpleasant realities. Professionals should be alert
to their reluctance to share distressing information with a client or patient.
Failures to disclose information are, all to often, for the benefit of the practitioner, who is reluctant to confront the facts together with the patient or client.

Provision of information to a child regarding his or her situation and
alternatives may, in itself, facilitate the positive goals related to the child's
welfare. This author is familiar with the case of a 7-year-old girl who was
enrolled in a speech therapy program at her school with parental consent.
Although she was removed from her regular classroom for the two hours week-
ly, it was not until two years later that she inquired as to why she was in speech
class when her friends were not. Her mother told her that she had a lisp. The
child had not been aware she had a speech problem. Shortly thereafter, the

child corrected her lisp on her own. The adults in this child's life may have presumed that she was aware of her problem. They therefore were unable to take advantage of the fact that children have tremendous capacity to utilize their resources and skills to achieve goals that are in their best interests. This author believes that this anecdote may be reflective both of the motivations and of the capacities of many children to help themselves and of the ways in which many adults inadvertently structure situations to impede such self-help.

Conclusion

It is suggested that professionals who work with children involve their clients, subjects, and patients in decisions regarding their own welfare to the maximum extent possible given the minor's own desire for involvement, the minor's capacity for meaningful participation, and the legal standards regarding consent requirements. The professional can and must play an active role in fostering the child's participation. Most children will not expect to have input into such decisions and, therefore, their preferences and ideas often must be solicited and encouraged. Minors, like adults, evidence significant variability in competencies relevant to decision-making contexts. Because competency is not an all-or-none concept, neither must involvement in decision making be all-or-none. Professional judgment and experience can promote the participation of each child in manner that is consistent with that minor's ability to take part. In most jurisdictions and in most decision-making contexts, minors are not legally authorized to make independent decisions. Yet practioners can foster their independent or shared involvement in decison making by advocating for the minor's participation. Representation of the minor's point of view and encouraging parents to share decision making with the child are roles for which the practitioner is ideally suited.

The rationales for involving children in decision-making affecting their own welfare are many. Such involvement is consistent with legal and ethical principles which respect the human right to self-determine. As noted earlier, theoretical analysis suggests that such involvement is an important social learning experience and generally contributes to adaptive and healthy psychosocial functioning. With respect to specific interventions, involving minors in decision making may facilitate their success by increasing their motivation and commitment to the identified goals. One may speculate that the functioning of the parent and child as a decision-making team, where appropriate, may serve to train family members in adaptive techniques of collaborative problem-solving, which may feed the development of a mutual acknowledgement of and respect for the perspectives of others.

The past decade, with its attention to children's rights, has forced us to examine our "benevolent paternalism" and to assess when and under what circumstances it actually is in the child's best interests for us to make proxy decisions for them. Social trends and technological advances have complicated the diversity of decision-making dilemmas that face minors and their families. The standards of various professions, as well as legal doctrines, have not, and probably never will develop a formula for balancing the professional's responsibilities to his or her client or patient—the responsibility to promote well-being and the individual's best interests and the responsibility to respect the individual's autonomy and right to privacy. Perhaps, rather than a formula, a new perpective would be most useful. We usually conceptualize the child's best interests and the child's right to self-determination as conflicting and antagonistic notions. Yet there may be more congruence between these principles than is typically attributed. The true balance between these concepts may be the belief that appropriate levels of self-determination are in the child's best interests.

References

American Psychological Association. *Ethical principles in the conduct of research with human participants.* Washington, D.C.: American Psychological Association, 1973.

Applebaum, P.S. & Roth, L.H. *Competency to consent to research: a psychiatric overview.* Paper presented at the National Institute of Mental Health Workshop on Empirical Research on Informed Consent with Subjects of Uncertain Competence, Rockville, Md., January 1981.

Bersoff, D. N. Representation for children in custody decisions: All that glitters is not *Gault. Journal of Family Law,* 1976–1977, *15*(1), 27–49.

Bersoff, D. N. *Legal issues in children's consent to psychological research.* Paper presented at the American Psychological Association Convention, New York, September 1979.

Brown, R. H., & Truitt, R. B. The right of minors to medical treatment. *DePaul Law Review,* 1979, *28,* 289–320.

Castillo, A. A Ukranian family and a question of juvenile law. *New York Times,* September 9, 1980, p. B8.

Curran, W. J., & Beecher, H. K. Experimentation in children. *The Journal of the American Medical Association,* 1969, *10,* 77–83.

Day, L., & Reznikoff, M. Social class, the treatment process, and parents' and children's expectations about child psychotherapy. *Journal of Clinical Child Psychology,* 1980, *9,* 195–198.

Ellis, J.W. Volunteering children: Parental commitment of minors to mental institutions. *California Law Review,* 1974, *62*(3), 840–916.

Ellsworth, P. C., & Levy, R. J. Legislative reform of child custody adjudication: An effort to rely on social science data in formulating legal policies. *Law and Society Review,* 1969, *4* 167–233.

Fellner, C. H., & Marshall, J. R. Kidney donors—The myth of informed consent. *American Journal of Psychiatry,* 1970, *126,* 1245–1251.

Ferguson, L. R. The competence and freedom of children to make choices regarding participation in research: A statement. *Journal of Social Issues,* 1978, *34*(2), 114–121.

Forer, L. G. The rights of children: The legal vacuum. *American Bar Association Journal,* 1969, *55,* 1151–1156.

Fost, N. Children as renal donors. *New England Journal of Medicine*, 1977, *196*, 363, 367.

Frank, J. D. psychotherapy and the sense of mastery. In R. L. Spitzer and D. F. Klein (Eds.), *Evaluation of psychological therapies*. Baltimore: Johns Hopkins University Press, 1976.

Friedman, P. R. Legal regulation of applied behavior analysis in mental institutions and prisons. *University of Arizona Law Review*, 1975, *17*, 40–104.

Gert, B., & Culver, C. *Valid consent*. Paper presented at the National Institute of Mental Health Workshop on Empirical Research on Informed Consent with Subjects of Uncertain Competence, Rockville, Md., January 1981.

Glantz, L. H., Annas, G. J. & Katz, B. F. Scientific research with children: Legal incapacity and proxy consent. *Family Law Quarterly, 1977, 11, 235–295.*

Grisso, T. *Psychology's role in policy on minors' informed consent*. Paper presented at the American Psychological Association Convention, New York, September 1979.

Grisso, T. *Juveniles' waiver of rights: Legal and psychological competence*. New York: Plenum Press, 1981.

Grisso, T., & Vierling, L. Minors' consent to treatment: A developmental perspective. *Professional Psychology*, 1978, *9*, 412–427.

Herman, D. *Blythe v. Seagraves*: North Carolina treats the issue of whether a minor and her parents may legally consent to the minor's participation, as donor, in a kidney transplant. *North Carolina Central Law Journal*, 1979, *9*, 216–226.

Holder, A. R. *Legal issues in pediatrics and adolescent medicine*. New York: Wiley, 1977.

Katz, B. F. Children, privacy and nontherapeutic experimentation. *American Journal of Orthopsychiatry*, 1975, *45*, 802–812.

Korsch, B. M. The Armstrong lecture: Physicians, patients and decision. *American Journal of Diseases of Childhood*, 1974, *127*, 328–332.

Leon, J. S. Recent developments in legal representation of children: A growing concern with the concept of capacity. *Canadian Journal of Family Law*, 1978, *1*, 375–433.

Lewis, C. C. School exit: When are adolescents ready to decide? In J. Simon & S. Stipek (Eds.), *Reconsidering compulsory schooling for adolescents: Studies in social science, education and law*. New York: Academic Press, in press.

Lewis, C. C. A comparison of minors' and adults' pregnancy decisions. *American Journal of Orthopsychiatry*, 1980, *50*, 446–453

Lewis, C. E., Lewis, M. A., & Ifekwunigue, M. Informed consent by children and participation in an influenza vaccine trial. *American Journal of Public Health*, 1978, *68*, 1079–1082.

Lewis, C. E., Lewis, M. A., Lorimer, A., & Palmer, B. B. Child-initiated care: The use of school nursing services by children in an "adult-free" system. *Pediatrics*, 1977, *60*, 499–507.

McGarry, A. L., Curran, W. J., Lipsitt, P. D., Lelos, D., Schwitzgebel, R., & Rosenberg, A. H. *Competency to stand trial and mental illness*. (DHEW Publication No. ADM77–103). U.S. DHEW, National Institute of Mental Health. Washington, D.C.: U.S. Government Printing Office, 1973.

Meisel, A. The "exceptions" to the informed consent doctrine: Striking a balance between competing vaues in medical decisionmaking. *Wisconsin Law Review*, 1979, 413–488.

Meisel, A. *What would it mean to be competent enough to consent to or refuse participation in research: A legal overview*. Paper presented at the National Institute of Mental Health Workshop on Empirical Research on Informed Consent with Subjects of Uncertain Competence, Rockville, Md., January 1981.

Meisel, A., Roth, L. H., & Lidz, C. W. Toward a model of the legal doctrine of informed consent. *American Journal of Psychiatry*, 1977, *134*, 285–289.

Melton, G. B. Children's participation in treatment planning: Psychological and legal issues. *Professional Psychology*, 1981, *12*(2), 246–252.

Melton, G. B. Children's rights: Where are the children? *American Journal of Orthopsychiatry*, 1982, *52*, 530–538.

Mnookin, R. *Child, family and state*. Boston: Little, Brown, 1978.(a)

Mnookin, R. Children's rights: Beyond kiddie libbers and child savers. *Journal of Clinical Child Psychology*, 1978, *7*, 163–167.(b)

National Commission for the Protection of Human Subjects of Biomedical and Behavioral Research. *Research involving children* (DHEW Publication No. OS 77–004). U.S DHEW. Washington, D.C.: U.S Government Printing Office, 1977.

National Commission for the Protection of Human Subjects of Biomedical and Behavioral Research. *The Belmont report* (DHEW Publication No. OS 78–00012). U.S DHEW. Washington, D.C.: Government Printing Office, 1978. Reprinted 44 FR 76 (April 18, 1979).

Pilpel, H. G. Minors' rights to medical care. *Albany Law Review* 1972, *36* 462–487.

Rodham, H. Children under the law. *Harvard Educational Review*, 1973, *43*, 487–514.

Rogers, C. M., & Wrightsman, L. S. Attitudes toward children's rights: Nurturance or self-determination. *Journal of Social Issues*, 1978, *34*, 59–68.

Roth, L. H., *Empirical study of informed consent in psychiatry* (Final report: Grant No. MH-27553, Center for Studies of Crime and Delinquency, National Institute of Mental Health). Pittsburgh: University of Pittsburgh, 1980.

Roth, L. H., Meisel, A., & Lidz, C. W. Tests of competency to consent to treatment. *American Journal of Psychiatry*, 1977, *134*, 279–284.

Schowalter, J. E. The minor's role in consent for mental health treatment. *Journal of the American Academy of Child Psychiatry*, 1978, *17*, 505–513.

Schowalter, J. E., Ferholt, J. V., & Mann, N. M. The adolescent patient's decision to die. *Pediatrics*, 1973, *51*, 97–103.

Skolnick, A. The limits of childhood: Concepts of child development and social context. *Law and Contemporary Society*, 1975, *39*, 38–77.

Stanley, B. H. *Informed consent and competence: A review of empirical research*. Paper presented at the National Institute of Mental Health Workshop on Empirical Research on Informed Consent with Subjects of Uncertain Competence, Rockville, Md., January 1981.

Sub–task Panel on Infants, Children, and Adolescents. Report of the Task Panel on Mental Health and American Families submitted to the President's Commission on Mental Health. Washington, D. C.: U.S Government Printing Office. (No. 040-000-00392-4), 1978, *III* (Appendix), 612–660.

Thoresen, C. E., & Mahoney, M. J. *Behavioral self-control*. New York: Holt, Rinehart & Winston, 1974.

Wald, M. S. Legal policies affecting children: A lawyer's request for aid. *Child Development*, 1976, *47*, 1–5.

Wald, M. S. Children's rights: A framework for analysis. *University of California, Davis*, 1979, *12* 255–282.

Wald, P. M., & Friedman, P. R. Brief for *Amici Curiae* submitted to the U.S. Supreme Court in the case of *Kremens v. Bartley* (No. 75–1064), 1976.

Weithorn, L. A. Drug therapy—Children's rights. In M. Cohen (Ed.), *Drug therapy and the special child*. New York: Gardner Press, 1979.

Weithorn, L. A. Developmental factors and competence to make informed treatment decisions. *Child and Youth Services*, in press.

Weithorn, L. A., & Campbell, S. B. The competency of children and adolescents to make informed treatment decisions. *Child Development*, in press.

Wilkins, L. P. Children's rights: Removing the parental consent barrier. *Arizona State Law Review*, 1975, 31–92.

Table of Cases

261

Author Index

263

Subject Index